"Jesus
I AM

Answere To my needs — Bob
Nissi Victory
Shalom Peace
Jireh Provider

EPHESIANS

Bill O'Warria

BOOKS BY DR. CRISWELL . . .

Expository Sermons on Revelation – 5 Vols. in 1

Expository Sermons on the Book of Daniel, 4 Vols. in 1

The Holy Spirit in Today's World

The Baptism, Filling and Gifts of the Holy Spirit

Expository Sermons on Galatians

Ephesians—An Exposition

Expository Sermons on the Epistles of Peter

Isaiah—An Exposition

Acts: An Exposition, Volumes 1, 2, and 3

Abiding Hope

Great Doctrines of the Bible, Volume 1

EPHESIANS
an exposition by W. A. CRISWELL

ZONDERVAN PUBLISHING HOUSE OF THE ZONDERVAN CORPORATION
GRAND RAPIDS, MICHIGAN 49506

EPHESIANS — AN EXPOSITION

Copyright © 1974 by The Zondervan Corporation
Grand Rapids, Michigan

All rights reserved. No part of this publication may be reproduced, stored in a retrieval system, or transmitted in any form or by any means, electronic, mechanical, photocopy, recording or otherwise, without the prior permission of the copyright owner.

Library of Congress Catalog Number 74-11852

Ninth printing 1982
ISBN 0-310-22781-X

Printed in the United States of America

To
a family — you;
or to
a couple — you;
or to
just one somebody — you
who have undergirded the pastor and our dear church with your prayers, your devotion, and your faithful attendance through the years, and who are truly the saints of God.

CONTENTS

	Foreword	
1	Where the Christian Lives	13
2	The Reality of God	20
3	The Doctrine of Predestination	27
4	Our Acceptance Before God	35
5	The Purpose of God for the World	44
6	Seeing With the Eyes of the Soul	52
7	Our Priceless Possession	60
8	Our Spiritual Resurrection	66
9	Salvation by Grace	72
10	The New Creation	78
11	The New Man and The New Humanity	85
12	Jesus, The God-Man	92
13	The Mystery of the Church	100
14	The Unspeakable Riches of Christ	109
15	When Angels Attend Church	117
16	The Eternal Purpose of God	125
17	The Ableness of God	134
18	The Family of God	142
19	God's Love in Four Dimensions	151
20	Taking Hold of the Abounding Ableness of God	160
21	The Glory of God in the Church	168
22	The True Ecumenism	177
23	The One Baptism	186
24	The Heavenly Ascension	196
25	Leading Captivity Captive	206
26	The Grace Gifts of Christ	215
27	Grieving the Holy Spirit	225
28	The Sweetest Verse in the Bible	234
29	Awake and Arise	242
30	Filled With the Spirit	249
31	Christ Loved the Church	257
32	The Heavenly Mystery	266
33	Honoring Our Parents	274
34	Strong in the Lord	282
35	War in the Spirit World	290
36	The Panoply of God	299

FOREWORD

There is such a vast difference between a sermon written out word for word and a sermon preached extemporaneously from the pulpit to a large audience. These messages on Ephesians are delivered sermons, spoken without notes, and designed first for hearers. There is, therefore, repetition to be found in them which would not be found in a written message. In reading, one can go back and reread what may not have been clear, but in speaking the preacher must sense in his soul that the people understand what he is saying as he goes along. This causes him often to repeat what has already been said or explained.

Through the years I have learned something that has helped me greatly in my study and preparation for sermons. It is this: a book of messages on a book of the Bible is the finest commentary I could ever hope to find on that portion of Scripture. I pray that this volume on Ephesians will enrich the preacher's and teacher's library on this epistle of Paul.

The delivered messages were so blessed of God to the people who heard them in our dear church. May the Holy Spirit no less bless them to the hearts of those who now read them.

My deepest, sincerest gratitude is herewith expressed to those who copied the sermons from tape recordings and who corrected them for grammatical errors. In the fury of preaching the pastor will often forget whether the subject was plural or singular!

Now may God bless the eyes that look upon these pages: this is the prayer of the author.

W. A. Criswell

First Baptist Church
Dallas, Texas

Chapter 1

WHERE THE CHRISTIAN LIVES

> Paul, an apostle of Jesus Christ by the will of God, to the saints which are at Ephesus, and to the faithful in Christ Jesus. (Eph. 1:1)

Let me begin by saying a word about the epistle as a whole. You will be quite surprised in reading the letter of Paul to the church at Ephesus that it is barren of personal references. This is an astonishing fact because he spent more time in his ministry at Ephesus than at any other place. Paul worked twice as long in Ephesus as he did in Corinth. The greatest ministry the world has ever seen was Paul's ministry in this capital of the Roman province of Asia. On the second missionary journey, returning from Macedonia and Greece to Syria, Paul stopped at Ephesus with Aquila and Priscilla. After speaking in the synagogue there he left Aquila and Priscilla and went on his way with the promise that in God's grace he would return. On the third missionary journey, after visiting the churches in the interior of Galatia, he went to Ephesus where he spent the majority of that journey. When he finally left Ephesus after three years it was only because he was forced to leave the town. His preaching created a riot and he left with his life in great danger. He went to Macedonia and later, on his way home, he stopped at Miletus, about eighteen miles from Ephesus. From there he sent for the elders (pastors) of the church at Ephesus, and here he delivered to them the pathetic, moving address that is presented in Acts 20.

Why is it that with all of the intimate, close, heartwarming, and God-blessed contacts with the people and with the church at Ephesus there are no personal references in the epistle? The answer is this: the letter to the church at Ephesus is an encyclical.

It is a general letter, a circular letter. Paul wrote it to all the churches in that day and to the churches in our day. The epistle is addressed to the churches of all times. When Paul dictated the letter, there were copies made of it and he placed those copies in the hands of Tychicus, a fellow worker and minister. Tychicus took the letters and wrote in the name of each church to which he delivered it. When he brought the manuscript to Ephesus there was already written these words: "Paul, an apostle of Jesus Christ, by the will of God, to the saints which are," then Tychicus added the phrase, "at Ephesus." When he took another copy of the manuscript to Laodicea, he wrote "in Laodicea." When he took another copy to Hierapolis, he wrote "to the saints which are in Hierapolis." That is why there is no personal reference to Ephesus.

The manuscript that came down to us is the one that was addressed to the church at Ephesus. In the last verses in the letter of Paul to Colosse, he says, "And when this epistle is read among you (Colossians), cause that it be read also in the church of the Laodiceans; and that ye likewise read the epistle from Laodicea" (Col. 4:16). Where is any letter to Laodicea? The letter to Laodicea is this one, but the manuscript that was sent to Laodicea had written in it, "To the Laodiceans," just as our present Ephesian letter has written in it the salutation, "To the Ephesians."

So the Book of Ephesians is a general letter addressed to all the churches and it contains some of the finest of all the doctrinal revelations and truth of God to be found in the Bible.

The Environment of the Christian Life

Let us begin with the first verse. "Paul, an apostle of Jesus Christ by the will of God, to the saints which are at Ephesus, and to the faithful in Christ Jesus." This is the environment of the Christian life. Environment means "to circle around," and we are encircled by three things. First, we are in Christ. Our Christian life is lived in Christ. Second, our life is lived in the fellowship of the saints. Third, our life is lived in Ephesus, in the world around us. That is our inescapable lot. We are not saints in heaven; we are saints in Ephesus. We are in this world with all of its evils, trials, challenges, paganism, and secularism. Our life is lived in those three categories; namely, in Christ, in the fellowship of the saints, and in this present world.

Where the Christian Lives

LIVING IN CHRIST

The Christian life is lived first in Christ. We do not use that expression anymore. It is strange to us. We hardly know what it means. That is because we are materialistic in all of our outlook on life. If I go up to a man and ask him, "Are you in business?" he knows immediately what I am talking about and he will answer in kind. If I go up to a man and ask him, "Are you in one of the professions?" he will know immediately what I am saying. But if I come up to a man and I ask him, "Are you in Christ?" he will be mystified and possibly embarrassed. That is the difference between us and these first-century Christians. They lived with that language and to them it was most familiar. "In Christ" meant to be girded and grounded in Him and in His faithfulness, as a vine is anchored to the bosom of the earth from which it receives its strength and life.

Paul uses the expression one hundred sixty-four times: "in Christ for forgiveness"; "in Christ for salvation"; "in Christ for assurance"; "in Christ for holiness"; "in Christ for direction"; "in Christ for service"; "in Christ forever."

For example, look at the wonderful verse in 2 Corinthians 5:17: "If any man be in Christ, he is a new creature; old things are passed away; behold, all things are become new." If a man is in Christ there is a new love, there is a new vision, a new dream, a new life, a new hope, a new dedication.

Thus Paul addresses the saints who are at Ephesus and who are "in Christ." As one of their number he uses himself in this introduction as being one "in Christ." In the first words of the first sentence he writes, "Paul, an apostle of Jesus Christ by the will of God." So his place of apostleship and his ministries are not in himself but they are "in Christ." Where he is and what he is, he says, is by the sovereign will of God. He did not put himself in Christ, in the ministry, in the apostolic work of the Lord. Nor was he chosen by those who were apostles before him. His place was chosen by an act of God. When we apply that divine principle to ourselves we find an immeasurable, unfathomable, illimitable source of strength in our lives. What we do and what we are attempting to do, becomes not a matter of our choice but of heaven's choice for us. Our place, our message, our work, and our assignment are from heaven.

16   *Ephesians: An Exposition*

I say that is a source of immeasurable encouragement, for if you are as I am, you feel overwhelmingly inadequate as you face your tasks and assignments from God. However weak, however frail, however faulty, however unable, or however ungifted we may be, has nothing to do with God's sovereign choice of us. I may not be as gifted as I would like to be, but God has assigned me the task. I may not be as holy and as strong as I would like to be, but God put me in the task. The result of such a doctrine in the Bible is this: in our work and in our place we take our minds and our eyes off ourselves. We are not looking at ourselves but we are looking to God. It is He who gives us strength and makes us adequate. It is He who makes us equal to what He has assigned us to do. It is God's work, and we are God's people. It is He who sees us through.

We are not all apostles, we are not even all pastors or preachers, but we all have an assignment — a calling. There is a divine pattern for every life and in that task it is God who makes us able and equal; it is God who blesses us. If my work is to be a doorkeeper in the house of the Lord, that is fine. "Lord, help me to be Your doorkeeper, or teacher, or singer, or worker with children, or whatever You have called me to do in this life." We are in Christ and in His will.

LIVING WITH THE SAINTS

"Saints." There is a word we will never retrieve. The idea of that word in the Bible is one of the sublimest that may be found in revelation. Yet it has been destroyed for us and there is no way in the world for us to get it back again. *Hagioi*, "saints." The minute I say that word you think of some artificial, technical designation of someone who is being elevated in a certain category. Well, there is nothing of that meaning nor is there any approach to that meaning in the Bible. The word *kadosh* in the Old Testament Hebrew and the word *hagioi* in the Greek New Testament are alike and refer to the same thing. The verbal form of the word is *hagiozo* and refers to something that God takes out of common use and consecrates to heavenly use, to God's use. The forms of that verb are numerous. *Hagion* is translated in the Bible "temple"; *hagia* is the holy place; *hagia hagion* is the holy of holies. The idea, whether it is *kadosh* of the Old Testament or *hagios* of the New

Where the Christian Lives

Testament, is that here is something or someone that God has set aside — for Himself.

No man can build a building and say this is *hagion* to God. God has to do that. The same is true regarding a priest. No man in the Bible could take another man and ordain him to be a priest. God had to choose him. He was a *kadosh* man, a holy man. As you know, in the Old Testament it was the household of Aaron. The altar was *hagios, kadosh*. In Exodus 20 God gave to Israel the Ten Commandments, but in chapter 19 He said to the people, "You shall be unto me a kingdom of priests and a holy nation." For what? They were to be a blessing to all of the families of the earth. God gave oracles to them that they might be the teacher to all the Gentiles of the earth. The exact nomenclature and revelation from heaven are found in the New Testament, for God is the same yesterday, today, and through all eternity. This is how God works. He chooses and sets aside certain things for Himself.

One of those certain things is you. "But ye are a chosen generation, a royal priesthood, an holy nation, a peculiar people; that ye should shew forth the praises of him who hath called you out of darkness into his marvellous light" (1 Peter 2:9). The body I live in is holy to the Lord. It is the *hagion* of the Holy Spirit. God dwells in this temple, this house. You are not your own; you are bought with a price. Therefore, glorify God in your body. For a man to be drunk, to defile the body of Christ, is a sin. Why? Not that it is a sin for a man to drink, or smoke. Not that it is a sin in itself for a man to dissipate his life by habits that are just debilitating and destroying. That is not the point at all. What God says is that my body is the temple of the Holy Spirit. It does not belong to me. God gave it to me to glorify Him.

That same thing pertains to the saints as such. When the word is used referring to us it always is in the plural, *hagioi*, "the saints." "The saints" love to be together and were thus together in the Bible. They were called the *ecclesia*, translated in the New Testament, "church." They were the called out people of the Lord and they were also the *koinonia*, translated "fellowship," "communion." They loved to be together. If you are in Christ, that is a part of your makeup. You love to be with God's people. When the time comes for the convocation of God's people you are there, you cannot help it.

Recently a man and his wife from Atlanta, Georgia, were in

our evening service. After the service was over, when I was visiting with him, he showed me two tickets to the Cotton Bowl. There was a football game there that night, and he had two tickets to the game. He said to me: "I'm from Atlanta and I don't belong to the church here at all. I'm not even a Baptist." "But," he said, "when time came to go to that Cotton Bowl game, I thought about your preaching the Gospel down there in that church and I just couldn't go." He attended the service. We had a heavenly, pentecostal meeting that night, and he said, "This is the greatest thing that I could have done." He is "in Christ." That is just the way you are. Why, I would be miserable sitting in a theater at church time. I would be miserable in the Cotton Bowl looking at a football game when my church was having services. That is the way you get to be. "If any man be in Christ, he is a new creation; old things are passed away, behold, all things are become new" (2 Cor. 5:17). It is a new life and a new love, a new dream, a new association, and a new fellowship. It is just something different.

While I was in the seminary in Kentucky I pastored a church in a village. One day a family moved to the village for the man had bought a large, spacious farm. One of those beautiful Kentucky homes was on it. The man and his large family joined the church immediately. I would see him in the congregation every time the doors opened. He was like a man who was hungry as he listened. As I preached, the tears would fall from his face. As the people would sing, he seemed so moved. I was his guest one day for dinner and as I visited with him I said, "I see you in the congregation and you are so moved, like a man who is hungry, seated at the table of the Lord; like a man who is thirsty, drinking from the water of life, and you cry." I asked, "Why do you do this?" He said: "Young pastor, for these past years I have lived way up in the mountains where there were few, if any, Christian people and no church at all. Up there, away and alone, my heart was so hungry and my soul was so thirsty. Now that we have moved here we come to church and it is just like heaven. I cannot help but cry as I sit there in the church and just thank God for the people of the Lord." That is the way you are when you are "in Christ." There might be a thousand organizations, many of them very fine, but my soul would thirst to death just being in a wonderful organization. I want to be fed the Bread of Life. That song, "Break Thou the Bread of Life, dear Lord to me," does not refer to the Lord's

Supper. It refers to this Book. "Beyond the sacred page I see Thee, Lord." That is what that Book is about. I want someone to open God's Book for me and speak to me the Word of heaven. I cannot help that.

A man may lecture beautifully. His so-called ethical sermon may be full of finest admonitions. But Socrates could have said the same things. Buddha doubtless could have said it better, and Zoroaster could have placed it in even more beautiful language. But it is not beauty of language and it is not ethical content my soul desires. What I want to know is, does God say something? My heart wants to hear and my soul is thirsty to know. If you are "in Christ" you are that way. You love to be with God's people, in God's house, listening to God's Word. These are *hagioi*, the saints of the Lord.

LIVING IN EPHESUS

The saints "in Christ" are also "in Ephesus." We are on the sea of this life. God said to the Church at Pergamos, "I know where you are, where you live, where Satan's seat is, where Satan has his throne" (Rev. 2:13). We are in that world, but do not be afraid. A ship may be on the Pacific Ocean, and the water may surround for millions of square miles, but all the water in that ocean cannot hurt that ship as long as the water stays on the outside. Though the ship is in the middle of the sea (and we are that way), it is only when the water gets in the ship that it begins to sink to the bottom. We may live in a floodtide of iniquity, of blasphemy, of unbelief, of spiritual scorn and ridicule, and we may live in a veritable floodtide of secularism, materialism, and darkness. But it will never bother us as long as it does not get on the inside of us. If you are "in Christ" the Holy Spirit is in you; there is no room in you for that floodtide of evil around you. Like a light shining in a dark place, like a ship smoothly sailing even in troublous waters, you are "in Christ" even "in Ephesus."

Chapter 2

THE REALITY OF GOD

> Blessed be the God and Father of our Lord Jesus Christ, who hath blessed us with all spiritual blessings in heavenly places in Christ. (Eph. 1:3)

When we read this letter of Paul to the church, we move into a different world. We live in a secular and materialistic society and one that increasingly finds no place for God in life, work, and play. But this world to which we are introduced by Paul begins with God. As he begins, he also closes the epistle. "Peace be to the brethren, and love with faith, from God the Father and the Lord Jesus Christ" (Eph. 6:23).

The secular, materialistic, skeptical world says to us: "We do not need God. We do not have any place for faith, and as for ethics and morality, the Sermon on the Mount and the Golden Rule are enough." To them God is unnecessary. The Golden Rule is good but morality finally fragments and frays without God. There must be motive back of righteousness, ethics, morality and that motive is not found in men. Men change and are unstable, but morality, ethics, righteousness, goodness is ever the same, for it is grounded in the character of Almighty God. Right, morality, truth are not what man says they are, but what God says they are, and God never changes. What was right yesterday is right today and right forever. There is no such thing as a changing morality except in perversion. There is no such thing as situation ethics which proposes that under these circumstances this is right for me now. Right, righteousness, morality, truth are grounded in the character of Almighty God and without Him we have nothing but dust and sand.

The cynical world will say that faith is a matter of gullibility.

The Reality of God

It is a hangover from superstition, the drag of our evolutionary rise from our animal ancestors. The concomitant and the corollary is also either expressed or implied; namely, that there is a contradiction between science and faith and to have science is not to have faith, for science is diametrically opposed to faith. But, my friend, all science is capable of is to observe, and it writes down what it sees.

For example, all that scientists can do is observe the law of gravity, they cannot explain it. The moon in which we are so interested has the power to move the entire ocean. Think of the power to move an ocean! In Panama I walked along the beach and looked at the tides which are sometimes twenty and thirty feet high. The bend in the continent, the scientists say, causes the water to pile up. All by the moon? Science cannot explain, it just observes.

It is a universal law in physics that when a thing gets colder it contracts; when heated, it expands. One can take water, contain it, build a fire under it, and the steam will drive a powerful engine. The thrust of that expansion of water is tremendous. However, as it becomes colder and colder, it condenses, it contracts. When it decreases in temperature to 32°, for some unknown and inexplicable reason, it turns around and does just the opposite. It expands as it freezes! But it is supposed to contract. One can see it but one does not explain it. Science does not explain, it just observes and writes down what it sees.

Where are the answers? Is there purpose in life? Why was I born? Is there a meaning to existence? Where did I come from? What am I? Where is my eternal destiny and home? The answers lie in God. What is inexplicable to my mind is why men who are skeptical will say, "This is a reality," pointing to a piece of brick or dust or rock. They say a star is a reality and the world on which we stand is a reality. But faith to them is not a reality. To me, however, faith is as powerful and as moving a reality as any other observable phenomenon in human life. If we leave God out of life, we have a different world, do we not? The world to which we are introduced in Christ and the world of a materialistic skeptic are two different worlds.

Paul begins with God and that is the way we want to start. This is the way Paul lived and concluded his life, and this is the way we want to live and conclude our lives, namely, in God. "Grace, peace from God our Father and from Jesus our Lord. Blessed be God." Isaiah said that God measures the waters of the earth and that He holds the vast oceans and seas in the hollow of His hand. The earth itself is like a piece of fine dust in His scales. Paul says that His ways are past finding out and that His wisdom is unfathomable.

In 1879 Sidney Lanier wrote in *The Marshes of Glynn:*

As the marsh hen secretly builds on the watery sod,
Behold I will build me a nest on the greatness of God:
I will fly in the greatness of God as the marsh hen flies
In the freedom that fills all the space 'twixt the
    marsh and the skies:
By so many roots as the marsh grass sends in the sod
I will heartily lay me a-hold on the greatness of God.

How Can I Bless God?

"Blessed be God," Paul writes. But how can I bless God? Hebrews 7:7 avows; "And without all contradiction the less is blessed of the better." God is so great and I am so small. How could I bless God? When God blesses us He bestows benefits upon us. He pours out of His abounding grace — love and gifts. He enriches our souls and our lives. But how can I bless God? I cannot add to His perfection. I cannot add to His blessedness. He said in the Psalm: "If I were hungry, I would not tell thee: for the world is mine and the fulness thereof. For every beast of the forest is mine and the cattle up on a thousand hills" (Ps. 50:12, 10). How can I bless God? I can do it in three ways.

By Praise and Prayer

I can bless God by my praises, prayers, words, deeds of gratitude, thanksgiving, and appreciation. Psalm 103:1-4 reads: "Bless the LORD, O my soul: and all that is within me, bless his holy name. Bless the LORD, O my soul, and forget not all his benefits: Who forgiveth all thine iniquities; who healeth all thy diseases; Who redeemeth thy life from destruction; who crowneth thee with lovingkindness and tender mercies." "Bless the Lord and forget not all his benefits." I can praise God in thanksgiving and gratitude, remembering the gracious hand from whence my blessings come.

BY FILIAL LOVE

I can bless God in filial love. "Hear, O Israel: The LORD our God is one LORD: And thou shalt love the LORD thy God with all thine heart, and with all thy soul, and with all thy might" (Deut. 6:4, 5). Jesus repeated the Biblical injunction in Matthew 22:37. We are commanded to love the Lord our God. We can bless God in filial love. We can love our Father in heaven with all our being. How great He is! But still He is our Father in heaven.

In my reading for this sermon I came across the story of the Earl of Asquith who was the Prime Minister of Great Britain in the early years of this century. He was a noble man, an appreciated man, a man who was highly honored. He received many citations and plaudits in the course of his illustrious political career. One day a servant was recounting to the Prime Minister's little girl the greatness of her father. He spoke of his citations and the honors bestowed upon him. The little wide-eyed girl broke in and said, "But sir, is he still my father?" God is so great, so mighty, but He is still our Father in heaven. I can bless God through filial love.

BY SERVING GOD'S PEOPLE

I can bless God in my service, ministry, and compassionate remembrance of God's people, God's children. "Inasmuch as ye have done it unto one of the least of these my brethren, ye have done it unto me" (Matt. 25:40). I can bless God in my love and friendship for His people, Israel. I can bless God in love and compassionate service and ministry to these for whom Christ died.

OUR HEAVENLY FATHER AND OUR LORD JESUS CHRIST

Let us read our text again. "Blessed be the God and Father of our Lord Jesus Christ, who hath blessed us with all spiritual blessings in heavenly places in Christ." It is in Christ that we come to know the Father and through whom we are blessed as His children.

What is our heavenly Father like? The Holy Scriptures say that no man can see God's face and live. To look upon the presence and glory of God would be like looking into the blazing sun. It blinds our eyes. Hebrews 12 concludes with this verse, "For our

God is a consuming fire." The earlier verses in that chapter describe Mount Sinai, the mount that burned with fire, and then quote from the Old Testament, "And Moses said, I exceedingly fear and quake." Who can look at God?

On the Damascus road the burning, Syrian sun at midday is dazzling. Yet in the brightness of glory of that shining orb the Lord appeared so much brighter, so marvelously iridescent, that He completely blinded Paul's eyes. They had to lead him by the hand into Damascus. This is the glory of God. It is like gazing upon the sun that blinds. Then how are we to know God? We know God in His self-revelation in Christ. He is God. He is the love of God and the mercy of God. He is the atoning grace of God. What is God like? Look at Jesus. He is Emmanuel, God with us. Jesus is one with God.

Yet the two, God the Father and God the Son, are distinct. How could such a thing be? We cannot know. It is a mystery. All of the works of God are mysteries. "Mystery" is the signature of the presence of God. Everything that God has done is mysterious, unfathomable, unknowable. One cannot see to the end of it nor can one grasp the inner meaning of it. The hand that flung this universe into space and made the world on which we walk is the same hand that wrote the Bible and that revelation is mystery. We cannot fully understand it. We cannot put the infinitude of God in our circumscribed and finite words. He is too beyond us.

When I read the Bible I see in the Book the same mystery that I see in the world of God's creation. I cannot understand it. God is one, yet He is three. We are told to baptize "in the name of the Father, and of the Son, and of the Holy Spirit." We know God as Father. We know God as Son. We know God in our hearts as the Holy Spirit. Yet the three are One in a mystery I cannot enter into. No man can grasp it.

When Jesus lived in the days of His flesh, He leaned on the promises of God, He trusted in God. His enemies said so (Matt. 27:43). He prayed to God His Father. In the institution of the Lord's Supper at the Passover they sang praises to God before they left the Upper Room. In Gethsemane He bowed in agony praying to the Father. When He was crucified on the cross He cried, "My God, *lama sabachthani?* Why hast thou forsaken me?" When He died, He bowed His head and said, "Father, into thy hands I commit my spirit." When He was raised from the dead

He said to Mary Magdalene: "Touch me not. The old relationship in the days of my flesh has passed, for I am here only because I have not ascended to my Father." The two, Father and Son, seem to be so distinct, yet the two are one. In John 10 our Lord avows, "He that hath seen me hath seen the Father." Would you like to know what God is like? Look at Jesus, for if you know Jesus you know God the Father. If you love Jesus you love God the Father. If you sit at the feet of Jesus you sit at the feet of God. If you follow Jesus you follow the Lord God. What an unfathomable mystery!

He was a man, the Word was made flesh, yet He was God. In church history the Christological controversies that raged through Christendom for the first several centuries were over the humanity of Jesus, not over His Godhead. Those ancients did not argue about the deity of Christ, but they were forever in controversy over the humanity of Christ. They had difficulty believing in His humanity.

Today our philosophical world has turned exactly around. No-one has any trouble today with the humanity of Jesus. He was a good man, like Socrates; a fine man, like Plato; a learned man, like Aristotle. All accept Jesus' humanity. But today we have trouble with His deity. How could a man who lived and died be God? And yet He is! The climactic conclusion to the fourth gospel is the cry of doubting Thomas, "My Lord and my God!" There is no sweeter or finer verse in the Bible than what Paul wrote in Titus 2:13, "Looking for that blessed hope, and the glorious appearing of the great God and our Saviour Jesus Christ." For whom are we looking from heaven? We are looking for God. It is God who is coming down. It is God who shall recreate this fallen earth. It is God, our Saviour, whom we shall adore and worship. He is coming!

ALL SPIRITUAL BLESSINGS ARE IN CHRIST

Blessed be God in the unfolding ages of all the eternities to come. Think of it! Our text exclaims, "Blessed be God, and blessed be the Lord, our Saviour Jesus Christ, who has blessed us with all spiritual blessings in the heavenlies, in Christ." The blessing is not something that is going to happen. It is not a future thing. It is God who has blessed us, *now*. If you are in Christ, right now you are in the heavenlies and you are blessed with all spiritual blessings. Ah, how rich we are! And how encouraged we ought to be! Why, if a first-century apostle or a first-century Christian were to see you today and find you discouraged and blue, pessimistic and down in melancholia, he would not understand. In confirmation of your spirit of defeat you point out to him the cross, "Oh, the death, the suffering, the blood, the agony, the cross." "Ah," he would say, "that is our sign of triumph and conquest and victory."

A little girl came into the church, brought by her father, for the first time, and saw a cross on the wall. She said, "Daddy, look, there is a plus sign up there on the wall." That is it; the cross is a plus sign. God has given us in Christ all of the riches of glory. It is better to have a new heart than a new coat. It is better to sit at the table of the Lord than to sit at the banquets of the most festive boards the world has ever provided. You are richer being an heir of God and a joint-heir with Christ than if you were the son of the wealthiest man on the earth. You have all of the answers in Christ. "Whether there be prophesies, they shall fail; whether there be tongues, they shall cease; whether there be knowledge, it shall vanish away. For we know in part . . . , we now look through a glass darkly" (cf. 1 Cor. 13:8b, 9, 12a). All things to the human mind are so shaded and so fuzzy, so unclear in outline and finality. But in Christ we have all of the answers. God has blessed us with all spiritual blessings in the heavenlies, in Christ.

Our lives ought to display these blessings. Whether we suffer, whether we are sick, whether we are in agony, whether we are discouraged because of others, whatever, the Christian is to be up, singing songs in the night. He is to be happy in the Lord.

I have read works from Christian psychologists who avow that the martyrs felt no pain when they were burned at the stake because of the glory in their dying for Jesus. Think of that! Thomas Cranmer, first Protestant Archbishop of Canterbury, was burned at the stake at Oxford. As he was martyred he put forth his right hand and held it in the flame and watched it burn to a crisp. He was so exalted in the Lord that he apparently felt no pain. The Christian is forever triumphant. If Paul and Silas are beaten and thrust into a dungeon, at midnight they are singing praises to God. That is what it is to be in Christ. It is to be in the heavenlies, blessed with all of the blessings of God. As Clement of Alexandria said, "He has turned all our sunsets into sunrise."

Chapter 3

THE DOCTRINE OF PREDESTINATION

According as he hath chosen us in him before the foundation of the world, that we should be holy and without blame before him in love:

Having predestinated us unto the adoption of children by Jesus Christ to himself, according to the good pleasure of his will,

In whom also we have obtained an inheritance, being predestinated according to the purpose of him who worketh all things after the counsel of his own will (Eph. 1:4, 5, 11)

According to the eternal purpose which he purposed in Christ Jesus our Lord. (Eph. 3:11)

We have a tendency to back away from the word "predestination," to hesitate before the word "election," but not so with God, and not so with the Word of God. They are words much used. It is a revelation much employed and it is a truth of God, functional, on which this earth stands and by which the kingdom of God abides forever.

All of us are introduced to this teaching, though sometimes we do not recognize it. It is a part of our everyday life. Not that we can explain it; we cannot explain anything. All we can do is observe. The great mysteries of life are to us inexplicable and unfathomable.

We are conscious in our lives of freedom of choice. One can put his hand up or he can choose to put it down. But at the same time we are also no less conscious that there are choices in which our lives are inexplicably involved that are over, above, and beyond us. Why was I not born one hundred years ago? Why am

I not a Hottentot? Who chose the color of my eyes? My whole life is bound up and enmeshed with a plan, a purpose, and a choice into which I do not enter at all. Freedom of choice belongs to moral accountability — I am morally responsible. But there is also a sovereignty in this world above my life, above history, and above all of the story of creation and mankind. Those two things, the sovereignty of God and the free moral agency of man, are two lines of development that we cannot reconcile. We only observe them. Charles Haddon Spurgeon said of those two lines, "I cannot make them meet, but you cannot make them cross."

John A. Broadus said that to look at the sovereignty of God and the free moral agency of man is like a man looking at a house. You can never see more than half of it at a time. I can stand and see two corners, but I cannot see the other two. I can walk around the house and see two sides at a time but two are hidden from me. I cannot see all four sides of the house at the same time. But someone above me could look down on that house and see all four sides at once. So it is with us. We cannot see but alternately one half of the house at a time. But the Creator who presides above us can see all of it at once.

The philosopher — theologian, Edgar Young Mullins, said that the problems of the freedom of man and the sovereignty of God have been problems that philosophers have wrestled with from the beginning of intelligence, but no philosopher yet has ever risen who can reconcile them. It is a mystery into which we cannot enter. Like everything else that God does, it is a mystery we cannot explain. But we can observe it, know it, and see it. The foundational fact in human life and in human history is that God is, that God rules, and that God is sovereign. It is a part of the perfection of God that He should have a purpose and a plan. The more the magnitude of the project, the more the necessity that there be a plan to be followed in it. The more the artist is a fine artist, or the architect is a fine architect, the more he will be sensitive to the necessity and to the use of purpose and plan.

Before a stone was laid in the construction of St. Paul's Cathedral in London, the idea was born in the mind of Sir Christopher Wren. He saw it in his mind and he purposed it in his heart. Before he struck a chisel against the heavy rock of marble, Michaelangelo saw the mighty Moses in his mind and purposed it in his heart. Before there was a stroke of the brush against the canvas, the dedicated young artist, Raphael, saw the spectacular picture of the Sistine Madonna in his mind.

It is thus in the perfection of God. It belongs to God that He has in His heart and mind a plan and purpose that lies back of the work that He has done and is doing in the universe and in human life. This revelation of the God of purpose, of planning, of activity, of expression is found all through the Word. Not just adventitiously or inadvertently; it is woven into the very apocalypse, the very revelation of God in ways that many times we do not realize.

For example, the gospel of John begins with these sentences: "In the beginning was the Word, and the Word was with God, and the Word was God. The same was in the beginning with God." What is the meaning of that? In the beginning was the *logos*, the Greek word for "word." Philo used the word *logos*, "word," in a technical sense to refer to the God of expression, the God of activity, the God who acts, the God who moves, the God who purposes, the God who plans and does, the God who executes. Under inspiration John the sainted apostle took that philosophical Greek word and applied it to Jesus. "In the beginning was the *logos*, and the *logos* . . . was God. The same was in the beginning with God." In the beginning there was purpose, activity, planning, and expression in God. What we see in this universe is the expression and activity of God. This is the plan and purpose of God and we are an inexplicable part of it.

PREDESTINATION IS FOUND THROUGHOUT THE BIBLE

In keeping with the revelation in God's Book, one will find God's purpose and plan all through the Bible. For example, in Galatians 4 Paul says, "When the fulness of the time was come, God sent forth his Son, made of a woman, made under the law." "In the fulness of time"; that is, God directed and purposed all history toward that exact moment when it should happen. John says, "The word, the *logos*, was made flesh." Before God was manifested in human life, God moved toward that end, and guided the entire civilization toward that one point.

We can observe some of the movements of God as we look at what God did through the centuries and the millennia in preparation for the coming of Christ. When that moment came, and the Word was made flesh, there was one language. The entire civilized world spoke Greek. At that time God moved in human history to create one universal empire. (Daniel said there would never be another.) The empire witnessed the building of Roman roads everywhere. There was Roman law everywhere. There was the Pax Romano, universal peace, everywhere. God was moving in human history. Religiously, in every city and in every part of the country there was a synagogue. The law of Moses in the Old Testament was known and preached. Toward the fullness of time God was working through human history to bring to pass the divine plans that were in His heart.

This working out of the sovereign purpose of God is mentioned so many times in Holy Scripture. For example, in Revelation 13 the Lamb is referred to as "the lamb slain from the foundation of the world" (v. 8). In 1 Peter 1 the apostle refers to the lamb who was foreordained and offered for us before the foundation of the world (vv. 18-20). The sacrifice of Christ our Lord was in the mind and heart of God before a star was flung into orbit or before this world was created.

A man may as well stack bricks to try to stay the Noahic flood, or try to turn the stars from their courses in their orbits as to try to interdict the sovereign will of God. That is predestination. That is election. That is the foundational truth of the Almighty God of human history. This is the world in which we live. The purpose and plan of God can never be finally or ultimately interdicted, never. Age or the passing of time are as nothing to God, for yesterday is as today, and today is as tomorrow, and a thousand years in His sight are no more than a watch in the night. Time and age do not waste away God's purpose or God's plan.

The Lord said to Abraham when he was a young man and to Sarah when she was a young woman, "Out of your loins shall he be born, the seed who shall be a blessing to all the families of the earth." But the days passed and they multiplied into years and yet no heir was born. In Genesis 15 Abraham went before the Lord and said, "Lord, the days are passing, the years are multiplying and there is no heir in my house. This Eliezer, a servant from Damascus, will inherit all my possessions. There is no fulfillment of the promise." And the Lord took Abraham out under the chalice of the sky and said, "Count the stars." Abraham said, "I cannot." And God said, "Neither will you be able to count the

The Doctrine of Predestination

nations and the people and the families that shall be born out of the seed that shall come out of your loins."

The days passed and the years multiplied and Sarah lost faith in God and said to Abraham, "Take Haggar, my maidservant, and have a child by her." So Ishmael was born. When Ishmael became a boy about twelve years of age, God renewed His promise, but Abraham bowed before the Lord and said, "Oh, that Ishmael might stand before Thee, that he might be the heir, the seed." God said: "No. Out of your loins and out of the womb of Sarah shall he be born, as I have faithfully promised in the years gone by." The days multiplied and the years passed by. Abraham is one hundred years old and Sarah is ninety years old. An angel messenger comes and says, "According to the time of life you should have a child." Sarah laughed: "My Lord is a century old and is as good as dead. I am ninety years old." And the angel said, "Sarah, you laughed." Sarah said, "My Lord, I did not laugh." The angel messenger said: "I heard you laugh. But is anything too hard for God?" And according to the time of life God laid in her arms a little boy and she called him "laughter," Isaac, because she laughed. God does not change nor is He hindered in His purpose.

When Pharaoh ordered that every male child born to the Hebrews should be drowned in the river, he did not know that five hundred years before he was born God had revealed to Abraham that the children should go through the fiery furnace in the land of Egypt. God the Almighty is never taken by surprise.

DEATH DOES NOT INTERDICT IT

Death does not interdict the sovereign, elective purpose of God. In Hebrews 2 we read that Satan has the power of death and from the beginning has been seeking to slay the righteous seed. He remembered that God said it would be the seed of the woman that should bruise and crush his head. Therefore, from the beginning Satan, who has the power of death, has sought to destroy that seed by death. He slew Abel, thinking he was the seed. He slew him through Cain. Centuries later Satan sought through Pharaoh to drown the righteous seed. Later, Satan tried again. In the 2 Chronicles 22 is recorded the story of Athaliah who was the daughter of Jezebel and Ahab. Because God had said that the seed should be in the line and lineage of David, Satan, moving through Athaliah, slew every male child in the family of David. But a nurse hid away a little baby called Joash, unknown to Athaliah, and this baby lived to be king. Centuries later Satan tried again. In the days of the coming of the Prince of Peace at Bethlehem, bloody Herod sought to slay all of the children two years of age and under. Finally, in the day of the cross Satan succeeded. He nailed the Son of God to a tree. In mind's imagination (and it is only in my imagination) I can see Satan and every demon in hell as they rejoice. They had slain the Son of God. They had done it through Israel's own hand. But a thousand years before, God, by His servant David, had written that His Christ would not see the corruption of death. God raised Him up from the dead for our justification to declare us righteous.

There could be no ultimate interdiction of the will of God. There can be no deviation. There can be no destruction of the purpose and plan of God for His people and for the world in which we live. That is the comforting truth in which God's people are ever to rejoice. Blind unbelief looks at the opposition of evil. But faith looks at the infallible faithfulness of Almighty God. Blind unbelief will look at the shifting sand of daily history, but faith looks at the immutable and unchanging Word of God. "Forever, O God, thy word is fixed in heaven."

The brothers may sell Joseph to the Ishmaelites; the Ishmaelites may sell Joseph to Potiphar; Potiphar may put him in a dungeon; but God says that he shall rule the nation. Nebuchadnezzar may come and destroy the nation of Israel, tear up the city and carry the people into captivity, but one hundred fifty years before Nebuchadnezzar was born and seven hundred fifty years before Christ was born, God called Cyrus by name and said that in the days of his Persian kingdom the wall of Jerusalem would be rebuilt and the temple would be remade.

Judas may sell the Lord for thirty pieces of silver; the captains of the guard may turn our Lord over to the chief priest; and the chief priest may turn Him over to Pontius Pilate; Pilate may turn Him over to a quaternion of legionnaires; the Roman soldiers may nail Him to the cross and you see Him die; but God says that this is the Saviour of the world. This is the fountain that cleanses from sin. This is the King of glory before whom every knee shall bow. The sovereign, immutable purposes of God—that is predestination. That is the election of the Almighty.

GOD'S ELECTIVE WILL AS I HAVE SEEN IT

The hand of God in history is upon us. I can remember World War I. I was pastor in the days of World War II. Listening on the radio and reading the newspaper, the entire free world and especially the Christian world was plunged into despair. A dictator arose in fascist Italy. A companion dictator arose in Nazi Germany. There was an emperor who was worshiped as a god across the sea in Japan. When Nazi Germany made a treaty with Stalinist Russia the whole world was plunged into impenetrable darkness and hopelessness. As one English statesman said, "The lights of the world are going out, out, out." Yet, in faith, and in commitment, we saw our people rise, rise, rise. I lived to see the day when the dictator in Italy, Benito Mussolini, was hung up by his heels like a slaughtered pig by the side of his brazen paramour. I lived to see the time when Hitler committed suicide in a bunker, underground. I walked in destroyed East Berlin to visit the place. For years, and it may still be that way, it was a vacant and empty area with a barbed wire fence around it, an unholy, desecrated site. Across the Pacific Ocean I lived to see the day and walked in front of the palace wall where the emperor walked out before the Japanese people and said: "I am no god. I am just another Japanese."

Who would have thought it? The moving hand of God in human history! Today, fear sometimes grips our soul and despair sometimes breaks our hearts. Surely the kingdom will be grounded in atheism, communism, and covered with a floodtide of iniquity. There is no hope for the future. There would not be except for the God of purpose, plan, election, and predestination. "Be of good cheer, little flock," Jesus said, "it is my Father's will that you should inherit the kingdom." "Be of good cheer," said our Lord again, "in the world ye shall have tribulation, trials, but I have overcome the world." Little flock, God's purpose is that we shall inherit the earth. That is predestination. That is election and that is the foundational fact upon which this earth stands and civilization moves.

Just let me speak personally of God's elective purpose. There were times and there were days when as a lad growing up I felt God had forgotten me, had left me out of the largest and most bountiful of His gifts and blessings. I belonged to a poor family. We had no car, no running water. As the days passed I was introduced to other boys and girls, many of them in affluent homes, and I could not understand why God was not good to me. As I look back over those days, the best thing God ever did for me was to let me grow up in a poor home. I thank Him for it.

When I began to preach, my first churches for many years were in the country. I would see young men with whom I went to school, called to famed pulpits and high-steepled churches. I was left out in the country. I used to wonder if God had forgotten where I was, if God even remembered my name. But as I look back over it now, my years in rural churches was the best thing God ever did for me as a preacher.

Romans 8:28 says, "In all things God works together for good to them that love God, to them who are the called according to his purpose." That is predestination. That is election.

> God moves in a mysterious way
> His wonders to perform;
> He plants His footsteps in the sea
> And rides upon the storm.
>
> His purposes will ripen fast,
> Unfolding every hour;
> The bud may have a bitter taste,
> But sweet will be the flower.
>
> Blind unbelief is sure to err
> And scan His work in vain.
> God is His own Interpreter
> And He will make it plain.

Back of your life, back of human history, and back of the whole universe in which we live is the sovereign purpose and will of God who guides us toward the ultimate and final consummation when we as joint-heirs with our Lord shall inherit the kingdom. Comforting and triumphant, it is victorious. We cannot lose!

Chapter 4

OUR ACCEPTANCE BEFORE GOD

Blessed be the God and Father of our Lord Jesus Christ, who hath blessed us with all spiritual blessings in heavenly places in Christ:

According as he hath chosen us in him before the foundation of the world, that we should be holy and without blame before him in love:

Having predestinated us unto the adoption of children by Jesus Christ to himself, according to the good pleasure of his will,

To the praise of the glory of his grace, wherein he hath made us accepted in the beloved.

In whom we have redemption through his blood, the forgiveness of sins, according to the riches of his grace;

Wherein he hath abounded toward us in all wisdom and prudence. (Eph. 1:3-8)

Our text reads, "Having predestinated us unto the adoption of children by Jesus Christ to himself, according to the good pleasure of his will" (Eph. 1:5). By nature we are alienated from God. We are dead in trespasses and in sins. We do not belong to the family of God by natural birth. We failed in our first parents and the repercussion of that sin is felt and experienced in all of our lives. The story of the fall of Adam and Eve is not just a story which we read in the first chapter of Genesis, but it is a story which all of us experience in our hearts. We are alienated from God. Being children of wrath and condemnation, we shall never be able to see the face of God by human nature or moral righteousness. There is a separation, an alienation, between us and God — sin. But we become children of God by adoption, by being born a second time. "He came unto his own, and his own received him not. But as many received him, to them gave he power [the privilege, the prerogative] to become the sons of God, even to them that believe on his name" (John 1:11, 12). We are adopted into the family of God through Jesus Christ when we open our hearts to the Lord and accept Jesus as our Saviour. He gives us the power, the right, the privilege to become the children of God. We are thereupon adopted into God's family.

ADOPTION

I am told that by law if one adopts a child, he can never disinherit the child. It is his child forever. I would suppose that law would exist because a family might adopt a child, become disgusted with him, disinherit him, then maybe want him back again, adopt him again, and then disinherit him again, and so on. Such a procedure is facetious, and it is no less so in the Bible with regard to our relationship with God. It is a fanciful doctrine when one believes that one can be a member of the family of God, and then not a member of the family of God, then come back and be a member of the family of God, and then not be a member of the family of God. It is a facetious teaching that one can be saved, and then unsaved, and then saved, and then unsaved, and so on. There is no such suggestion of anything like that in the Bible. God's Word says that when we are saved, God gives us everlasting life. If you have ever been born again, if you have ever been saved, you are saved forever. There is a new heart and a new life. There is a new love. There is a new creation in you and you never get away from it. God's seed remains in you. That forever salvation is illustrated precisely in this doctrine of adoption. When we are adopted into the family of God, we are adopted forever.

God purposes for us a far greater gift than that we should be sons of God just by creation. God purposes some finer thing for us, even though our first parents fell, and even though we have fallen. The Lord's purpose for us is that we shall be joint heirs with Christ. Whatever the Son of God possesses, we are to possess. We are to sit with Him on His throne. His great riches, all that God has, are ours. Every grace, every mercy, every gift, every possession, every reward, every authority, every rule over principalities and powers, things present, things to come, height, depth, everything is ours. That is the purpose of God. He does this not because we are meritorious or worthy, but He does it because it is the good pleasure of His will to do it. It is not because of anything that we do or any worth that we possess that God bestows upon us such incomparable riches and such marvelous blessings, but we are adopted children of God through Jesus Christ according to the good pleasure of His will.

Sometimes when I think of where I have been and the people I have seen, my heart overflows with unspeakable, abounding gratitude for the mercies of God toward me. I could have been born in a Muslim home. I could have been a Mohammedan, brought up worshiping Allah and Mohammed, his prophet. Why was not I born in a Mohammedan home and why was I not raised a Muslim? Why am I not a son of Islam? Why am I not trying to make that lifetime pilgrimage toward Mecca? I thank God for His good grace extended toward me according to the good pleasure of His will. I was not born in a Muslim home; instead, God put me in a Christian home.

Why was I not born in the heart of Africa living all my life on a dirt floor under a thatched roof, worshiping animistic gods, gods of trees, rocks, and stones? I have walked in the heart of Africa and seen blood on a tree, or on a stone, or on a rock, or on a stick. I asked the missionaries, "Why is this blood?" They replied, "Someone offered chickens and other animals to the animistic spirits that live in the rocks, trees, and stones." Why was I not born on one of those dirt floors and why was I not raised in an animistic religion? The grace of God was extended toward me, thus to place me in a Christian home.

I think of the homes in America and of the ungodliness of so much of life in America. But I was born in a Christian home, in a godly home. The Lord's Day to us was a day of worship, Wednesday was a prayer meeting night. Thursday was a choir practice night for us, and I used to attend when I was a little boy because my father took me with him and I loved to hear the people sing. I have ten thousand precious memories as a child, growing up in the heart of the church. Why was I not born in a godless and worldly home in America, and why was I not brought up with all those diabolic attitudes toward God and God's people and toward God's holy day? It was due to God's mercy that I was born in a Christian home and brought up in the love and nurture of the Lord. He adopted us into the family of God and made us joint heirs and brothers with Jesus Christ according to the nature of His will.

That is why when we get to heaven we shall sing praises to Christ alone. No one of us will brag, "Look at how far I have come; I have even climbed up here to heaven!" There is not going to be any suggestion of an approach to a doxology like that. When we get to heaven, the praise and the glory will be to Him who loved us and washed us from our sins in His own blood. It is He who has made us kings and priests to God His Father. To Him be riches and honor and dominion and glory and power and strength forever and ever, Amen and Amen. Jesus paid it all. That is what we are going to sing when we get to glory. That is what we ought to be singing here.

Redeemed

Adopted, placed in the family of God, according to the good pleasure of His will, to the praise of His glory and grace, "in whom we have redemption through his blood" (Eph. 1:7). That is what the Bible is about, and that is what the life of our Lord is about. He came to die for us, to redeem us through His own blood. "This is my blood of the new covenant shed for the remission of sins." The theme of the Old Testament and the theme of the New Testament is that Christ came into this world to die for our sins. All of those typologies, those old sacrifices of the ancient ritual, and all of the ancient prophecies were pointing to the coming of Jesus our Saviour. The story of the life of our Lord, along with His miracles and His parables, illustrate that grace and love. The epistles of the New Testament expatiate upon it and expound it. The glorious Revelation is the consummation of our praise to God forever because of what Jesus has done for us. The theme of the whole Bible is Jesus coming to die for our sin, or Jesus here to die for our sin, or Jesus in eternity being praised because He redeemed us from our sin.

One year when New Year's Eve fell on a Sunday night I started at 7:30 and preached past midnight, preaching through the entire Bible. The title of the sermon was, "The Scarlet Thread Through the Bible." From the shedding of blood of an innocent animal in the Garden of Eden to clothe the nakedness of our father and mother, even to the Revelation, where we see those who washed their robes and made them white in the blood of the Lamb, the whole theme and story of the Bible is Jesus dying for our sins according to the Scripture, and Jesus raised for our justification; that is, to declare us righteous according to the Scriptures.

How does the cross of Christ save us? We are certainly redeemed through His blood, but how does the suffering of Jesus purge us from sin? How does the blood of Christ wash the stain of sin out of our souls? How are we saved in the blood of Christ? In my doctoral work I had a major and two minors. One of those minors concerned the theories of the atonement, how the cross of Christ saves us. After faithfully studying the atonement for two years and after I came to the conclusion of the study and passed a doctor's examination concerning it, I hardly knew any more about the doctrine than when I first started. The theories of the atonement change from age to age and generation to generation. Some of those theories are technical and artificial. Some of them are positively grotesque. Some of them are intellectually incredible. How does the blood of Christ save us? In my humble judgment it is a divine wisdom inaccessible to human understanding. One cannot enter into it. It is beyond our comprehension. All we can do is just see the results of it, what the death of Christ does for us. One can see the effects of it in human life.

For example, the effect of the atoning grace of Jesus will correspond to the effect of a slave who has been ransomed and set free. Therefore, some of the theories of the atonement will refer to Jesus as a ransom for our sins. Our Lord thus spoke of it Himself. "The Son of man came not to be ministered unto, but to minister, and to give his life a ransom for many" (Mark 10:45).

Again, the effect of the atoning love of Jesus corresponds to the effect of a God who was angry and His anger has been turned to favor. So we refer to the atonement of Christ as a propitiation, a rendering favorable. God is made favorable toward us in the death of Christ.

Sometimes one can look at the effect of the atonement of Christ and that effect will correspond to the effect of a worshiper who has been excluded from the temple because of his sin, and he brings a sacrifice for expiatory purposes. The effect of the atonement is then described as an expiation. It is a taking away, an "at-one-ment" with God concerning our sins.

Sometimes the effect of the death of Christ will correspond to the effect of one who has been separated. There is an abyss between, and a reconciliation is effected. They will speak of the atoning death of Christ as an instrument of reconciliation. In the death of the Lord we are reconciled to God. God is reconciled to us in the death of Christ as an instrument of reconciliation.

One could spend hours and days speaking of the grace and the mercy of Jesus and its effect upon us. Propitiation, expiation, atonement, reconciliation, ransom — whatever it is, we will never understand it and we will never be able fully to describe it. All we can do is just look upon the marvelous, incomparable results of the atoning grace of God in Christ Jesus, and see that they are legion. The effect of the preaching of the cross of Christ, the effect of the atoning grace, love, and mercy of God in Christ Jesus is manifold. I will not belabor the point, but for us to get into the feeling of it, I might cite some of the things that all of us read and experience.

George Whitefield was one of the preachers out of Oxford who was denied the pulpits of England and therefore preached outside in the Commons or on a riverbank. One day when George Whitefield came to preach at Exeter in southwest England, a ruffian came there whose pockets were filled with rocks. He was going to break up the meeting. He stood there and began listening to George Whitefield. He said, "I don't want to throw these rocks at him in the prayer so I'll wait until the prayer is over." Then Mr. Whitefield read his text. The ruffian said: "I'm not going to throw these rocks at him while he is reading the Bible. I'll wait until the text is read." And when he had read the text, George Whitefield began to launch into his message about the grace of God in Christ Jesus. The ruffian never threw the rocks. After the message was over, he made his way to the preacher and said, "I've come here with my pockets full of rocks to break up this meeting but instead God has broken up my heart." The man was saved, gloriously converted right there on the spot. That is the effect of the preaching of the Gospel of the grace of God in Christ Jesus.

T. DeWitt Talmadge was one of the most unique preachers of American history. He described one day how his family became Christians. He said his grandparents went to hear Charles G. Finney preach, were wonderfully converted, and came back home seeking to win their children to Jesus. The children smiled. We say today that there is a generation gap. There has always been a generation gap. Their children smiled and went off to a party. As they left the house the mother said, "I'm going to stay on my knees, praying for your salvation until you come back." When they came back, there was that dear mother, who had found the Lord, down on her knees, praying for those children. The next day they heard the daughter weeping in her room. They went upstairs, opened the door, and there she was under deep conviction. She said, "One of my brothers is in the barn, and one is in the wagon shed, both under deep conviction." They went out to the barn and there was Elijah Talmadge, who later became a preacher, bowed down before God. They went to the wagon shed and there was David, the father of T. DeWitt Talmadge, under great conviction from God. The entire family was saved. They lived in a little village, and word soon spread of the marvelous grace of God upon the Talmadge family. When Sunday came for services in the church, there were more than two hundred people that Sunday who accepted Jesus as their Saviour. The effects of atonement are incomparable. They are indescribable. They are beyond what tongue, pen, poem, or song could ever tell.

Look in your own life and look all around you and you will see the effects of the preaching of the Gospel of the Son of God. Whatever your explanation or theory of the Atonement, it will never encompass it, or explain it. The atonement is something that partakes of the very infinitude of the presence, character, love and grace of Almighty God Himself. Is not this a glorious Gospel we preach?

Forgiven

Finally, there is "the forgiveness of sins, according to the riches of his grace" (Eph. 1:7). There are three ways to that forgiveness of sins. All of us come before the Lord asking God to forgive us our sins. Most of our prayers will close like that — "forgive us our sins." There are three ways in which God forgives our sins.

First, there is personal forgiveness, a cessation of the moral indignation and righteous resentment of God because of our personal sin. Second, there is ethical forgiveness, the alleviation of the awful burden and oppression of guilt in our lives and on our souls. And third, there is legal forgiveness, the commutation of the sentence of judgment and damnation and death.

Personal Forgiveness

God is a Person. You are a person; you can feel, you can love, you can be angry, you can be grieved, you can be hurt. All of those personal attributes are in God and in Christ. "And he . . . looked round about on [the crowd] with anger," the Scriptures say of our Lord (Mark 3:5). Or He picked up cords and made a whip out of them and drove the money-changers out of the Temple (John 2:15). Or He denounced the Pharisees for their hypocrisy and covetous unrighteousness (Matt. 23). All of these things which you feel, God feels.

When the prodigal came back having wasted his life and his substance in riotous living, the father could have refused to forgive him. He could have been like the elder brother: "Now you have chosen your way. Having made your bed, you can lie in it. We do not want to see your face, we do not want to hear your name; we buried you. We have had your funeral and want you out of our sight." The father could have done that and God could do that with us, but the sweet story of the parable of the prodigal son is that when the boy came to himself in humility and repentance and bowed before his father, the father said: "Why, raise him up and put shoes on his bare feet and take off those old, dirty, tattered garments and put a robe around his shoulders and put a ring on his finger. Kill the fatted calf and rejoice! For this my son was dead and is alive again; he was lost and is found!" That is personal forgiveness, and that is God's way with us. However we have wronged Him, and whatever we have done, when we come back home God rejoices and accepts and forgives us. That is personal forgiveness.

Ethical Forgiveness

Do you remember how John Bunyan begins his *Pilgrim's Progress?* We see Pilgrim with his back to his house. As he stands in rags he is reading a book, the Bible. As he reads he weeps because the Holy Scriptures describe to him his lost estate. He has a great burden on his back, the weight of his sins. All of us know what that is. That is the sense of wrong and guilt, the drag of human sin. As Pilgrim progresses, the burden rolls away at the cross. We sing songs that describe that experience:

At the cross, at the cross,
Where I first saw the light
And the burden of my heart rolled away.

That is the ethical side of forgiveness. God takes away the burden of the guilt of our sins.

Legal Forgiveness

Because we have sinned and wronged God, we deserve all of those judgments that fall upon us. But God blots them out — and not just some of them but all of them. You can rest assured that when Noah's flood covered the highest mountains, it also covered all the little molehills. That is what God has done with our sins. He has covered them. The word for "atonement" means "covering." Jesus paid for our sins. We are not going to die. Jesus died in our stead. And all that awaits us now is some coronation day, when we close our eyes upon this world of death and open our eyes in Glory.

Chapter 5

THE PURPOSE OF GOD FOR THE WORLD

> Having made known unto us the mystery of his will, according to his good pleasure which he hath purposed in himself:
>
> That is the dispensation of the fulness of times he might gather together in one all things in Christ, both which are in heaven, and which are on earth; even in him:
>
> In whom also we have obtained an inheritance, being predestinated according to the purpose of him who worketh all things after the counsel of his own will:
>
> That we should be to the praise of his glory, who first trusted in Christ.
>
> In whom ye also trusted, after that ye heard the word of truth, the gospel of your salvation: in whom also after that ye believed, ye were sealed with that holy Spirit of promise,
>
> Which is the earnest of our inheritance until the redemption of the purchased possession, unto the praise of his glory. (Eph. 1:9-14)

First, we shall exegete some of the words in these verses. "Having made known unto us the mystery, the *musterion*...." A *musterion* is a secret hid in the heart of God until the day comes for Him to reveal it.

"That in the dispensation, the *oikonomia*...." An *oikon* is a house, an *oikonomos* is the manager of the house. The word can be translated "steward." An *oikonomia* is the "management" of the house. God's management of the universe is the *oikonomia*.

The next word that we are going to exegete is *anakephalaiosasthai*, translated here, "gather together." Literally it means "to head up." The Greek word *kephale* is "head." The Greek word *ana* is "up." Place them together and they mean "to head up." In the *oikonomia*, in God's management of the times, it is

His purpose to gather together in one, to head up everything in Christ.

THE MYSTERY OF GOD'S PURPOSE

"Having made known unto us the *musterion*. . . ." The secret hidden in the heart of God until the time came for Him to reveal it is this: namely, that all things are to head up in Christ. This is the revelation that was not made to the prophets in the Old Testament, nor was it revealed to the former saints, the generations that had preceded. It was the secret that God kept in His heart; namely, His great intention, in this universe — to make our Lord Christ the head of all things.

There is the greatest division imaginable today in present philosophy. There are two ways one can believe. First, one can be an existentialist, a philosopher of despair. This philosophy has overwhelmed this present world. Existentialists believe that there is no meaning and no purpose back of what one sees in life, in creation, or in the universe. Life is without goal, reason, or purpose. That is modern philosophy — that there is no meaning or purpose in life and that there is no goal toward which human history is moving.

But there is another philosophy, the one which is inspired and revealed by God. There is a purpose which lies back of all that one sees in creation and in human life. That purpose was a *musterion*, a secret hid in the heart of God until the day came for the Lord to reveal it to his apostles. The revelation of that *musterion* did not come to pass before Paul's day. It was not hidden because of any unforeseen development in human history or in creation, but it was a purpose that God hid in His heart and mind from the beginning. It is not changed nor has anything developed that has altered it or impeded it; rather, it is a purpose that has been dominant in the heart of God from the beginning of creation. There is a purpose in the will of God for the whole course of history in which our lives are inexorably bound, and there is a great consummation and goal toward which all time and tide inevitably move.

THE MANAGEMENT OF GOD'S PURPOSE

Paul now defines and describes the mystery of God's will and purpose. In the *oikonomia*, in God's management, He will gather together in one, in Christ, all things.

Paul says that the great goal toward which time, life, and creation move is in the hands of almighty God. This is a management, a stewardship which God possesses. Some of this we can see and some of it we hope for. Some of this dispensation of the fullness of time we can see: this *oikonomia* guides and sustains through all of history. We can see the management of God in the preparation of this world for habitation. Wind, fire, smoke, vapor, snow, ice, and rain all have had their part in preparing this world through the ages for human habitation, all under the directed sovereignty, the *oikonomia* of God. It took millions of God's little creatures to make the limestone rock and the coral reefs. It took millions of God's ferns and forests to make the beds of coal and the pools of oil. It took volcanic eruptions, the glacial ages, and the alluvial deposits of the rivers to make the rich valleys that feed God's people. Geologists sometimes seemingly overwhelm us by putting a billion years here and five trillion years there, but that is a part of the management of God through the ages, preparing this earth for human habitation.

Now we can see that same thing, the *oikonomia*, in the preparation of the world for Christ. First, there were hints and adumbrations and faint echos. As the days passed and the years multiplied, these adumbrations became clearer and more vivid. As the days multiplied the Lord began to teach us the language of heaven that we might understand His revelation. There is a visible temple, there is a human priesthood, there are rites and rituals and ceremonies. In them we are learning what an "altar" is, what a "sacrifice" is, what "propitiation" is, what "atonement" is, and what "expiation" is. We are being taught the language of heaven.

Then the prophets arise. As the days pass, their prophecies become clearer, more specific, and finally, to the smallest detail, they outline the coming of the great King and Lord. As the days pass a family is chosen, a tribe is chosen, and a king and kingdom are chosen. And one day a forerunner's path crosses the history of God's revelation and he lifts up his voice and his hand and says, "Behold!" and the Lamb of God, the Saviour, is introduced to the world!

This is the *oikonomia,* the getting of the world ready for the coming of Christ. The world is prepared with a language, with a law, with a universal civilization all under one government, and with a Bible known and read in every city and hamlet.

The Purpose of God for the World

We stand in the midst of that *oikonomia*. Has God's purpose stopped? Been thwarted? Perverted? Is this all, what we now see and experience? Generations have gone before us and yet the great goal of the kingdom and the consummation is not reached. We groan; we are a perishing people. As Paul writes in Romans 8: "For we know that the whole creation groaneth and travaileth in pain together until now. And not only they [the earth tormented by tornadoes and hurricanes, the deserts that blot the landscape, the winds, the cold, the storms, that afflict the earth; the cattle, moaning in calving, and the trees that are imperfect, and the fruit that is not ripened; all give evidence that the world is cursed as it groans and travails], but ourselves also, which have the first fruits of the Spirit, even we ourselves groan within ourselves, waiting for the adoption, to wit, the redemption of our body" (Rom. 8:22, 23). Paul avows in Ephesians that the redemption of the whole purchased possession is yet beyond. We are still in these ages, these millennia of years of suffering and trial, of heartache and disappointment, age and senility and finally death.

That is where we stand now in the *oikonomia* of God. It is like the opening of the fifth seal in Revelation 6: "And they cried with a loud voice, saying, How long, O Lord?" And God replied, "Yet for a little season" (vv. 10, 11). So it is with us in the great sweep of God's hand through human history and the reaching out toward that ultimate consummation. We must wait, we must trust, we must believe. God's purposes will not fail. There may have been generations before us in sorrow and trial, and there may yet be generations to follow us who know nothing but sorrow, tears, and death, but the promise of God will surely come, and the King will suddenly some day appear.

Do you remember how the Book of Genesis closes? Joseph is one hundred ten years old and the time has come for him to die. He calls the elders of the children of Israel to come around him and makes them swear an oath that they will bring his bones, his embalmed body, out of Egypt into the Promised Land. "And Joseph said unto his brethren, I die: and God will surely visit you, and bring you out of this land unto the land which he sware to Abraham, to Isaac, and to Jacob. And Joseph took an oath of the children of Israel, saying, God will surely visit you, and ye shall carry up my bones from hence. So Joseph died, being an hundred and ten years old: and they embalmed him, and he was put in a coffin in Egypt" (Gen. 50:24-26). A hundred years passed and there was no keeping of God's promise. Yet Joseph had said, "God will surely visit you." Two hundred years passed, and three hundred. Three hundred ninety-five years passed. Still there was no evidence of God's visitation. But at the end of four hundred years, according to the Word of God to Abraham, His friend and servant, God appeared to Moses on the backside of the desert in a bush that burned unconsumed, and He sent Moses down to deliver His people.

The promise may be long and delayed but it will surely come. For the universe, the whole world, and the flow of human history are in the *oikonomia* of God.

God's Purpose Revealed in Christ

The purposes of God for His world, for us, and for His universe are three that are listed here in this passage in Ephesians. First, it is the purpose of God (not a late development but in the heart of God from the beginning) that all things shall find their meaning and their reason and their purpose for being in Christ. Paul says that all the things are to find their ultimate place and meaning in Christ. Outside of our Lord there shall be no meaning to existence. All outside Christ shall perish. All existence that continues shall find its meaning in the Lord Christ. Outside of Him there will be no life and no purpose for being.

Whatever is outside Christ is to be like the chaff. The chaff is burned with fire. Whatever is in Christ is to be like the wheat. We belong to Christ and as such we are the bread that represents His body. It is the same thing as when the Lord talked about the vine and the branches. The branches that are not in the vine shall wither, die, and shall be burned. All things that are not in Christ shall perish.

It is the same thing as the Lord said in Matthew 16:18 concerning His church. "Upon this rock (that is, on the great foundation of Peter's confession of the deity of the Son of God) I will build my church: and the gates of hell shall not prevail (*katischuo*, be able to hold it down) against it." That verse is erroneously interpreted when we say that the gates of hell are going to storm the kingdom of God but the attack will not be able to overcome the church. I do not know where such an interpretation came from, but it seems to be universal. The interpretation has been repeated

The Purpose of God for the World 49

ten thousand times. But gates do not attack. What Jesus said is that the power of Hades will not be able to hold down, imprison, His church.

The gates of Hades are the gates of death. Hades refers to the region of death. Death has been universal since the days of our fallen parents, and the gates of death seem to prevail. We have seen people whom we love fall into that awful abyss. Everything in human life is dissolved in death. When I marry a couple, the phrase is repeated, "until death do you part." The marriage vow and the marriage home is dissolved in death. There is no marriage in heaven. We are to be like the angels in heaven. Christ is saying this, "The only relationships that abide, that sustain beyond the grave and beyond death, are those that are made in Me." Outside of Him there is no life and there is no existence. Outside of Christ there is nothing but the fire, the worm, and the second death. The horror and terror of what it means to be cut off from God I am unable to enter into. The vivid imagery by which it is described in the Bible is a horrible thing to contemplate. Outside of Christ there is no life, there is no hope, and there is no presence of God.

This is the purpose of God: Whatever He cannot sum up in Christ is to be taken away, it is to be burned, it is to die. Lord, our existence and our life, our hope and our future are in Thee alone.

What is the purpose of God? It is, first, that all things that continue shall find their meaning in Jesus our Lord. All things are to be summed up under the sovereignty of Christ.

The Purpose of God for Us

The second purpose of God that is written in the text is "that we should be to the praise of his glory." The order of the words in the Greek sentence is most unusual and most emphatic. The verb "to be" is first (*eis to einai,* "that we should be.") God would herein assure us that our full, true life is beyond the grave. What a marvelous revelation and promise that is! What do you think will happen to us when we die? Do we go out like a light, like a candle? What is beyond the grave and what is beyond death? Is there existence and if there is what kind of an existence? That we should be, that we should exist, that we should live, is the purpose of God for us beyond the gates of death.

What is it beyond death and beyond the grave? There are numerous answers for that. The atheists believe that there is nothing beyond. One dies like a pig or like a dog. The Buddhist will believe in a Nirvana. One is reincarnated until finally he comes to that state where there is no more reincarnation, but the soul enters the great limbo of nothingness, an absolute limbo of emptiness. The materialist says that after one dies, after life has ceased, there is nothing remaining but the ceaseless tide of the eternal sea. Nothing remains but the unending orbit of the spheres around their central sun. Nothing remains but the empty silence of the universe.

But God reveals to us that in the eternity of the eternities and in the ages of the ages "we shall be to the praise of his glory." We shall be, that is, God is to have someone to love Him. God is to have someone to praise Him, and God is to have someone to live in His presence. That someone is you and that someone is me — we who have trusted in Jesus.

In Ephesians 2 Paul says that we shall "sit together in the heavenlies." He emphasizes that we shall be alive. We are to form a community, a gathering of God's saints. We shall be to the praise of His glory.

The Purpose of God in Faith

The last purpose of God is revealed in the phrase, "we . . . who first trusted in Christ." The important Greek words are *pro* (before) *elpizo*, (to hope, to trust in). The purpose of God for us is that we achieve this final consummation through our faith, hope, trust in Christ. What Paul is talking about is this: that without any sign of the ultimate consummation, we just believe God for it. Our total dependence and the weight and the burden of our souls are upon Jesus. We have done away with all other confidences in order that we may rely wholly upon Him whom we trust. We rest by faith alone upon Jesus. God has in store for us all of those marvelous things which He has prepared for those who love Him, for those who believe in Him, and for those who trust in Him.

Why did God do it that way? Why is His kingdom to be made up of those who trust Him and believe in Him without any particular evidence of all of those incomparable events that God says are yet to come? Why does God give it to those who just trust Him for it, and who believe Him for it?

For one thing, it honors God just to trust Him for it. In John 6 the people came to Jesus and said, "What shall we do, that we might work the works of God?" And the Lord replied, "This is the work of God, that ye believe on him whom he hath sent" (vv. 28, 29). The greatest work whereby a man can glorify God is to believe in Him. Such faith honors God.

Second, faith, hope, and trust open the very foundations of blessing and of assurance and of God's benedictory rewards. Do you remember the sweet passage in Hebrews 11? The author is following the roll call of the faithful, those who have trusted in God, the heroes of faith. Speaking of Abraham and Isaac and Jacob who dwelt in tents, who had no permanent abiding place, and who confessed to be strangers and pilgrims in the earth, the author of Hebrews said, "For they looked for a city which hath foundations, whose builder and maker is God" (11:10). Then verse 16, "wherefore God is not ashamed to be called their God: for he hath prepared for them a city." Strangers and pilgrims in the earth, they were looking for a city which has foundations, whose builder and maker is God, and they died having never received the promises. But God has prepared for them that city. God rewarded their faith with an answer from heaven. They trusted God for it and God did not let them down. Faith opens vistas of God's blessings and God's rewards.

I read one time that a man talking about faith made this observation. He said so great was the faith of Columbus that had there been no American continent, God would have created one just to reward his trust. I like that, whether it is true or not, because it reflects the faith that we are to have in God in the Word. When we believe God and trust God for the answers to all of life's questions, God opens up the fountains of blessings to reward us.

Third, when we trust God and believe in Him, such faith leads to open commitment as in the life of Nicodemus, or the Apostle Paul, and as in your life. When you begin trusting God, believing in Him, looking up to Him, you are going to find your life more and more openly committed to the blessed Jesus. It is a benedictory commitment, sweeter, more precious with each passing hour and day.

Chapter 6

SEEING WITH THE EYES OF THE SOUL

> Wherefore I also, after I heard of your faith in the Lord Jesus, and love unto all the saints,
> Cease not to give thanks for you, making mention of you in my prayers. (Eph. 1:15, 16)

Then follows the first prayer in the Book of Ephesians, a book which contains some of the most beautifully meaningful prayers of all literature.

> That the God of our Lord Jesus Christ, the Father of glory, may give unto you the spirit of wisdom and revelation in the knowledge of him:
> The eyes of your understanding being enlightened; that ye may know what is the hope of his calling, and what the riches of the glory of his inheritance in the saints,
> And what is the exceeding greatness of his power to us-ward who believe, according to the working of his mighty power,
> Which he wrought in Christ, when he raised him from the dead, and set him at his own right hand in the heavenly places. (Eph. 1:17-20)

Let us look closely at the text, "That the God of our Lord Jesus Christ, the Father of glory, may give unto you the spirit of wisdom and revelation in the knowledge of him: The eyes of your understanding being enlightened . . ." (Eph. 1:17, 18). The "eyes of your understanding." *Dianoia* (the Greek word which refers to the cognizant man) is translated here "understanding." The Revised Standard Version translates it "heart," but "heart" only in the sense of *dianoia*. Whatever you are consciously, sensitively, understandingly, responsively, intelligently, is included in this word.

Seeing With the Eyes of the Soul

Paul continues the text by writing that "the eyes of your soul may be enlightened." The Greek word translated "intelligent" is *photizo*, which means "illuminated," "filled with light." The "eyes of the soul" expression is found nowhere else in the Bible. However, the expression is found in secular Greek literature often. Plato will use the exact phrase, "The eyes of the soul." Describing Pythagoras, Ovid said (and I copied the sentence exactly), "With his mind he approached the gods so far removed in heaven and what nature denied to human sight he drew forth with the eyes of his soul." And one of our great English poets wrote, "The seeing eyes see best by the light in the heart that lies."

Seeing with the eyes of the soul — this is the intuitive insight (which is the highest of God's exalted and heavenly gifts) that God has confirmed upon the man He made. To see with the eyes of the soul, that is what the painter does. He paints what his soul feels and sees. The great English painter, Turner, was famed throughout the world for his gorgeous sunsets. A woman came up to him one time and said, "Mr. Turner, I never saw a sunset like that." And the artist replied, "Ah, but do not you wish you could?"

To see with the eyes of the soul — that is what the architect does. I have been in some of the great cathedrals of Europe such as Saint Isaac's in Leningrad. Ah, those incomparable expressions of the exaltation of the human spirit! The architect saw it first with the eyes of the soul before it became a reality.

Seeing with the eyes of the soul — that is what an engineer does. While I was down in Panama, the man who built the bridge across the canal, the Pan-American Bridge, took me to his office and showed me a little model of it. Before a span was swung, that great engineer had seen it with the eyes of his soul. For you see, facts and things are meaningless in themselves. It is the principle of meaning and purpose that is all pervasive and significant.

I am just pointing out to you what the Bible is teaching us. The great truth of life is what lies behind the facts, that which is invisible, that which you cannot see, namely, the principle, the idea that gives to facts meaning and purpose. In the pursuit of truth we seek to find the idea and the principle and the purpose, and those you must see with the eyes of the soul. Whoever saw a principle? Whoever saw a purpose? These are seen and recognized only with the eyes of the soul.

The Illumination of the Spirit

The Apostle Paul prays that the eyes of our understanding may be enlightened. He prays that we can see and hear and comprehend, the eyes of our souls being filled with light. He writes in 2 Corinthians 4:6, "For God, who commanded the light to shine out of darkness, hath shined in our hearts, to give the light of the knowledge of the glory of God in the face of Jesus Christ." God has illuminated our hearts. He has opened the eyes of our souls to give the light of the knowledge of the glory of God through faith in Jesus Christ. The great assignment of the Holy Spirit is to enlighten our inward souls. It is only the Holy Spirit who understands the things of God, and He takes those things of God and reveals them to us.

A natural man cannot understand like that. Paul wrote in 1 Corinthians 2:14 that the natural man, the unconverted man, cannot receive the things of God, neither can he know them because they are foolishness to him. A man has to be enlightened before he can see and comprehend the things of God. But the Holy Spirit can speak the things of God to us for He knows God and He understands God — He is God. He opens to view the things of God and shows us their meaning and their purpose. He fits together all of the providences of the Lord. He knows the mind of God, He illuminates us, and He places life and history before us in such a way that we can see purpose and reason. We can see the building fitly put together in the revelation and in the illumination of the Holy Spirit.

God's work in us and in history is like the building of the great temple under Solomon. Solomon's accomplished architect, Hiram, fitted every piece and when the building was put together there was not the sound of a hammer nor the ringing of a ponderous axe. So it is with the Holy Spirit. He takes the things of God and puts them together. They fit, and He reveals to us the tremendous purpose, the principle, behind them.

What a tragedy that there are so many whose eyes are closed, whose ears are stopped, and who cannot see and cannot understand. The Lord said in Matthew 13, "Because they seeing see not; and hearing they hear not, neither do they understand. And in them is fulfilled the prophecy of Esaias, which saith, By hearing ye shall hear, and shall not understand; and seeing ye shall see,

Seeing With the Eyes of the Soul

and shall not perceive: For this people's heart is waxed gross, and their ears are dull of hearing, and their eyes they have closed; lest at any time they should see with their eyes, and hear with their ears, and should understand with their heart, and should be converted, and I should heal them. But blessed are your eyes, for they see: and your ears, for they hear" (vv. 13-16). This is a gift of the Spirit of God. For a man can see and yet never see. He can hear and yet never hear. He must be illuminated by the Holy Spirit of God, and when he is, he suddenly sees! He suddenly hears! He has found the glory of God that shines in the face of Jesus Christ. That is why the psalmist's prayer in Psalm 119:18 reads: "Open thou mine eyes, that I may behold wondrous things out of thy law." The law is found in the world around me and in the book of God's revelation that I hold in my hand.

THE SPIRIT OF WISDOM

When the Holy Spirit illuminates us, when He opens our eyes and we can see, He gives us the spirit of *sophia*. There was never a word in the Greek language or in Greek literature that has been used so meaningfully as *sophia*. When one visits Istanbul, ancient Constantinople, he will see the greatest church that has ever been built. It was erected by the Roman Emperor Justinian in A.D. 500, and named St. Sophia in keeping with the text, "that God will give you the spirit of *sophia*." In 1 Corinthians the first gift of the Spirit of the nine named in that Corinthian letter is the gift of *sophia*, the gift of "wisdom." *Sophia* means "wisdom."

Logic and reason can explain in part, but of itself logic fails miserably and dismally. For a man to shut himself up to reason or to logic is to blot out of his life the spectacular revelations of Almighty God.

The Greeks played around with logic and with metaphysics and loved doing it. An author named Zeller wrote a book called *Outlines of Greek Philosophy*. In that book he presents a Greek sophist by the name of Gargius. By metaphysics Gargius proved that motion is impossible — logically, reasonably, intellectually. First, a thing cannot move from where it is because if it does, it is not there. Second, a thing cannot move from where it is not; that is obvious. And third, where it is, and where it is not are the only possible places that there are. Therefore, a thing cannot move. Now one can think about that forever. That is logic.

Logic by itself takes you nowhere. There are people who want to live by logic, but they are always illogical. There are people who want to live by reason, but they are always unreasonable. They reduce the world to an illogical and irrelevant fact.

What God has done for us is to give us another faculty, and that faculty is what exalts and raises up a man in the likeness of God. Reason can take one only so far. It cannot soar, it cannot rise. The eyes of the soul, the inward faculty that God has given a man makes him go on and on.

That is why in Hebrews 11 we read: "By faith we understand." One does not understand any other way. "That God may give us the gift of *sophia* (of inward, intuitive wisdom, of understanding), seeing with the eyes of the soul."

Paul continues with the prayer "That God will give us the spirit of . . . revelation. . . ." The Greek word for revelation is *apocalupsis*. "Apocalypse" means "the unveiling," "the uncovering." For you see, everything of God is a *musterion*, a mystery. One cannot explain anything about God. One just sees and observes. If we understand anything God must unveil it to us.

Now the Holy Spirit unveils God for us. He unveils the purpose and meaning of God for us, and we see it with our eyes, and feel it with our souls, and hear it with our ears, and understand it with the inward, intuitive gift God has bestowed upon us from heaven. And if the Holy Spirit does not do it, we cannot comprehend it.

Paul, for example, will say about a people that they have a veil over their hearts and even when the Gospel is preached to them they do not understand.

The Lord said in John 6, "No man can come to me, except the Father which hath sent me draw him," reveal Me to him. One does not become a Christian by logic or by reason. One does not get to heaven because he is shrewd or smart. Now the vehicle and the instrument by which God reveals the truths of heaven to us is in the enlightenment of our inward souls. How wonderful it is when God uncovers Himself! One cannot know Him any other way.

"Seeing with the eyes of the soul." A man can walk out under the firmament of the sky and look at that glory forever, and all he could ever know is that wherever it came from it must have been done by an omnipotent hand. Or he could look at a glorious sunset or a beautiful rainbow and he could deduct that whoever did

Seeing With the Eyes of the Soul

it and however it came to pass, it must have been someone who loves things beautiful. What good is there in the gorgeous autumnal colors, or a sunset and just what utilitarian purpose does a rainbow serve? Whoever created it must have loved things beautiful and pretty. But one would never know who did it unless He unveils Himself and reveals Himself.

We could look on the inside of ourselves and find ourselves highly moral. We are most sensitively made. We are moral creatures. Whoever created us must have been someone who had a keen sensitivity to what is right and what is wrong. But what is His name and what is He like? You could never ever know except God discloses Himself. God does reveal Himself, and that is what you call the apocalypse, the unveiling of the Lord. It is the work of the Holy Spirit. He presents God. He uncovers the Lord. He shows you what His name is and what He is like, and who He is, and all about Him.

There are powerful truths that cannot be intellectually substantiated because the intellect, the reason, the logical part of a man cannot grasp it. Many things that we receive by faith we cannot intellectually defend. For example, Plato said a man can salute the truth by force of instinct as something akin to himself before he can give intellectual account for it. One can receive it and believe it because it is something like him. And yet, as Plato says, one cannot give an intellectual account for it.

I do not know of a better illustration of that than something which happened in the life of a deacon in a church which I pastored in a college town. The deacon taught psychology and one day he brought to me a textbook in his field of science. At the end of that book the author had said something about himself. Briefly, the scientist said: "I have been an unbeliever. I have not believed in immortality and I have not believed in the resurrection. But since I began writing this book my father died, and my mother died, and though I cannot explain it, nor can I intellectually defend it, I cannot believe that my father has ceased to be and that my mother is altogether gone. I believe my father is somewhere and my mother is somewhere and though yesterday I denied both immortality and resurrection, today after the death of my father and my mother, I believe in both of them." God had intuitively enlightened his inward soul and he began to see with the eyes of his soul, looking at the invisible. This is the work of the Spirit of God.

Paul says that God will give us the Spirit of *sophia*. The Holy Spirit opens to us the "apocalypse," so that we can see the unveiled Christ, the veiled God.

EXPERIENTIAL KNOWLEDGE

In this text in Ephesians 1:18, Paul writes, "that ye may know, . . ." The Greek word is *epignosis* (our word "know" comes from it), and it means "to know experientially." The Holy Spirit will lead us into experiential knowledge. That knowledge is not philosophical, it is not metaphysical, nor is it second hand. We know the truth ourselves. We have felt and experienced. That is the only kind of knowledge that really matters. One does not know what he has not experienced. We are not just to take our religion for granted. Our faith, if it is real, is something that we have experienced. It is an *epignosis*.

Look at this for a moment. Whatever noise music is, whatever sound music is, one can mathematically write it out. One can put it on a screen and see it in picture frame. The wave lengths and the overtones can be presented by mathematical formulae. But one can read those formulae forever and read those mathematical equations world without end and still not know music. The way to know sound is to sit and listen to a glorious oratorio or to a great anthem of praise, and then one will know what it is like. One must experience it in *epignosis*.

It is the same thing with color. One can describe color mathematically, but one will never really know color until he looks at a glorious sunset, at a beautiful rainbow, or at a marvelous painting.

It is the same with taste. Taste can be anatomically demonstrated but one will never know how an orange tastes until he eats it.

Logic cannot demonstrate to us a sunset, and cannot demonstrate to us a noble character. One must see someone noble and say, "That is it." It is the same way about God. Neither logic nor reason can demonstrate God. One has to experience God. He must know Him in his soul and in his heart. That is what the psalmist meant when he said, "O taste and see that the LORD is good . . ." (Ps. 34:8). One has to try Him for himself.

One evening a sweet family sat in my study. The man in this family was an engineer. Brilliant as he was, his mind had begun to disintegrate. He was verging upon a nervous collapse. But he

Seeing With the Eyes of the Soul

was married to a glorious Christian girl and she brought him to the Lord. She laid him at the feet of Jesus. The man said to me: "I was dreading those long, interminable sessions from psychiatrist to psychiatrist when my dear wife brought me to Jesus. I found the Lord and my mind is healed and I am sharper today than I have ever been and doing better work today than I ever have." And I said to him, "In Exodus 15 the Lord says, '. . . for I am the LORD that healeth thee,'" (v. 26). It is a trust, a coming to God. If we have that faith He heals us. He heals our hearts, our souls, our minds, and our bodies. But we must come, we must *epignosis*.

Bring yourself to Jesus and lay yourself at His dear feet. Look in faith upward and let the Holy Spirit reveal to you the knowledge of the glory of God in the face of Jesus Christ. Let the Holy Spirit illuminate your soul and fill you with light so that you can see with the eyes of your heart. Let God lead you to that holy place of trust in Jesus. He will take the veil away from your heart. He will take the scales away from your eyes, and you will find that holy rest and peace in Jesus. Make the decision now in your heart. Try Him and see if God is not good. Try seeing with the eyes of the soul, "illuminated by the Holy Spirit."

CHAPTER 7

OUR PRICELESS POSSESSION

>Which he wrought in Christ, when he raised him from the dead, and set him at his own right hand in the heavenly places,
>Far above all principality, and power, and might, and dominion, and every name that is named, not only in this world, but also in that which is to come:
>And hath put all things under his feet, and gave him to be the head over all things to the church,
>Which is his body, the fulness of him that filleth all in all. (Eph. 1:20-23)

There are two extraordinary revelations the apostle presents by inspiration in these verses. One is the exaltation of Christ. God has raised Him, exalted Him, and set Him at His own right hand in the heavenlies, far above all angelic orders, and above all of the created beings in this world and in the world that is to come. He has put all things under the feet of our Lord. This is the theme that Paul will delight to dwell on as he so beautifully speaks of it in Philippians 2. "Wherefore God also hath highly exalted him, and given him a name which is above every name; That at the name of Jesus every knee should bow, of things in heaven, and things in earth, and things under the earth; And that every tongue should confess that Jesus Christ is Lord, to the glory of God the Father" (vv. 9-11). All creation some day, even that part of God's creation that is in rebellion and in sin, shall acknowledge the Lordship of Christ.

God has not only purposed, ordered, and ordained that Christ shall be exalted above all of the creation, but God also has done something else. He has given this living, exalted Lord to be head

Our Priceless Possession 61

over all things to the church which is His body, the fullness of Him that filleth all in all. God has given to us a priceless possession, and that gift is made to the church, the body of our Lord. I speak first of that church.

THE CHURCH

The word "church" in the dictionary has several meanings. The first meaning is a building where a Christian congregation gathers. But there is no hint or even approach to such a meaning as that in the Word of God. It was almost three hundred years after Christ before there was such a thing as a church building.

In the New Testament, the church is an *ecclesia*. It is a "called out people of God." For three hundred years it was known by no other word or description than an *ecclesia*. But when Constantine was converted, the word was changed from *ecclesia*, referring to the people, to a *kyriakos*. An impressive, massive temple that a Roman emperor would erect for a pagan god was called a *kyriakos*. Thus the word for "church" came to refer, not to the people, but to the building. So much did that change affect us that even in our imagery, when we think of the church, we think of a building: a spire, a colonade, glass windows beautifully stained. But the church in the Holy Scriptures is the *ecclesia*, the called-out, separated, dedicated people of God.

The word *ecclesia* is used in the New Testament sometimes in a generic sense, but most of the time it is used to refer to a local congregation of Christ's believers. Paul will refer to the churches of Judaea, the churches of Macedonia, the churches of Achaia, the churches of Galatia, the churches of Asia. He will address his letters to the church at Philippi or the church at Colosse. In the last apocalpytic revelation, the Lord addressed his letters to the church at Ephesus, at Smyrna, at Pergamos, at Thyatira, at Sardis, at Philadelphia, at Laodicea. The generic idea of the church includes all of the believers in Christ of all ages. The Lord said in Matthew 16:18, "On this rock I will build my church." He was speaking of the important fellowship that shall endure forever, the believers of all ages and all times. It is in that sense, which is unusual for the apostle, that he uses the word "church" here in the Book of Ephesians. He will say in 3:10 that Christ is exalted above all principalities and powers and the heavenlies that it might be known *by the church* the manifest wisdom of God in Him. He closes His most beautiful prayer, "Unto him be glory *in the church* throughout all ages, world without end, Amen." And Paul will say in Ephesians 5 that Christ loved *the church* and gave Himself for it. Paul avows that a man ought to love his wife as Christ loved *the church*. He says for this cause shall a man leave his father and mother and be joined to his wife and they two shall be one flesh. The apostle defines this relationship as "a great mystery." It is a deep secret hid in the heart of God but revealed to us now, because the apostle speaks concerning Christ and His *church*. Christ loved *the church*. In the management of Christ's stewardship of the whole universe, in the dispensation of the ordering of all time and event, He always consults the best interests of His people, of His *church*.

It is sometimes difficult for us to see that relationship between Christ and His people or to persuade ourselves of it, but it is true. According to the revelation of the Word of God all things move, however they turn, toward that great consummation when Christ shall be married at the Marriage Supper of the Lamb, to His bride, *the church* (Rev. 19:9). Even when troubles, rebellions, and turbulences rise among us, it is ordered of God for our good. In 1 Corinthians II Paul says it is needful that heresies be among us. What an astonishing thing to say! Yet the apostle declares that heresies are needed among us so that they which are approved may be manifest. It is only in the confrontation of evil, denial, and unbelief that a man can stand up like a light, like a giant. Paul avows that even the troubles that we have and the confrontations that are thrust upon us are for our good. It makes a true man of God stand up and stand out. Also, in furthering the highest interests of the church, our defeats, our troubles, our sorrows, and our sometimes overwhelming disappointment also have a part. They move us toward an ultimate and final glory.

Living through that day, who would have ever thought that the envy of the priests, the treachery of Judas, the cowardice of the Roman Procurator, Pontius Pilate, and the mad fury of the mob that led to the crucifixion of the Lord would result in the resurrection and the exaltation and the glory of Christ? Born in sobs and tears, in blood and in sacrifice is the church of God (Eph. 5:30). Our sorrows and trials in this world are but a preview, an introduction to the glory that God has purposed for us.

The church, the fullness of Him that filleth all and all, is the body of our Lord.

Christ Jesus, the Son of God, has a body. There must needs be a body for sacrifice and in the secret part of the virgin Jewess Mary, God formed the body, the humanity of our Lord. That mantle, that robe of humanity, Christ possesses forever with the wound prints in His hands, His feet, and His side. The Lord of all the universe who sits upon the throne of majesty and glory is a man. He is a man like us, and He has a body like ours, only His is already changed and glorified. The mighty God of all the universe is incarnate in a human body. Let us read again the incomparably precious passage in Hebrews 4:15, 16. The Lord of the universe can be touched with the feeling of our infirmities for He was tried in all points such as we are. He is a Man among men, and that humanity that He assumed in the incarnation He bears forever. The God of the universe is Christ, the Man, Christ Jesus.

But Christ has another body. He has a spiritual body and He is incarnate in the body of His church. He is the Head and we are the members. All of the members are activated by the Head. We move in the fullness of the life and the strength and the glory of Christ. It is Christ who thinks with our minds, who sees with our eyes, who hears with our ears, who talks with our tongues. He actuates our joints and He moves in our limbs, for we are His body. Our life is directed by Him. If we have understanding, it is He who gives us comprehension. If we have will and volition, it is He who gives us strength in its use and activity. If we have affections and feelings, it is He who makes them sweet, precious, and beautiful.

The most precious and incomparably meaningful gift that God has given to us who belong to His church and are members of His body is Christ our Lord Himself. God gave Him to the church. This is the colossal difference between the Christian faith and all other living religions in the world.

I think of the Jewish religion. I have so many close Jewish friends whom I love in the Lord. But it seems to me, though they cannot see it (Paul says there is a veil over their hearts), that their faith and their religion is broken. It has no consummation and no completion. Reading in the Old Testament Scriptures, I find that the Book of Genesis begins with these words, "In the beginning God." But how does it end? The Book of Genesis ends with these words, "in a coffin in Egypt." How does the Pentateuch end? It ends with the weeping over the death of Moses. How does Joshua end? It ends with the lamentation over the death of Eleazar the high priest, the son of Aaron. How does the Book of the Kings end? It ends with the tragic imprisonment and death of Jehoiachin in the Babylonian captivity. And how do the prophets end? How does the old covenant end? How does the Old Testament end? It ends with these words, "Lest I come and smite the earth with a curse." The Jewish faith, the Jewish religion has no Christ. They have no Messiah. They have no fulfillment of those glorious promises in the Old Testament. It does not go on Godward, heavenward, and victoriously Christward.

Once when I stayed at a hotel in Jerusalem I visited a Jewess who had a gallery of paintings. She had on display there in her shop a painting of what was the Wailing Wall, now the Western Wall. If one visits there he will see soldiers with their guns, their fatigue uniforms, and their belts of cartridges mingling with those old orthodox rabbis with their felt hats and the little bells around their hats, the little fur bells that mark them out as being faithful worshipers of Jehovah. After the Six Day War there was such incomparable jubilation on the part of God's people that they joined hands, the orthodox rabbis and those armed soldiers, and danced together in circles in the presence of God at the Western Wall. There was a painting of that picture. I bought the picture and brought it home.

As I bought it, I visited with the Jewish lady. Her name is Maria Nura Sonis. She was born in Moscow and reared in Budapest. She is one of the most gifted and intellectually perceptive and discerning women I ever talked with. She spends eight months in Israel, four months in Boston just for the cultural life of our American city. To my astonishment (I cannot describe to you how surprised I was) I learned that she is a Christian. When she learned that I was a Baptist minister, we had much in common. Every Sunday she drives to Tel Aviv and teaches a Sunday school class. She is a Jewess who has found the Lord. She told me about a dinner at which she sat with the general who led the Israeli Army to vistory in the Six Day War and who is now Minister of Defense for the Israeli government. They were eating dinner together and he asked her what she was doing. She answered that it was Christmas time and she was preparing to go to Bethlehem and rejoice in the festivities, the season's holiday of all holidays when Christ was born. She witnessed that Jesus is the Messiah of God, the King of the Jews, the King of the Gentiles, the King of the nations, and King of all Kings. As she spoke so victoriously of the meaning of Christmas, she said that the man bowed his head and put his face in his hands. Lifting up his face after a long, meditative period he said to her, "My dear, you do not know how much I envy you." There never has been, there shall never be, there could not be, a gift from God that approaches the incomparable preciousness of the gift of God to us in Christ Jesus.

Christ is God's peculiar gift and our precious possession. The Muslim has his prophet named Mohammed. What kind of a prophet was he? The last part of his life he was vile, villainous, treacherous, and lecherous. Yet Christ, the Son of God is so separate, pure, and apart.

I cannot but admire the rich nobleman who forsook all that he might find some kind of an answer to the suffering of human life. But his final answer was only in his personal enlightenment. His name was Buddha. His answer for human suffering was to escape it by denial of it, to live oblivious to it. So you see Buddha with his fat, rotund belly and his hands clasped over his navel, grinning in a sea of indescribable poverty and human misery. Krishna of the Hindus is no better. There is no religion as filthy as the Hindu religion worshiping cows and animals. Ah, Lord Christ — what you mean to us! Our Lord is wisdom when we want to know the way. He is strength for our weakness, forgiveness for our sins, comfort in our sorrows.

In that final and ultimate hour of death Jesus will receive us to Himself. Everywhere in God's Book, Christ is pictured as seated at the right hand of glory. There is one exception. In Acts 8 when Stephen, the first martyr, was beaten to the ground by stoning, he lifted up his face and saw heaven opened, and there standing on the right hand of glory was Christ the Son of God. Jesus stood to receive the spirit of His martyred saint.

It shall be thus with us in the days of our translation. He will be there to receive us to Himself and to glory. Christ is our most precious possession. No wonder we try to sing about it, preach about it, praise God for it. What Jesus means to me!

Chapter 8

OUR SPIRITUAL RESURRECTION

And you hath he quickened, who were dead in trespasses and sins,
Wherein in time past ye walked according to the course of this world, according to the prince of the power of the air, the spirit that now worketh in the children of disobedience:
Among whom also we all had our conversation in times past in the lusts of our flesh, fulfilling the desires of the flesh and of the mind; and were by nature the children of wrath, even as others.
But God, who is rich in mercy, for his great love wherewith he loved us,
Even when we were dead in sins, hath quickened us together with Christ, (by grace ye are saved;)
And hath raised us up together, and made us sit together in heavenly places in Christ Jesus:
That in the ages to come he might shew the exceeding riches of his grace in his kindness toward us through Christ Jesus. (Eph. 2:1-7)

The passage now under consideration concerns our total victory in Christ. When I walk down the streets of glory, I cannot boast, saying, "I made it." I will get there by the grace of God. The glory, the honor, the dominion, and the praise are all His.

Dead in Sin

Now let us expound the text. "And you hath he quickened who were dead in trespasses and sins . . . and were by nature the children of wrath, even as others." All of us are alike. Unregenerate nature is fallen, it is corrupt. By nature a man is lost. He is not a

Our Spiritual Resurrection

child of God. Paul refers to unregenerate nature as one refers to death. A cadaver is a solemn sight wherever it is seen. Death is a formidable enemy.

There are no degrees in death. We are not somewhat dead in our trespasses and sins. We are completely dead. The daughter of Jairus, the twelve-year-old girl, looked as though she were asleep but she was dead. When the Lord said to roll the stone away from the grave of Lazarus, Martha, sister of Lazarus said, "Oh, Lord, no, for he has been dead four days and by now he is corrupt." The sleeping child or the decaying Lazarus are both alike — cadaverous. In our day at a funeral service the embalmer will make it look as though the loved one is asleep. He will have flowers and music to cover the harsh face of death. But it is there in all its tragic sadness just the same.

When I began my ministry years ago among very poor people, they did not embalm their dead. They had no money so they put them in a cheap, box-like coffin. In the cemetery it was the custom for the family to stay and listen to clods of dirt being shoveled on the box below. Death had a harsh visage and those dear, poor people to whom I ministered wept and cried. But whether I hold the funeral today in beautiful surroundings, in a marble chapel, or whether I conduct it in a rural cemetery, it still is the same. There are no degrees in death. God says by His Holy Word that this is an exact picture of our fallen nature.

We look at two men and we say that one is a fine man, but the other is an evil man. But by the Word of God they both are dead. All of us by nature are fallen. The Holy Spirit calls us here the children of wrath. That is Hebraism. If someone is poor, he is a child of poverty. All of us are children of wrath, of condemnation. The judgment of death is born with us. We do not learn it. It is not something that we have acquired by practice. We were born in sin and shapen in iniquity.

In Psalm 51 the poet David says, "Behold, I was shapen in iniquity, and in sin did my mother conceive me." I have heard men quote that passage in a terribly wrong misinterpretation. They make it mean that the act of love that would result in conception was in itself sin. That is not true. The act of love that resulted in the conception of the child David was not an act of sin nor did David refer to it as that. What David was saying is that when he was conceived, when he was born, there was in him, coursing in his veins, the black drop of death. The old-timers would call that original sin. A child does not have to be taught to be selfish, he will be selfish. One does not have to teach him to misrepresent, he will tell you an untruth. All of us are alike in the course of human life. Sin is ever present in our members. Nor can all of the education in the world eradicate it. We are ignorant sinners if we are unlearned. We are learned sinners if we are academicians and taught. There are no differences. All are alike God says in the text. We are fallen by nature, and that nature always will exhibit itself in our lives.

I read of a hunter in India. While he was hunting, the river overflowed and there was a great flood. He escaped to a little island of high ground. While he was there a tiger swam out of the swift, moving current and came to the little island with the hunter. The tiger was wet, afraid, and cowed like a domestic cat. Nevertheless the hunter took his gun and shot it. One might have thought what he did was an unhuman and cruel act on his part, but the hunter was wise. He had sense enough to know that while the flood raged and while they were on that little island together, if the hunter went to sleep or turned his back, or as the days passed and the tiger became hungry, being carnivorous he would eat that man. It was the nature of the beast. The tiger was born that way. So we are born in a certain way and the way leads to sin and to death.

There is the latent ability of any kind of a sin in any man's life. He can murder. I would say that most murders are not premeditated. They are done in anger, fury, emotion, or in fear. We are capable of anything. We are a fallen people, "but God, who is rich in mercy, for his great love wherewith he loved us. . . ." What a marvelous change in tempo to turn from death and corruption and to lift our faces and hearts upward, Godward. "But God. . . ."

Resurrected in Christ

Now you are going to read about one of the most dramatic doctrines in the Bible. How could a dead man, a corpse, believe? How could he repent? How could he be saved? And the answer from the Word of God is this: the man *cannot*. He cannot save himself. He cannot resurrect himself. He cannot even repent of

Our Spiritual Resurrection

himself. In Acts 11 it says that repentance is a gift of God. How is this man ever to see, to hear, to feel, to breathe, to repent, or to be saved? The answer is that it is the work of God. A man who is dead toward God in his heart, in his spirit, could see but never see; or he could hear but never hear. He could feel but never feel. He is dead.

Soon after the Second World War, I was in a bombed-out shelter in Munich, Germany. The refugees there were having a Christian service. They were Baptist people. First, the service was in Ukrainian. It meant nothing to me, I could not understand. Then the service was in German. Again I could not understand. Then the service was in English and I could understand. My mind was touched and moved in enlightenment. A dead man is like that. He can be in the presence of the Word of God, but if he is dead it means nothing to him.

In a journey to Alaska I sat in the plane by the side of a Belgian atheist. He was proudly an atheist as were his wife and children. He spoke to me of the freedom of being an atheist. He was absolutely unbound and free. You would think I had found true glory, listening to him, but actually, he described a panorama of death. He does not see, he does not hear, he does not feel, and he does not know. He is not quickened.

How does a dead man save himself? How does a dead man hear? How does a dead man feel? All the preaching in the world will not resurrect a dead man. If you would like to try it, go to the cemetery. There are many dead men out there. Preach to them. Preaching does not resurrect the dead. All the tearful, heartbroken cries and intercession of parents for their children will not resurrect the dead. Resurrection is a gift of God. God must touch the heart. God must unstop the ears. God must quicken the soul. It is as great a miracle as when God created life and created you. It is as great a miracle as when God resurrected us from the dead to our spiritual life in Christ. Paul describes it: "And [he] hath raised us up together, and made us sit together in heavenly places in Christ Jesus: that in the ages to come he might shew the exceeding riches of his grace in his kindness toward us through Christ Jesus." It is something God does. A man in Christ Jesus is a new creature.

Down the aisle came a man giving his heart to Jesus and he said: "I do not understand. Either I am a new creation or the whole world is altered, for everything is different." A man came down the aisle confessing Christ as Saviour and he said: "For fifty years I have lived and have not felt the presence of God. But for these last fifty seconds the greatest fact in the world to me is God." A man lives, and then suddenly God quickens his soul and he is really alive and conscious of the Lord God Almighty. Like Jacob, he says: "Surely the LORD is in this place and I knew it not. . . . This is none other but the house of God, and this is the gate of heaven" (Gen. 28:16, 17). God had raised him up.

A baptismal service is beautiful and meaningful. God's Holy Word says we are dead in trespasses and in sins, and we are buried with Christ. Then we are raised in the likeness of His glorious resurrection. Dead, buried, and raised — that is what God has done for us. He has made us sit together in the heavenlies in Christ Jesus, living with the Lord. Enoch walked with God and was not for God took him. We who are quickened now and forever sit in heavenly places in Christ in order that in the ages to come, God might show the exceeding riches of His grace and His kindness toward us in Christ Jesus. This is the grace and mercy of God. We are God's redeemed and we are to show that forth.

I cannot but be overwhelmed as I listen to these scientists as they take the lunar material brought back by the astronauts, chemically analyze it, look at it through microscopes, weigh it, and study its chemical formulae. The papers say that these scientists are amazed and are overwhelmed by the component parts of that lunar material. They say, "To our amazement, the moon is covered with little beads of glass." Then they say that it has great amounts of titanium which, in its oxide form, can bend light more beautifully and more gloriously than a diamond. On the moon there are no trees, no vegetation, no ocean, no clouds, no mist, but there are craters and irregular features like the channeled glass on the lamp on the headlight of your automobile. The moon is a perfect reflector. That is what makes it shine. The scientists, as they analyze the material of the moon, say that it is the most glorious reflector that man could imagine. They did not have to go to the moon to find that out. They did not have to analyze the material to learn that. For God said in Genesis 1 that He made the moon a giant reflector to give light over the earth by night. It reflects the light of the glory of God.

That is what we are going to do. In the ages to come we will reflect the exceeding kindness, goodness, and mercy of God. No longer will it be said then that the Lord God who made heaven and earth did thus and so, but it will be said then that the Lord God who redeemed a fallen and corrupt humanity into the glorious image of His son, Jesus Christ, did thus and so. He is to be praised forever. Ah, what a prospect! Glory, majesty, honor be to God through Jesus, forever and ever, Amen.

Chapter 9

SALVATION BY GRACE

> For by grace are ye saved through faith; and that not of yourselves: it is the gift of God:
> Not of works, lest any man should boast. (Eph. 2:8, 9)

There are two ways in which a man might be saved. First, he can save himself. Or second, God can save him. In this chapter we are going to take those two contingent possibilities, and look at them.

Ways Men Try to Save Themselves

First, look at the possibility that a man can save himself. This alternative is the dedication of practically all humanity. There are four different ways by which men suppose that they can save themselves. As I go through and discuss them, you will see them in history and in the present record of human life.

By Self-affliction

First, some men suppose that they can save themselves by self-affliction, by the tormenting of the body. There is the hope that we can deliver our souls from death by the torture of this physical frame. You have seen pictures of the Hindus as they seek to expiate their sins. Some of them will hold their hands up toward heaven, and do it so long that their arms become so rigid they cannot lower them. Some of them will lie on beds of nails and spikes. Others will starve themselves to death. Some will make long pilgrimages on their knees. They afflict their bodies in order to save their souls.

This is particularly and unusually a concomitant of a twisted understanding of Christianity. It is one of those strange aberrations

Salvation by Grace

of the truth. Martin Luther, when he was a monk, flagellated himself with a whip of many thongs. He would lie down at night covered in blood. The church father, Origin, one of the most gifted theological minds that ever has appeared in the human family, destroyed his own manhood and flung away by self-emasculation what it is to be a man. The torment, the grieving, and the afflicting of the body in order to be delivered from the penalty of death and sin is one way men seek to save themselves.

BY HUMAN SACRIFICE

Another way that men have proposed to expiate their guilt is in human sacrifice. The sacrifices that God pronounced acceptable in His sight were types of the supreme sacrifice for our sins on the cross. But the distortion of that purpose of God has been heart-rending through all of the millennia. In a museum in Mexico are displayed sculptured carvings of ancient Aztec pyramids. On an altar will be laid a warrior for human sacrifice with a priest holding high a knife sharpened to cut out the warrior's heart. The sacrifice had to be warm in blood, and the heart carved out of the victim had yet to be pulsing with life when presented to the gods. The Ganges River once was the scene where mothers came to fling their children into the hungry mouths of crocodiles in order to save their own souls. They offered the fruit of the body for the sin of the soul.

In reading through the Old Testament one will find that Ahaz, king of Judah, made his son pass through the fire to Moloch. That is the way of saying that he offered up his son to the heathen god, Moloch. In the Valley of Hinnom a large, brass god was heated, and those who sought to save their souls threw their children into his burning arms. Manasseh did that. During the revival under Josiah, he defiled and polluted that valley forever and made it a place where the dead animals, garbage, and the filth of the city was poured. That is the New Testament word for hell, Gehenna, the Valley of Hinnom. In Jerusalem it is one of the most noticeable of all the topographical features of the land. There they offered their own children for the sin of their souls.

I would suppose that there have been literally rivers of blood poured out in an attempt to cover over sin. Walking through Africa one will see blood on the trees, blood on the sticks, and blood on the stones. The missionary will say these objects are smeared with blood by animists who believe that spirits live in all inanimate objects and thus they offer to them blood sacrifices.

By Good Works

There are those who hope to save themselves by good works. If I am good, I will go to heaven. They look upon their lives as a ladder with rungs that are good, better, and still better. They leave off one vile thing and another iniquituous thing and they cast yet another unmentionable sin out of their lives, and they go up and up and finally they think they will place that ladder against heaven itself. The Lord says that in His sight all of our righteousnesses are as filthy rags. But we do not think so. We think we will be good enough to be saved.

There are those who keep the Golden Rule. It is surprising to me how shallow is the understanding of the human race concerning the depth of its depravity. Sin has entered every faculty of our mind, of our emotions, of our wills. Even when a man may be the most altruistic and philanthropic, at that moment he may be the most selfish and the most prideful. There is nothing that we do perfectly. There is always the element of mistake, of shortcoming, of human error in everything that we do. The Lord says no man can be saved by his own righteousness. He is never good enough.

By Religious Ritual

The fourth way that men have sought to save themselves is by religious ritual. The more I read the Bible and think about what it reveals, the more I am convinced that Satan, Lucifer, is the most dedicated religionist of all of God's creation. He is the most sensitive to religion. He desires it the most eagerly and provokes it the most astutely. The Scriptures say he transforms himself into an angel of light. One of the reasons that I think of him as being a religionist is this: In the fourth chapter of Matthew, in the third temptation when Satan took Jesus on a high mountain and showed Him all the kingdoms of the world and the glory of them, Satan said, "This will I give thee if thou wilt bow down thyself, fall down, and worship me." Satan covets worship. His masterpiece is religion. He perverts men's minds and men's lives by false, ritualistic hoax. He persuades us that by ceremony and sacrament we can save ourselves. If I get myself baptized, I will be saved. The ceremony of ablution, washing, will cleanse the stain of sin out of my soul. The truth is that even if one were scrubbed with lye soap it could never suffice to wash the stain of sin out of the soul. But men still believe that ceremony will cleanse iniquity. Many believe that they can be saved by the sacraments. Oh, how Satan blinds our eyes to real faith and to real religion!

The Way God Saves Us

The alternative for a man saving himself is that God alone can save us. This is the theological thrust and impact of this marvelous sentence written by the Apostle Paul, "By grace are ye saved through faith; and that not of yourselves; it is the gift of God: not of works, lest any man should say, 'I did it.'" By grace are ye saved through faith.

Saved by Grace

The Greek word for "grace", *chanis* is one of the most beautifully meaningful words. It is a word that the Greeks admired. It refers to that indescribable something that causes one to love someone, to be attracted to someone. In some instances the Greeks would use it to refer to that burst of generosity that would bestow a lavish gift, unmerited, without thought of reward or return on a loved one. The Christians took the word as beautiful as it already was, and exalted it. They dedicated it to the love and mercy of Christ Jesus. They used it in so many ways. A *charisma* is a gift of God's grace, a charismatic gift.

Charis originally referred to a gift. Then it referred to the forgiveness of a debt. A man could not pay another, and in grace, in *charis*, the owner forgave the debtor. Finally, it came to mean the mercy of God in forgiving us and saving us. This is how God does it. All of us were perishing like falling, autumnal leaves, but God in His goodness and mercy lifted us up and saved us. *He* did it. According to God's blessed revelation, He is not like a tideless sea, blissful, holy, undisturbed, separate, apart. Rather, according to the revelation of this Holy Book, God is like a living stream of mercy, love, grace, and affection.

The song says that everybody loves somebody sometime. You may be as hard as nails, made out of cast iron. No one ever gets to you. But on the inside you are just as soft and tender as you can be, and you can fall in love. That is because you are like God. We are made in His image and God is a veritable stream of love, concern, and affection.

Because God is gracious, therefore sinners are welcome. Because God is abounding in infinite love, He forgives us. Because His mercy endures forever, we are not destroyed. Because He is all compassionate, therefore we are saved. Grace is in God. That is why Paul would say that our part in salvation is one of acceptance, of trust, of hope, of surrendered yieldedness. He will say it both positively and negatively. "By grace are ye saved through faith (this is the positive side); and that not of yourselves (that is the negative side): it is the gift of God; not of works, lest any man should boast." It is something God has done for us. It is in His mercy and love that we are delivered. But the apostle is careful to speak of its mediation to us. How are we saved? The apostle says that God does it through the channel of faith.

SAVED THROUGH FAITH

There is a common denominator in every life: we live by trust, by belief, by faith. How do I know that the sun is going to rise in the morning? I have no way in the earth to prove that to you, but I believe it. How do I know that my money is safe in the bank? I could not prove it to you, but I believe it. How do I know the bridges are safe over which I drive my car? I never get out to examine one of those bridges before I drive a car over it. I take it by faith. I believe it is safe. I do not get out and examine the posts, pillars, foundations, and beams up there when I go underneath a roof. I just take it by faith that the thing is not going to fall on me. We live by faith. The food we eat, the roof above us, the bank in which we do business, the whole fabric of life is woven throughout with faith and trust. There are three parts to saving faith.

First, I must hear, I must listen. Paul wrote in Romans, "So then faith cometh by hearing, and hearing by the word of God" (10:17). That is why a man ought to preach the Bible when he is in the pulpit. Faith cometh by hearing; hearing the Word of God. When a preacher stands up in the pulpit and expatiates upon economics or talks about politics and the current events of the day, the people can hear him forever and never be saved, never be convicted. They can hear the commentators on television talk about current events and read in the newspapers all about politics. But faith cometh by hearing, and hearing by the Word of God. If a man will stand in the pulpit and preach this Book, someone will be saved. Maybe not all, but someone will be saved. Faith comes by hearing, and hearing by the Word of God. Saving faith begins with hearing.

Saving faith is also accepting. I hear it, I accept it as true — the testimony of the Book and the testimony of other Christians. I come to believe that testimony. I have never been to Tibet, but I believe there is a Tibet. I have never been to Afghanistan, but I believe there is an Afghanistan. I have talked to people who were there. I believe this testimony and that it is the channel by which God's grace comes to me. Your heart is made like your hands. Your hands are made on purpose to receive, to take. Your soul is made to take, to receive. It is like those aquaducts in Rome. From those Appian Mountains living water comes down to the eternal city. The aquaduct is a channel of life-giving water.

The other part of saving faith is committing yourself to it. When the sower sows his seeds in the fields, he believes they will grow and bring a harvest to God. The mariner in the trackless sea trusts the stars and the mariner's compass. A man who is sick trusts the hands of the surgeon. The one riding in an airplane trusts the pilot. That is the way we are saved — we trust Jesus for it. We hear His voice, we accept the offer, and we give ourselves to it. That is it. When you do that, you are in. You have crossed the threshold. You have gone through the door. You are saved. "For by grace are ye saved through faith; and that not of yourselves: it is the gift of God: Not of works, lest any man should boast."

Chapter 10

THE NEW CREATION

> For we are his workmanship, created in Christ Jesus unto good works, which God hath before ordained that we should walk in them. (Eph. 2:10)

When Paul opens the verse with the word "for," that word refers to the argument that has preceded. The words that follow are his deduction, his conclusion. So I look above to see what Paul has said. What he has said in this second chapter is that our salvation is not by our good works. We do not win it through personal merit. Salvation is a gift of God. It is something that God does for us. Thus this second chapter begins with the avowal that we were dead in trespasses and in sin, by nature the children of wrath. "But God," he says, "who is rich in mercy. . . . hath raised us up together, and made us sit together in heavenly places in Christ Jesus." (vv. 4, 6). Then he avows that same thing again. "For by grace are ye saved through faith; and that not of yourselves: it is the gift of God: Not of works, lest any man should boast" (vv. 8, 9). No man will be able to say, "See, I did it." Salvation is not of our merit or of our good works, but it is by grace mediated to us through faith. Having said that, Paul then adds "For we are his workmanship" (v. 10). We are God's creation in Christ Jesus and God purposed beforehand that we walk in those good deeds that glorify our Lord.

WE ARE GOD'S WORKMANSHIP

This chapter will be almost entirely an exegesis of the verse, "For we are his workmanship." The Greek word is "His poem." Our salvation is not the product of some evolutionary development.

The New Creation

We are not saved by rearranging our environment or controlling the circumstances and providences that press us in this life. Salvation is not by human development whereby we become spiritual, godly, or Christian. But we are saved by the workmanship of Almighty God. Never by nature or by development do we become Christians. By nature we are iniquitous, vile, and evil. The famous preacher George Whitefield once created an outcry against himself when he avowed in one of his eloquent sermons that man is half beast and half devil. I do not think there would be such an outcry against the great evangelist were he to say that today, because we are increasingly sensitive to the fact that the development of humanity is in a veritable ferment of violence, evil, and iniquity. We are now looking askance at a floodtide of crime in our own nation. We can hardly believe our ears or our eyes as we hear and read a record of atrocities that have characterized the generation to which we belong. In our day tribes and nations of people have been massacred literally by the hundreds of thousands. There is no day in some tragic places of the world but that godless predators are not maiming hands and ripping open women and exposing the corpses in public squares. This is the development of humanity politically.

Body and soul we are depraved and lost. Our bodies continually and finally fall into decay and disintegration. It is the same spiritually. The human soul moves toward a pit and in that abyss, as vile as it is, there is nothing so vile as those who are in it. By development there is never spiritual life, only spiritual death. There is no birth of light out of darkness. There is no birth of purity out of filth. There is no birth of grace out of degeneration and depravity. Such a regeneration must come as a workmanship of Almighty God. *He* must speak resurrection to the dead, for the dead cannot raise themselves. Life would be filled with muck and mire forever were it not for the genius of God that could raise out of it a soul as beautiful in glory as the lily. This God has done for us in our salvation. Our Christian life is from His gracious hands. He goes to the mountain side, He marks out the stone, and He quarries it. His genius of masonry shapes us and sets us in His holy temple. If a man is a Christian, it is by the grace of God that he becomes what he is.

I sometimes think of the creative workmanship of God in the life of a child. I went to the zoo one day, stood there for a long time, and watched a chimpanzee with her newborn babe. It was an astonishing thing to me to watch that mother. She fondled her baby, played with it, loved it, and caressed it with her long, hairy, bony, animal hands. She held it, pitched it up, played with it. It was a pleasant sight to see the lavishment of love that that beast poured upon the little animal. As I stood there, looking and thinking and watching, I thought what is the difference between that little animal born and loved there, and a little child laid in your bosom, growing up in your home. The difference lies in the creative workmanship of God. God breathed into man's nostrils the breath of life and man became a living soul. When that child was born into this world and laid in your arms, God breathed into the life moral sensititivy. God quickens him as he grows up and he becomes sensitive to right and to wrong. The child, if brought under the influence of the Gospel, will respond to the loving grace of Jesus, our Lord. The moral sensitivity is a gift of God, "For we are his workmanship." Our continuation to our final glorification is in God.

Paul wrote to the church at Philippi, "Being confident of this very thing, that he which hath begun a good work in you will perform it until the day of Jesus Christ" (Phil. 1:6). I am not to interfere with or to interdict the place and purpose of God. God has a program, a work, a plan for every life. If I let God have His way and His will, I will come to that place in my life where I am completely in the will and service of my Master, doing what God wants me to do, serving in a place where God wants me to serve. Oh, how precious and how wonderful to know, to realize, to have the assurance that we are God's workmanship, and that God has a program and a plan for us. My part is just to walk in it. As God shall lead, I am to follow as a servant in obedience to the great King. It is God's work, it is God's day, and it is God's hour. This life is God's life, and my will is God's will. What a wonderful way to be! "For we are his workmanship, created in Christ Jesus."

Paul uses another word to describe the identical thing. "We are his creation." The word "create" is to bring something out of nothing. That is why actually the word "Creator" can be applied only to the great Jehovah God. We can create nothing. Creation is a divine prerogative of the Almighty. All the genius of man, every scientific achievement, advancement, and instrument that we know could not create one little gnat, one little sunbeam in which it dances, or the eye that beholds it, or this voice that speaks of it.

The New Creation

It is all of God. So it is with this new nature of ours. Sometimes people think that the grace of God takes the old nature of man and reforms it, remakes it. No, not according to God's Word or the experience of human life. We who are Christians do not possess just an old nature that God is ameliorating and beautifying. No. God gives us another nature, a new nature. If you are a Christian there are two natures inside of you. The old nature so often wars against the new nature. The old nature is there. You will feel the drag of it until you die. The old heart is there, the old life is there, but God gives us a new heart, a new life, and a new nature. That new nature is called "a creation in Jesus Christ." It is something that God has done.

GOD RECREATES THROUGH HIS WORD

The Christian is a new creation at the hands of our gracious Lord, and He does it by the Word. Through the Word, God recreates us, remakes us, regenerates us. In the beginning God flung these worlds and starry spheres into space by fiat, by word. The Scriptures so often mention that. In 2 Peter 3, the apostle writes, "... by the word of God the heavens were of old, and the earth ..." (v. 5). In one of the Psalms the poet says: "For he spake (God spake), and it was done; he commanded, and it stood fast" (33:9). So it is with this new nature that God gives to us. It is created in us by the Word of God. "Being born again, not of corruptible seed, but of incorruptible, by the word of God, which liveth and abideth forever.... And this is the word which by the gospel is preached unto you" (1 Peter 1:23, 25). "Of his own will begat he us with the word of [God]." (James 1:18). "Now ye are clean through the word which I have spoken unto you" (John 15:3). "That he might sanctify and cleanse [us] with the washing of water by the word" (Eph. 5:26). "Verily, verily, I say unto you, He that heareth my word, and believeth on him that sent me, hath everlasting life" (John 5:24). "So then faith cometh by hearing, and hearing by the word of God" (Rom. 10:17). We are regenerated, we are made Christians by the word of God.

"For we are his workmanship, created in Christ Jesus unto good works." "In Christ Jesus." God does this great work in the cleansing and atoning mercy of the Lord. The Word magnifies Him, presents Him, describes Him, preaches Him. That is the

Word of God. When a man is delivering the Word of God, he is delivering the glory, the majesty, and the all-sufficiency of the grace and atoning mercy of Jesus. That is what the Gospel is. That is what saves us. That is the instrument God uses to regenerate us.

In the old Adam, the first man, this natural body possessed a natural proclivity and affinity for evil. In the fall of our first parents, who are the federal heads of the race, all of us alike have suffered. We have fallen also. The sins of my father, the sins of his father, the sins of the generations past are the sins that I know. They are the drag of my life. There are no manifestations of life that do not have that shortcoming, that sin and failure. It is a concomitant with everything we do.

When I turn back to the moralists like Plato, Seneca, or Marcus Aurelius, I find that they are my brothers in calamity and damnation. All of us are alike yesterday, today, and until God shall rid us of this body of evil and death. Even when I rise to the highest mountain peak of my finest moral achievement, I still have not touched the stars nor have I wings to mount up to the sky. My feet are still on this earth. I am a brother to the worm and a sister to decay, disintegration, and corruption. I cannot escape it. In myself I am helpless. As the dead cannot raise themselves so I cannot give myself a new nature, a heavenly disposition. I am a lost sinner. But there is another Adam, another federal head. There is a second Adam and in Him there is a creation of a new race, a spiritual race that is sublime and without spot or blemish and that knows and loves God. When we are regenerated and born again, that new nature, the seed of God in us, is one that aspires to heaven, that loves the Lord, that seeks God's will and is identified with Him forever. In our second Adam we have died and are dead to sin. We were buried with Him and the third day raised with Him from the dead. We who are dead in trespasses and in sins are raised with Him to a spiritual sensitivity and new life in Christ. We ascended with Him into heaven, and we are with Him at the right hand of God. There is no separation between the Head and the members of His body. We are one. He is there in heaven and we are here in earth for awhile. But in our new nature, in our Christian spirits, we are forever one in Christ Jesus.

One may say: "Would to God that I could be like that. I would love to be a Christian. I would love to go to heaven when I die. I would like to be saved, but how can I?" Why, you can be saved.

The New Creation

You can become a Christian by being born again, by being re-created in Christ. "But how can I recreate myself? How can I give myself a new nature? How can I reenter my mother's womb and be born again?" That is where the Gospel comes in. If you come to the place in your life where you say, "I cannot save myself; I cannot born myself again; I cannot regenerate or re-create myself; I am helpless," then take yourself to Jesus, to God, and let Him do it. That is what it is to be saved. That is what it is to be born again. We take our helpless selves to God, and we cast ourselves upon His kind arms. We are dependent upon His mercies and His grace, and God does something for us that we cannot do for ourselves. What a verse is Isaiah 45:22, "Look unto me, and be ye saved, all the ends of the earth: for I am God, and there is none else."

Take yourselves to God, and He does the regenerating. "But there is such a helplessness in me, there is such a pulling down in me. I lack so much. There is so much of sin and evil in my nature. I am like a bird trying to fly, held down by a heavy trap." But God releases us from the drag of sin. "But I have such a withered hand." What is a withered hand when Jesus bids us stretch it forth and be well? "But pastor, I do not have any man to put me in the pool when the water is troubled." What is that when Jesus of Nazareth passes by and says, "Take up your bed and walk; be healed?"

When the cripple was expecting only alms, and the apostle said, "In the name of Jesus Christ of Nazareth, rise up and walk," his feet and ankles and bones immediately received strength and he walked. That is what God does for us. Our spirits have withered arms and hands. Our spirits have crooked and broken bones and weak parts mostly out of joint. But God is abundantly able to bring to us recuperation, strength, and length of days that last forever and ever. It is nothing for God to do it. It would be something for us, for we cannot. But it is as nothing for God who is so all sufficient and so able to save us and to keep us forever.

GOOD WORKS ARE THE FRUITS OF THE NEW NATURE

"For we are his workmanship, created in Christ Jesus unto good works, which God hath before ordained that we should walk in them." We do not see fruit making a tree. The tree makes the fruit. So the works of our lives do not regenerate us. They do not give us a new nature. God gives us a new nature, and the new nature bears the fruit that honors the Lord. That good fruit was in the purpose of God. Our good works were in the mind of God before we were saved. He saved us unto those blessed ministries. When God made the first Adam and placed him in the Garden of Eden, He gave him an assignment. He was to dress and to keep the garden. So also in the new Adam, and in the new paradise, we have work to do. The Lord said, "Go work in my vineyard." He said: "The fields are white unto harvest. Pray that God will thrust forth workers into His harvest." As God saves us there is a task and an assignment for our lives. Maybe it is to sing, God bless *you*. Maybe it is to play, God bless *you*. Maybe it is to teach, God bless *you*. Maybe it is just to be a doorkeeper or to raise a window or to sweep the floor. It does not matter. Whatever God shall will for our lives, it is our sublimest joy to do it. For we are saved to that purpose, to do good and to honor God in our lives.

That is why we give the appeal and the invitation. Give yourself to Jesus. Make that decision now. Say: "I shall give my heart to Jesus. I will let Him save me and keep me. I will let Him regenerate me. I cannot save myself. I will just cast myself upon the mercies of God. I will look to Him in faith that God is able to do it, and here I come." Let God create within you a new being, a new creation. And let Him do it now.

Chapter 11

THE NEW MAN AND THE NEW HUMANITY

> Wherefore remember, that ye being in time past Gentiles in the flesh . . . without Christ, being aliens from the commonwealth of Israel, and strangers from the covenants of promise, having no hope, and without God in the world:
> But now in Christ Jesus ye who sometimes were far off are made nigh by the blood of Christ.
> For he is our peace, who hath made both one, and hath broken down the middle wall of partition between us;
> Having abolished in his flesh the enmity, even the law of commandments contained in ordinances; for to make in himself of twain one new man; so making peace;
> And that he might reconcile both unto God . . .
> Now therefore ye are no more strangers and foreigners, but fellow-citizens with the saints, and of the household of God. (Eph. 2:11-19)

In this passage is found the basic persuasion of all of the Word of God that there are only two classes of people. We are either dead or we are alive. We are either in Christ or we are in the world. We either are saved or we are lost. We are one or the other. The Apostle Paul presents this message on that basic assumption of the Scriptures.

First, he describes the old life and the old man, the one that was lost, condemned under the judgment of God. "Remember," he says, "that in time past . . . ye were without Christ." Nor is there any poverty more destitute than to be without a Lord to pray to, a Saviour to help, and a God to whom to make an appeal. "Ye were without Christ." There is nothing that can take the place of our Lord: wealth, success, fame, fortune, anything and everything is a poor thing compared to the riches of the glory that we

86   *Ephesians: An Exposition*

have in the Christ Jesus. "Though I speak with the tongues of men and of angels and have not [Christ], I am become as sounding brass or a clanging cymbal. And though I have the gift of prophecy and understand all mysteries and all knowledge, and though I have all faith so that I could remove mountains and have not [Christ], I am nothing. And though I bestow all my goods to feed the poor, and though I give my body to be burned and have not [Christ], it profiteth me nothing." "Ye were without Christ." This is a poverty, a destitution incomparable and beyond description.

Aliens and Strangers

Not only that but we were "aliens from the commonwealth of Israel, and strangers from the covenants of promise" (2:12). This refers to the true worship of God which the Lord revealed to His chosen people, Israel. We were outside of that covenant, aliens and strangers to the household of faith. There is no temple unless it is ordained of God. There is no sacrifice and no altar except they be appointed of God. There is no priest, no mediator, except he be chosen of God. There is no fire that falls down from heaven except God sends it, all of which is but another way of saying that a man cannot invent his own religion and have it be a true religion. True religion is a self-revelation of God. It is an ordaining and an appointing of God, or it is nothing at all.

While reading on a plane recently, I found that two of the most popular American magazines contained extensive articles on religion. I was not surprised at that, for it is my judgment that there is working in the hearts and minds of Americans today birth pangs of faith and religion beyond any other time in American history. One may think that it is almost absurd for me to voice such a judgment, but I think almost all of the pangs that one sees in modern American life are basically a manifestation of the spiritual hunger and longing of our people. As we have become more affluent, as the necessities of life recede in their pressures upon us, we are becoming increasingly conscious that our souls are empty and our lives meaningless. We live without purpose. That is why the young people are taking drugs, looking for some kind of a trip or experience or answer. That is why they dress and act as they do. That is why there are so many "isms" and so many far-out expressions of religious faith as are beginning to appear in

American life. The two magazines contained articles which were concerning these far-out, unusual reachings for God, and, of course, including in it, the established church. One article that I read had pictures depicting numerous religious approaches in comparison to previous delineations in religion. The article concluded with this sentence: "Try these religions. Try them. You might find something in them that you like."

As though religion were a matter of something that I liked! As though the true God was someone I could define in categories that please me! As though faith and religion were nothing other than a human seeking and a human searching after an unknown factor in life! I am just avowing to you that God's temple, God's worship, God's altar, God's sacrifice, God's mediator, God's Saviour, and God's true religion is a revelation from Him, and not a human speculation. Without the appointments of God, all of our religious forms are just so many chains of slavery. All of our gatherings and meetings are so many burdens. All of our professions are so many words of empty futility, and all of our efforts are nothing but carnal strivings in the flesh, unless God is in them. That is what Paul meant when he said that we are aliens when we were lost, aliens from the commonwealth of Israel and strangers from those covenants. We were outside the realm of the promises. We did not belong to the chosen family of God. We were pagans as were our forefathers. They worshiped and bowed down before all of the idols that their hands had made.

WITHOUT HOPE

Not only that, but in times past we were without hope. No hope. If you have read Dante's *Divine Comedy*, you have seen hell described as having a giant door that leads down into the pit to the abyss. Above this door are inscribed these words, "Despair of hope all ye who enter here." That is a description of all outside the Lord — without hope. Our lives without God are like a shipwrecked mariner thirsting to death in a sea of brine, looking up to a burning sun, looking down to the bottomless pit, and looking around to barren decay. Our lives are like that without Christ; we are without hope.

Sometimes I think of life as a race with death on a great track. When one is young, the grim, skeleton, monster of death seems to be far behind. But as the days go on and the race continues, he approaches closer and closer until finally, if one looks over his shoulder, he can see him breathing down his neck. I do not need to speculate who wins. He always wins, like a stag-hound that drags down the deer. Ultimately, inexorably, and inevitably, death drags us down without hope. You are not going to win. Some day it will be with you as it has been with those who have preceded us.

When I was a young preacher we laid our dead away unembalmed in crude coffins. Today I bury our dead in carefully-built caskets. They are beautifully washed, groomed, and laid out, but no less dead. Without God and without Christ we are without hope. That is the end of all life as the lost know it. Without hope in Christ we fall into the arms of decay, corruption, and disintegration. "And ye were without Christ . . . and without God." Oh, what an isolation! What a separation! What a damnation, and yet without annihilation. Without God, separated from Him. This is Paul's description of the man without Christ, outside of the household of faith.

But Now

Then Paul turns, "But now in Christ Jesus ye who sometimes were far off are made nigh by the blood of Christ" (2:13). We were far away. There was a mountain of debt that we could never pay, separating us from God. We were on one side and God on the other. There was a time when there was a whole mountain range of sin in our lives. There was a time when there was an entire ocean that separated us from God. While God was on the other side, we were on this side. God was far away, as far away as the heavens are higher than the earth. He was as far away as the east is from the west. But now, we who are in Christ Jesus, who sometimes were far off, have been made nigh, brought close by the blood of Christ. He has paid that debt and taken it away. He has forgiven our sins and moved them away. He has lifted us up from the miry pit, from the depths of the abyss, and set us in the heavenly places close to God. He has redeemed us, saved us, suffered for us, died in our stead, and lifted us out of sins and raised us up to God.

An old Indian in Oklahoma was asked: "How did Christ save

you? You say that you are saved, that He saved you. How did He do it?" The old Indian took some dead leaves, laid them in a little circle, and took a worm and put it inside that circle. Then he set fire all the way around those leaves. As the fire burned, that caterpillar crawled one way seeking a way out, then turned another way back again, this way, that way, and another way. Finding himself encompassed in the flames, the worm drew as far away from the fire as he could and curled up to die. The old Indian then reached down his hand, picked up the worm, and placed it safely out and away from the fire. The Indian said: "That is what Jesus did to me. I was perishing and dying, and He lifted me up and saved me."

> From sinking sand He lifted me.
> With tender hands He lifted me.
> From shades of night to plains of light,
> Oh, praise His name, He lifted me.

This has God done for us. When Christ died, we died. The life that shall inevitably some day die is already dead in Him. When Christ was buried in that tomb, our sins were buried. One of the most graphic of all of the scenes to be found in *Pilgrim's Progress* is when Pilgrim, weighed with the great burden of sin on his back, comes beyond the wicket gate, and there at the cross the burden falls off his back and rolls away into the empty sepulcher where Christ had once been. Our sins were buried when He was buried. When our Lord was raised from the dead, we were raised in righteousness, in justification, in sinlessness, in purity, and in forgiveness. We are joint-heirs with Him, and God's Book says some day we shall be like Him.

NEW MEN IN CHRIST

Now we who were far off, in Christ have been made nigh through His atoning grace. Not only that, but He has made us new men. There are two ways to interpret that. The first is personal, the new man, you in Christ Jesus. The other is the new man collectively, the new humanity.

First, the new man, you in Christ Jesus. God does not have an assignment of grooming cadavers. He does not try just to touch us up, to reform us, or to change us. God does not take the dead and put on a little rouge here, and comb the hair there. God says the old man dies, is dead, and is buried. Then God creates a new man. If any man be in Christ Jesus, he is a new creation. You have a new heart, a new life, a new vision, a new love, a new dream, a new ambition, a new purpose, and a new commitment. That is what God does. He makes us new men.

THE NEW HUMANITY

Now if I were to exegete these passages exactly as Paul is saying it here, he is referring to a "new humanity." For he says, ". . . to make in himself of twain one new man" (Eph. 2:15). In Christ the Jew and the Gentile are made one. That would include us all, would it not? He makes all of us, the Jew and the Gentile, one new humanity, one new household of faith, one new body of Christ, one new worshiping congregation of the Lord. The Lord Jesus has broken down the middle wall of partition that long has separated us. What are those walls of partition and separation?

Had one gone to the holy city to worship God in Biblical times to worship the true God, he would have found as he entered the city and approached the holy temple a gigantic wall or partition. Had he passed through that wall into the Court of Gentiles, he would have found again a gigantic wall of partition. Had he gone beyond that wall in the Court of Gentiles into the Court of Israel, there again he would have found another wall of partition. Had he gone beyond that wall from the Court of Israel into the Court of the Women, there again he would have found a wall of partition. Had he gone through the wall of the Court of Women into the Court of the Priests, there he would have found again a wall of partition. Had he gone beyond the Court of the Priests and approached the Sanctuary itself, there he would have found another wall. Had he entered the Sanctuary itself as only the priests could do, there again he would have found a veil separating him from God.

But in Christ all of these partitions are broken down. There are no walls with Jesus. The whole concourse is broken down. In Christ we can walk directly into the presence of God Himself — just stand in His presence and talk to Him face to face as a man would talk to his best friend. Christ has broken down those walls of partition.

There is so much of that union mentioned in Paul's writings, such as Galatians 3:28: "There is neither Jew nor Greek, there is neither bond nor free, there is neither male nor female." We are all one in Jesus, a common brotherhood. No big and little in Jesus, no rich and poor in Jesus, no learned and unlearned in Jesus. We are all alike before the Lord.

THE HOUSEHOLD OF GOD

Paul concludes, "Therefore ye are no more strangers and foreigners, but fellow-citizens with the saints, and of the household of God" (Eph. 2:19). Sometimes God will say in His Book that we are temples; and again that we are stones in His temple making up the household of faith. Sometimes God will say that we are the members of His body. He is the head and we are the members of His body. How close is my hand to me — a part of me. How close is my foot to me — a part of me. How close is my heart to me — a part of me. How close is my breath to me — a part of me. Just that close are we who once were far off. No walls or partition separates us.

When I am alone, I am by myself and yet I am with God. I ought never to be discouraged for He is there. There are no walls of partition between us. I ought never to be full of fear or anxiety for He is there. I ought never to lack wisdom, for He knows. I ought never to be weak, He is there in strength. I ought never to live a life of lack and poverty. Jesus is there, strength for me, working for me, help for me, kindness for me, mercy for me, forgiveness for me, encouragement for me. And He invites me to come boldly to the throne of grace. I just walk right up to Him and say what it is on my soul and on my heart. Is not that wonderful? What a godly religion, what a boon and what a blessing is ours who know the Lord Christ Jesus, our Saviour!

Do you know Him? You can know Him today.

Chapter 12

JESUS, THE GOD-MAN

> Now therefore ye are no more strangers and foreigners, but fellow-citizens with the saints, and of the household of God;
> And are built upon the foundation of the apostles and prophets, Jesus Christ himself being the chief corner stone. (Eph. 2:19, 20)

Of all the wonderful themes that one can find in the Christian religion, the most incomparable theme is Jesus Himself. Of all the glorious miracles in the Bible, the greatest miracle is the Lord Himself. Of all of the wonders of wonders in the Christian faith, the most wonderful wonder is the Lord Himself. He is incomparable. He is without peer. He is unique, separate, and apart. In all history and from all humanity, there is none like Him. In every other area of human life and achievement, however great, grand, and glorious any man may have been in his chosen field, yet there is another just as fine, just as great, and just as grand. In the field of literature if one names Homer, another will name Shakespeare. In the field of music if one names Mozart, another will name Beethoven. In the field of artistry and painting if one names Raphael, another will name, Michaelangelo, etc. But in the field and in the world of God and God's creation and the revelation of God, if one names Jesus, we are silent. There is none other comparable to the name that is above every name, and at whose name some day every knee shall bow in heaven and earth and under the earth. There is none like Him. There is no mind, there is no genius, and there is no human power that could ever present another personality like Jesus. How could one take the two incongruities of God and His perfection, and man and his imperfection, and put them together

Jesus, the God-Man

in congruity in one life? There are those who look upon the four gospels as being spurious and without authentication. Wonderful! Let us see these critics write a fifth and show us how it was done. Whoever would attempt such an assignment to create another personality like Jesus would find himself in utter frustration. Jesus is alone. He is unique. There is none other like Him in all of the story of humanity. Paul says of Jesus in his letter to the Colossians, "In whom are hid all of the treasures of wisdom and knowledge" (2:3). It is Jesus only we preach.

Theology is a glorious science. The scholastics called it the queen of the sciences. It is a marvelous and incomparable study and revelation. But when Jesus is not there, religion and theology tend to be cold and hard. It is the glorious person of Jesus, who reveals to us God, that makes religion, faith, and theology the glory that it is before God and man. Would you know this Jesus today? Would you see God? Then look at the Lord. When a man preaches Christ, he is preaching the Gospel of God.

JESUS IS THE GOSPEL

In Corinthians 15, there is meticulously defined what the Gospel is. Paul says, "Moreover, brethren, I declare unto you (I define for you) the gospel . . . by which also ye are saved" (1 Cor. 15:1, 2). And what could it be? If a man preaches the Gospel on a foreign field or if he stands in a pulpit in America and preaches the Gospel, what does he preach? Paul says, "I define it for you." Namely, "How that Christ died for our sins according to the scriptures; and that he was buried, and that he rose again the third day according to the scriptures" (vv. 3, 4). When a man preaches the Gospel, he preaches Jesus, and when a man ceases preaching Christ he is finished preaching. It would be better were he not to attempt to preach at all if he leaves Christ out of his message, for the life, the light, the power, and the salvation in a man's sermon lies in his exaltation of Jesus. When we push our Lord into the background, there is nothing left but a darkness and a despair that can be felt, but in preaching Christ Jesus Himself, there is in the sermon light, life, power, and salvation. Our souls reverberate and respond like a harp that is plucked with a hand.

So often the people that go to church will leave and say: "You know, our minister gives himself to wearisome tautologies and boring redundancy. He is taken up with certain things and like an organ grinder, he has five or six tunes that he grinds out Sunday after Sunday." Psychology and sociology, current events, book reviews, the political complexion, the things of the passing ephemera of the day are the themes of many messages. The misguided preacher speaks of those things to the wearisome boredom of the congregation. No one is saved, no one is moved, no one is encouraged, no one is enheartened, no one is lifted up out of the pit of despair. But did you ever hear a man go to church and after the benediction go out the door and say to his wife or to his friends: "You know, our minister exalts Jesus too much. He praises the Lord too zealously and too joyfully and too triumphantly. He preaches Jesus and exaggerates His ableness and power too much"? Or did you ever hear a godly Christian seated by the radio or by the television set, listening to a minister preach Christ, say to the members of the family, "You know, that minister speaks too much about the power of Jesus to heal and to save"? When we go to church we seemingly and unconsciously ask, "Is there something from the Lord? Tell us." It is like the song we sing, "More, More About Jesus." As the Scriptures say in John 12, "If I be lifted up from the earth, [I] will draw all men unto me" (v. 32).

This is the substance and the content of our message, Jesus Christ Himself. He is the means of our salvation. If a man is saved, he is saved by the power of the Gospel of Jesus, the Son of God. The text of the great theological book in the New Testament called the letter to the church at Rome is in the first chapter, "For I am not ashamed of the gospel of Christ: for it is the power of God unto salvation to every one that believeth; to the Jew first, and also to the Greek" (v. 16). The power of salvation is in Jesus Christ Himself. He is the means of our salvation, the occasion of the remission of our sins, the avenue of our entrance into glory.

What Christ Has Done

Paul says so wondrously, "[For he] loved me, and gave himself for me" (Gal. 2:20). That is what Jesus has done for me. That is what Christ has done for all lost sinners. He gave up His throne. He gave up His crown. He gave up the adoration of the angels

Jesus, the God-Man

and the hosts of glory and came down into this cursed world. And coming down, He took upon Himself the form of a man, and being found in fashion as a man, He humbled Himself and became obedient to death, even the death of the cross. This He did for me. What language could describe the hatred that tore His soul and the anger that mutilated His body. When Satan desired Job, God said to him: "He is in your hand, but only thus far can you go and no further. Touch not his body." Finally the Lord said: "He is in your hands. You may afflict his body, but spare his life." But when our Lord was delivered into the hands of sinners and into the hands of Satan, God gave no such interdiction. There were no boundaries to the grief suffered by our Lord.

John says in 1:11, "He came unto his own, and his own received him not." There is no hurt or sorrow like the rejection by those whom you love. Why did He lay upon the heart of the Apostle John the care of His mother as He died on the cross? Because His own brethren did not believe on Him. Who was it who delivered Him to be crucified? His own nation and His own people. When He was delivered into the hands of the Gentiles for execution, they spit upon Him and plucked out His beard. They beat Him with thongs. And finally, they nailed Him to a tree and watched Him die in agony. The earth itself drank up the crimson blood of His life. This He did for me. And the Lord looked upon it, and God said, "It is sufficient for the remission of sins."

The suffering of Jesus, God's Son, is equated in God's eyes with all of the iniquity of all of the world. I could conceive of an angel coming down out of heaven seeking to assume the burden of our transgressions and dying for our sins, but I could not conceive of it being efficacious, of it being able to wash our sins away. The Atonement of Christ is virtuous, it is powerful, it is efficacious because of the Person of the One who suffered and died. He is Prince Emmanuel, God in the flesh. His atoning grace is equal and above what we were when sin did abound. In Him grace did much more abound above the mountains of the iniquities and transgressions of all humanity. When God looks upon us, God says the blood and the suffering and the cross of Jesus are able and powerful, saving to the uttermost those who come to God by Him. "For I am not ashamed of the gospel of Christ, for it is the power of God unto salvation." He is the object of our faith.

COME TO JESUS

There is a marvelous invitation in Isaiah 45:22, "Look unto me, and be ye saved, all the ends of the earth: for I am God, and there is none else." The prophets pointed to Him, the apostles pointed to Him, and all of the leaves of all of the pages of the Bible point to Him. "Look unto me, and be ye saved, all the ends of the earth: for I am God, and there is none else." The invitation of our Lord is just that. "Come unto me, all ye that labour and are heavy laden, and I will give you rest. Take my yoke upon you, and learn of me" (Matt. 11:28, 29). "In all the scriptures he expounded unto [the disciples] the things concerning himself" (Luke 24:27). The object of our faith, of our adoration and our worship is Jesus Christ Himself.

This is the subject of the ministry of the Holy Spirit. Whenever a congregation or people are magnifying and seeking the Holy Spirit above what the Scriptures say, they are that much away from the great purpose of His presence and His coming, the outpouring of God into the earth. For the Lord said that when He, the Spirit of Truth is come, He will not speak of Himself. He will never present Himself. Jesus said, "He shall glorify me: for he shall receive of mine, and shall shew it unto you" (John 16:13, 14). When I hear of a man or a church under the power of the Holy Spirit, I know exactly what the man and his church are doing. They are glorifying and magnifying the Lord Jesus. The instructor is the Holy Spirit. The lesson is Jesus. When we sit at the feet of the Master, the Holy Spirit guides us into that sublime, celestial wisdom, knowledge, grace, power, and salvation hid in the illimitable depths of God in Him. Jesus is our precept — He is the way. Jesus is our doctrine — He is the truth. Jesus is our experience — He is the life. That is why we love the things of God. We are looking to Jesus, the Author and Finisher of our faith. Looking at Him we love the types in the Book because they foreshadow and harbinger Him. We love all the ordinances because they picture Him. We love every page of this Book, because they tell about Him. Were the whole earth and all God's creation an alabaster box it would be in our heart to break it that it might anoint Him. He is the object of our faith.

Look at Jesus

That is why I love an objective expression of religion. I have never felt that a subjective expression of our faith honors God. When I turn my voice, my mind, and my eyes inward I think I am dishonoring the great truth of God in Christ Jesus. I am not denying that there is value in introspection. I remember when I was a student in the seminary there was a movement in the religious world called the Oxford Movement in which the devotee wanted you to draw aside and he would tell you about himself — all of his weaknesses and his sins. He would talk about his religious introspection and self-examination. It was offensive to me then, and now that I have studied through the years, it is even more offensive. Paul says, "Examine yourselves, whether ye be in the faith" (2 Cor. 13:5). There is profit in self-examination, but if you want to fall into despair and to face defeat and failure, just continue looking at yourself and examining yourself.

What I love is to try to lift up my soul and face to gaze upon the Lord Jesus. I may be an epitome of faults and failures, but I know He is all right. I may live in a world of blasphemy and rejection, but I know He is all right. I may face in this world defeat and failure, losing one battle after another, but He will never fail or be discouraged or know defeat. Our church may be filled with all kinds of weaknesses that reflect the carnality and the humanity of the pastor and his people, but I know Jesus is all right. If I can just keep my eyes upon Him, I can walk then on the water like Peter. I can be true to a commitment like Paul and his heavenly mandate. I can die triumphantly like Stephen who saw Him when the heavens opened, if I can just keep my eyes upon Jesus. When you look around, you take your mind, your eye, and your heart off the Lord. When you look around, what discouragements you see in your family, in the circle of your friends, in the world in which you live! Brother, look up! Look at Jesus. The object of our faith is the Lord Jesus.

Jesus Is Comfort

He is not only the content of our message, not only the means, the instrument of our salvation, not only the object of our faith, He is also the comfort of our souls. There is no sweeter verse or admonition in all God's Book than when the author of Hebrews writes, "For in that he himself hath suffered being tempted, he is able to succour them that are tempted" (2:18). He is a high priest who can be moved. He is sensitive to the feeling of our infirmities, for He Himself bore our iniquities and carried all our sicknesses. This is the blessedness and the comfort of our Lord Jesus. He understands and He knows. No tears but that He shed them. No suffering but that He bore it. No disappointment but that He lived through it. No agony of spirit but that He also agonized just like you. To know that the Lord understands and is with us, oh, what a bond and what a comfort!

When I went to the funeral of my father I sat in the little chapel, my mother by my side, leaning against me, and the preacher said: "Late, late one night I went by the hospital to see Mr. Criswell. I stood by his bed and said, 'Mr. Criswell, how are you?' And my father replied, 'Sir, the nights are long and lonely, but Jesus is with me, comforts me, and helps me.' " What a wonderful thing to say! The comfort of the blessed Lord Jesus. Sometimes when people will bury their dead they will be hesitant about coming to church. If church is just another liquor party, just another social gathering, I say burn it up, tear it apart, dismiss it, be done with it. But if church is a place where Jesus is preached and the Lord is lifted up and God is named, then in the midst of my sorrow and grief, make a place for me to be present, for I need God's comfort and God's help. That is Christ to us.

How many of us have been encouraged by His triumph over death as He suffered on the cross! There have been saints in dungeons who were in spirit free as though they walked on the earth. There are godly men who have been stretched on the rack but have said: "It is like a bed of ease, like lying of soft down. Jesus is here." And how many martyrs have clapped their hands when all ten fingers have been dipped in pitch and burned like flaming candles crying out "Christ is all!"

> I saw the martyr at the stake,
> The flames could not his courage shake,
> Nor death his soul appall.
> I asked him whence his strength was given,
> He looked triumphantly to heaven and answered,
> "Christ is all."

When in the fiery furnace, the three young men walked around free with the fourth who was the Son of God. The fire but melted their bonds and set them free.

> When through fiery trials thy pathway shall lie,
> My grace all-sufficient shall be thy supply;
> The flames shall not hurt thee; I only design
> Thy dross to consume, and thy gold to refine.

With Him — whether in the furnace, in the fire, in the pit, in the valley, or in the grave — it is all light and hope, joy and salvation; for Jesus is all that to us. Jesus alone is all-sufficient.

Chapter 13

THE MYSTERY OF THE CHURCH

For this cause I Paul, the prisoner of Jesus Christ for you Gentiles,
If ye have heard of the dispensation of the grace of God which is given me to you-ward:
How that by revelation (not by reason) he made known unto me the mystery (musterion)....
Which in other ages was not made known unto the sons of men, as it is now revealed unto his holy apostles and prophets by the Spirit;
That the Gentiles should be fellow-heirs, and of the same body (the body of our Lord, the Church) and partakers of his promise in Christ by the gospel:
Whereof I was made a minister....
Unto me, who am less than the least of all saints, is this grace given, that I should preach among the Gentiles the unsearchable riches of Christ;
And to make all men see what is the fellowship of the mystery (musterion), which from the beginning of the world hath been hid in God, who created all things by Jesus Christ:
To the intent that now (up in heaven where it was not even known) unto the principalities and powers (those orders of heavenly beings) in heavenly places might be known by the church the manifold wisdom of God,
According to the eternal purpose which he purposed in Christ Jesus our Lord. (Eph. 3:1-11)

Without the truth of this passage, the Bible is a locked, unknown, unsearchable, fragmented Book, but in the explanation of this text every part of the Bible becomes a significant, beautifully integrated part.

A Secret Revealed

In verse 3 we read, "How that by revelation he made known unto me the mystery (the *musterion*)." Then in verse 9 Paul says God called him "to make all men see what is the fellowship (the dispensation) of the mystery, which from the beginning of the world hath been hid in God . . ." but now is made known to the angels in heaven as well as to the saints on the earth. The English Bible translation of the Greek word *musterion* sometimes presents to us an incorrect idea. A mystery to us is an enigma; it is something that we cannot ferret out. A mystery to us is unsearchable or is incapable of being understood. But a *musterion* in the days of the Apostle Paul, and as it is used here in the New Testament, is not anything like that. In the days when Paul lived the Roman Empire was covered with what they called mystery religions. Only the initiates, only those who were inducted into the mystery understood it. It is the same kind of thing as that found today in the Masonic Lodge. In the Masonic Lodge one is inducted into its mysteries; things about it one learns only when he is initiated into it. That is the way the word *musterion* was used in the days of the Roman Empire, and that is the way Paul uses it here. It was an ordinary Greek word referring to secrets that were made known only to those to whom they were revealed.

Paul says there is a *musterion*, a secret, that God kept in His heart. Even the angels did not know it and the prophets did not see it until the day that He revealed it to His holy apostles.

What The Secret Is Not

What is that *musterion*? What is that secret that was kept in the heart of God? Is it that the kingdom of God would include the Gentiles? No, for the old dispensation, the Old Testament, is filled with promised blessings to the Gentiles. The Old Covenant begins with God's promise to Abraham that "In thee shall all families of the earth be blessed" (Gen. 12:3). Over and over again will one find in the Old Testament the prophecies that the Gentiles are going to be blessed. God is going to use Israel to bring that blessing to the whole world. As we read newspaper headlines today, we cannot help but be amazed at the fulfillment of this prophecy. For example, in the last verses of Isaiah 19, Isaiah prophesies:

> In that day shall there be a highway out of Egypt to Assyria, and the Assyrian shall come into Egypt, and the Egyptian into Assyria, and the Egyptians shall serve with the Assyrians.
> In that day shall Israel be the third with Egypt and with Assyria, even a blessing in the midst of the land:
> Whom the LORD of hosts shall bless, saying, Blessed be Egypt my people, and Assyria the work of my hands, and Israel mine inheritance (vv. 23-25).

Now what do you think about that? Just look at the headlines today. The fact that the Gentiles are going to be blessed and that the Gentiles are going to be saved is no mystery, no *musterion*. It is written all through the Bible. That is what the Bible is about — that God is going to take Abraham and then his seed (Isaac, Jacob, and Israel), and is going to use Israel to be a blessing to the whole world. That is no mystery. That is what the Bible reveals.

Is the mystery the suffering and the glories of Christ? No, the prophets predicted that clearly. In the most beautiful, glowing, and dramatic terms in the Bible the suffering of Christ is predicted. In Isaiah 53, seven hundred fifty years before it came to pass, Isaiah described the passion of our Lord as though He were standing on the top of Mount Calvary watching Him die. The same prophet in the same breath will describe the glories of the Lord. We read in Isaiah 9, ". . . and his name shall be called Wonderful, Counsellor, The mighty God, The everlasting Father, The Prince of Peace" (v. 6). Isaiah 11 describes the glories of the Lord and the kingdom. So it is no mystery that Christ should suffer and that He should be glorified.

WHAT THE SECRET IS

What is the mystery that was kept in the secret heart of God until the day He revealed it to His apostles? The secret was this: that between the suffering of our Lord and the kingdom appearance of our Lord there was to be a long period of time, an age of grace, a dispensation of mercy, and that in that period of time God was going to form another entity. It would be made up of Jews and Gentiles alike and they would be of the same body belonging to the same household of faith. That was the mystery. Even the angels did not know it. First Peter says, ". . . which things the angels

The Mystery of the Church

desire to look into" (1:12) wondering what God was doing. To show you that the angels did not know it, when the Lord ascended to heaven, as we read in Acts 1:11, the apostles stood there looking up into heaven, and the angels came and said to those men, "Ye men of Galilee, why stand ye gazing up into heaven? this same Jesus, which is taken up from you into heaven, shall so come in like manner as ye have seen him go into heaven." He shall ascend, and then He shall come down. They said it as though He were ascending and then coming right down. Even the angels did not know that between the passion and ascension of Christ and His coming back again was to be this great period of time.

The prophets also did not know it. It was a *musterion* that was revealed to the later apostles like a hidden valley between two great mountain peaks. When one examines the mountains from afar they look like one mountain range with two giant peaks side by side, but on closer examination one finds that the two mountain peaks are far apart. Here is one and there is the other. There is a wide valley between. That is exactly what the prophets saw and that is all that the angels knew. They saw the coming of Christ in suffering. They saw the coming of Christ in His glory. But they never saw the wide valley between, and in that valley God says He is going to create something new: the Jew and the Gentile alike should belong to the household of faith. Is not that a remarkable thing!

A New Age Revealed

What is this age and this new creation, this church that God hid in His heart until He revealed it? Let us say what it is not. It is not the continuation of the old dispensation, of the Old Covenant. The church in this age is a new dispensation.

In Matthew 9 the Lord says that this church age is not a new patch on an old garment. It is not new wine put into an old wineskin. When the patch shrinks, it tears the rend bigger. When the wine begins to ferment, it breaks up the old bottle, the old skin. One has to put the wine into a new skin so that as it ferments and expands, the pliable skin will expand also. Christianity is not a new patch on an Old Covenant. It is something new. In Luke 17 the Lord said that the law and the prophets were "until John." But when John the forerunner came he introduced a new dispensation.

The first chapter of the fourth gospel says, "For the law was given by Moses, but grace and truth came by Jesus Christ" (John 1:17). There is a complete break there between the old and the new. That is what Romans 9, 10, and 11 are about. The Lord was working with His chosen people, the Jewish people. When they rejected their Messiah, the Lord took out of that era, that dispensation, the natural olive branch (the Jews) and He grafted in a wild olive branch which Paul says is the Gentiles. But, Paul also says, God is going to put back that native olive branch, the one that belongs. He is going to graft it back into the tree and it is going to flourish and grow. We are not a continuation of the so-called Jewish church. We are a new dispensation, a new covenant. We are in a New Testament, under a new government. It was something new that God has done. In other words, the church is one thing, and the kingdom is another thing. They are not the same.

In the Holy Scriptures Jesus is the head of the church and the church is His body. Jesus is the head of the church but one will never find any such nomenclature as that Jesus is the king of the church. It is not in the Bible, for a king must have a kingdom. The church has a head, a Lord, and we are His body. Now there is to be a kingdom. When John the Baptist came he said, "Repent ye: for the kingdom of heaven is at hand" (Matt. 10:7). But the Jews rejected their King and now He is an exiled King. He has gone away, but some day He is coming back and He is returning to be the King. He is coming back to establish His kingdom, to reign over the whole creation. But between now and then is this hiatus, this valley in between. This valley is the dispensation, the age of the calling out of this people, the church. It is the day of creation of this new body, the church.

What Is the Church?

The church is not a continuation of the old dispensation, it is something new. It is not the kingdom, for the kingdom is coming, but the church is right here. I belong to a church. What is the church? The church is the called out people of the Lord through the years, and now through the centuries. Of all the families, tribes, and people under the sun — the Jew, the Gentile, the northerner, the southerner, the easterner, the westerner — God is creating a new something and He calls it (it is a tragedy that we have lost the word) His *ecclesia*.

For three hundred years after Christ what our Lord created was called the *ecclesia*, but when Constantine was converted and built those gorgeous temples they changed it from *ecclesia* to *kuriakos* — a lordly house. The same word moved through the languages: *kuriakos, kirkus, kirk, church*. But the Bible knows nothing about this, for the church in the Bible is an *ecclesia*, the called out people of the Lord. The church can be anywhere. It can be in a barn, it can gather on a sawdust floor, it can be in a den or a cave, it can be in your house. The church can be anywhere, for the church is you; it is the people of the Lord, the called out people of God.

These buildings are nothing else but instruments, a facility. Like a mason needs a trowel, like a carpenter needs a hammer and saw, and like a solider needs arms, so the church needs a place to gather. I look upon these facilities like that. As the school system has facilities to teach reading, writing, and arithmetic, so I have facilities to teach about Jesus and about the Bible, about our souls, about heaven, and about glory. These are only facilities, but the church is you. I could preach just as well under a tabernacle as I could in a church with fine carpet and cushioned seats. In fact, I did it for years. The church is not a building. It is God's ecclesia. He is calling out His people.

What a glory that He calls us! God chose us and put it in our hearts to respond. The church is His bride; the church is His body. In the Book of Ephesians Paul turned to the second chapter of Genesis and took out of the story of the creation of Eve these words: "For we are members of his body, of his flesh, and of his bones. For this cause shall a man leave his father and mother, and be joined unto his wife: and they shall be one flesh" (Eph. 5: 30, 31; See Gen. 2:24).

What Paul is saying is this: that as Eve, the bride of Adam, was taken out of Adam's side, even so also the Bride of Christ, the church, was taken out of the side of our Lord. We are born in His tears, in His sobs, in His cross, in His suffering, in His blood, in His wounds, and in His death. That is where the church came from. We are His bride. God took us out of the body of our Lord and that is where we belong, close to the heart of our Saviour even as Eve belonged in the arms of Adam. God made her that way. "For this cause shall a man leave his father and mother, and shall be joined unto his wife, and they two shall be one flesh. This is a great mystery: but I speak concerning Christ and the church." Look what the Lord has done for us! That we should be His bride, His church, that is the mystery that was hid in the secret heart of God until the Lord revealed it to His holy apostles and to us.

THE DESTINY OF THE CHURCH

What is the destiny of the church? If we are on shouting ground when we talk about where we came from, out of the love of our Lord and out of His riven side, born in His blood and in His cross, then we are on hallelujah ground when we think of the glory we behold when we contemplate our destiny. What is the destiny of the bride of Christ, this new thing that God has created? What is the destiny of the Church? Paul again calls that a mystery.

> Now this I say, brethren, that flesh and blood cannot inherit the kingdom of God; neither doth corruption inherit incorruption.
> Behold, I shew you a mystery; We shall not all sleep, but we shall all be changed,
> In a moment, in the twinkling of an eye, at the last trump: for the trumpet shall sound, and the dead shall be raised incorruptible, and we shall be changed (1 Cor. 15:50-52).

The destiny of the church is seen in the word *rapture*. The word is an old Anglo-Saxon word that describes the meaning of "caught up" (1 Thess. 4:17). The church is to be raptured. It is a word meaning "to snatch away, to catch away." The destiny of the church is to be "caught up" with the Lord, to be taken out of the world. As the Lord said, "Then shall two be in the field; the one shall be taken, and the other left" (Matt. 24:40, 41). The rapture, the catching up of God's children to the Lord at the great consummation of the age, is the destiny of the church.

A duality of response to the coming of the Lord is found all through the Scriptures. Some of us will be raised up from the dead and others of us who are alive at the coming of the Lord will be raptured. Of the two Old Testament saints who were talking to

The Mystery of the Church

our Lord at His transfiguration, Elijah went up to heaven in a whirlwind of fire. When the chariots of Israel came for him, he was raptured; he never died. But Moses was there talking to Him also. Moses died and was buried. He represents those who are resurrected from the dead. Such is the destiny of the church. The church is to be with Jesus in His coming glory. Those who have died in Christ shall be raised to be with Him when He comes, and those who are still alive when He comes will be caught up, raptured, to be with Him.

In John 11 we find the profoundest sentence in human language. Jesus said, "I am the resurrection and the life" (v. 24). The duality of resurrection and rapture are here again. To those who have fallen asleep in the Lord and are buried in the earth Jesus says, "I am the resurrection." He shall speak and they shall live again. But Jesus also says: "I am the life. And whosoever liveth and believeth in me shall never die." Those who are alive and remain unto the coming of the Lord shall be changed and raptured to be with the Lord. They shall never die. This is the destiny of the church.

In 1 Corinthians 15 Paul says, speaking of the great consummating date, ". . . then shall be brought to pass the saying that is written, Death is swallowed up in victory. O death, where is thy sting? O grave, where is thy victory?" (vv. 54, 55). "O grave, where is thy victory" is the resurrection cry of these who have fallen asleep in the Lord, "O death, where is thy sting?" is the glorious cry of those who are raptured. "For this we say unto you by the word of the Lord," writes the apostle, "that we which are alive and remain unto the coming of the Lord shall not prevent (precede) them which are asleep. For the Lord himself shall descend from heaven with a shout, with the voice of the archangel, and with the trump of God: and the dead in Christ shall rise first (that is the resurrection): Then we which are alive and remain shall be caught up together with them in the clouds, to meet the Lord in the air" (that is the rapture) (1 Thess. 4:15-17). Always it is those two side by side — the resurrection and the rapture. Those who have fallen asleep in Jesus and we who are alive and remain to His coming shall all be with the Lord. Not the least of the saints who has trusted in Jesus will God forget. He marked the place where the missionary fell on a foreign field. He saw it. The humblest servant of Jesus who lives to the appearing of the Lord will also be remembered. We all have a part. We all will be there. This is the destiny of the church. This is the secret God has revealed to us. This is the mystery of the church.

Chapter 14

THE UNSPEAKABLE RICHES OF CHRIST

> For this cause I Paul, the prisoner of Jesus Christ for you Gentiles,
> If ye have heard of the dispensation of the grace of God which is given me to you-ward. . . .
> Whereof I was made a minister, according to the gift of the grace of God given unto me by the effectual working of his power.
> Unto me, who am less than the least of all saints, is this grace given, that I should preach among the Gentiles the unsearchable riches of Christ. (Eph. 3:1, 2, 7, 8)

A remarkable trait is the personal attitude of the Apostle Paul toward his ministry. He felt and expressed it repeatedly. It was a grace of God that he was permitted to preach. It was an unmerited remembrance and favor of heaven. "Unto me, who am less than the least of all saints, is this grace given (this unmerited, undeserved favor), that I should preach . . . the unsearchable riches of Christ." By man's measurements Paul's ministry was anything but attractive. His gains were his losses, his honors were his dishonors, and his glories were only in his sufferings, his privations, his stonings, and his imprisonments. Yet he gloried in the offering of a life that was beaten, bludgeoned, and finally destroyed. He gloried in the offering of a suffering life under God. He did not look upon the sacrificial cost of his ministry as something that he was driven to, like a galley slave to his seat. It was not a servitude of grievous and burdensome character, but it was something that he accepted in gratitude and looked upon as a special gift from God.

The Privilege of Preaching

One time the angels preached the Gospel at a midnight hour. They pointed to the little Babe in Bethlehem as the Saviour of the world. Likewise, in the midnight hour, beaten and bloody in stocks and chains in a dungeon, Paul and Silas prayed and sang praises to God. Paul's whole ministry was received as a gift of grace from heaven's hands. Not only that, but he looked upon his ministry as one for which he was not worthy to embrace or to share. "Unto me, who am less than the least of all saints, is this grace given, that I should preach . . . the unsearchable riches of Christ." That is not very grammatical is it? "Less than the least." Yet there is a grammar of the heart and of the soul that all of us understand. "I am less than the least of all of the saints," Paul, the greatest of all the apostles, said.

In Romans 16, saluting the saints in Rome, he calls them by name, saying, "Salute Andronicus and Junia, my kinsmen (they were Jews), and my fellow-prisoners, who are of note among the apostles, who also were in Christ before me" (v. 7). When Andronicus and Junia were preaching the Gospel, Paul was persecuting the church and wasting the household of faith. This was a burden to his heart and a bitter memory to his mind as long as he lived, so he says that he was less than Andronicus and less than Junia. He says, "I am the least of the saints, and yet to me is the place given that I should preach the unsearchable riches of Christ."

That has been my judgment of the true men of God. The deeper the vessel and the more laden it is, the further down in the water does it sink. Empty cans clatter and jostle on the surface of the sea. Those who are empty and self-conceited are loud, cheap, and empty. But the true man of God is like Paul, less than the least. In the nineteenth century there were two famous preachers in London, Joseph Parker and Charles Haddon Spurgeon. One day a man came to Joseph Parker and asked him: "Why did the Lord choose Judas, one of the twelve who betrayed him?" The humble preacher replied, "I am not able to answer, but the great mystery to me is not why he chose Judas, but why should the Lord have chosen me." Charles Haddon Spurgeon one time exclaimed in a sermon, "In the wonder of the elected love and grace of God, my heart cries out, 'Why me, O Lord, why me?' " This is the apostle.

The Unspeakable Riches of Christ

God's Glorious Goodness

It is a remarkable quality, not only Paul's personal attitude toward his ministry, but also how the splendor and wonder of the glory of God's goodness in Christ was ever fresh in his writings and in his life and ministry. Paul will be dictating along in his thirteen letters, plowing through some deep theological argument, when suddenly without any argumentative or apologetic reason at all, he will burst into some glorious, laudatory praise of the wonder and splendor of God's love in Christ Jesus.

For instance, in Romans 9, 10, and 11 we find a deep theological discussion concerning the problem of Israel's unbelief. In the midst of that doctrinal argument, Paul includes an interjection of praise.

> O the depth of the riches both of the wisdom and knowledge of God! How unsearchable are his judgments, and his ways past finding out. . . .
> For of him, and through him, and to him, are all things: to whom be glory for ever. Amen" (11:33, 36)

The burst of praise has nothing to do with the argument at all, but as Paul writes of those deep theological discussions in the Book of Romans he suddenly breaks into an exclamation of praise as though he were standing in the very presence of a dazzling revelation.

The entire writing, as well as the whole life of the Apostle Paul, was like that, as if a man were standing with his arms raised beholding the splendors of the revelation of God. Wherever he turned, there were other views of the glory of God just as majestic, just as iridescent, just as unspeakable, and just as unsearchable. It is as though a man has gone to the gate into the new Jerusalem and cries out in wonder, awe, and amazement at the glory of the sight that he sees here, there, and all around him. It is as though a man were going down a highway of supernal glory and beauty and every bypass that he took was no less wondrous. So it is with the explanation of the Apostle Paul concerning his ministry and his life. The wonder just kept advancing and expanding until finally it covered all heaven and earth. "Unto me, who am the least of the saints, is this grace given, that I should preach . . . the unsearchable riches of Christ."

The Riches of His Person

The riches in Christ are in His person, in the man Himself. Paul preached doctrinal truth, but he never preached it apart from the person of the Lord Himself. If Paul is preaching the doctrine of justification by faith, it is always as a part of the great atoning, suffering Christ. If Paul is preaching sanctification by the Spirit, it is always that we might be conformed to the image of God's Son. Paul never delivers the doctrine as though it were a cold stone rolled upon the sepulcher door where the Saviour is hidden within. Always when Paul preached the doctrine, it was as a herald of the living Lord Himself.

Paul's abounding awe before the presence of the Son of God is worshipful in itself. He would speak of the Lord as the express image of the invisible God. He would speak of the Lord as the One in whom all the Godhead dwelt bodily. Deity was clothed in human flesh in Jesus. Even in the story of His life in the earth, that deity shone through. O Lord Jesus, the wind knew Thee and was still at Thy voice. The waves knew Thee and kissed Thy feet. The angels knew Thee and administered unto Thee. The demons knew Thee and fled from Thy holy presence. Disease turned to health and strength at Thy voice, and the dead were raised when Thou didst speak. Oh, the unsearchable riches of God in Christ Jesus in His person!

The Riches of His Atoning Power

Paul preached the riches of God in Christ Jesus in His atoning grace and power to save. Did you ever think of this? Before the Lord came, before He died on the cross, all of the myriads of Old Testament saints before the day of the cross were saved by His promise and pledge to die for their sins. If the power of Christ's promise availed to save the myriads before the cross, think of the power of the day of the cross itself! Think of the abounding overflowing righteousness of that atoning hour when Jesus died for our sins. That was the Gospel Paul preached that brought such wonder and awe to his soul. Paul stood in reverence before the Lord, treasuring every groan, tear, sob, and drop of blood that God's Son poured out into this earth for our atonement, for the expiation of our sins, for the forgiveness of our transgressions, for the washing out of the stain in our soul.

Oh, the sufferings of our Lord! While He was in the agony of prayer they arrested Him. He was betrayed by one who had just broken bread with Him. His back was cut with many stripes, yet He deserved no stripes. He was carried in ignominy through the streets of Jerusalem, a city over which He had wept. He was crucified outside its walls as though He were not fit to be inside the city itself, put to death by those who should have worshiped Him and adored Him. He who merited the adulation and reverence of kings was spat upon and nailed to a tree like a felonious criminal. To so many His atoning death is nothing. But in God's sight, the tears, sobs, cries, sufferings, and blood of Christ are infinitely precious, so much so that God says to those who will love His Son: "For His sake I will write their names in the Book of Life. I will give them eternal glory. I will forgive their sins. I will save them forever." This is a part of the riches of God in Christ Jesus, His atoning grace.

THE RICHES OF HIS ASCENSION

Paul preached that the riches of God in Christ Jesus can be seen in His ascension into heaven and intercession for us there before the throne of grace. We are joint heirs with Him there. He is my friend and advocate before the Father. His presence there is a guarantee and a pledge that some day I shall stand there also. Look at Him. My Saviour and my friend is standing at the right hand of the throne of glory.

> The golden sun, the silvery moon,
>   And all the stars that shine,
> Were made by His omnipotent hand,
>   And He's a friend of mine.
>
> When He shall come with trumpet sound
>   To head the conquering line,
> The world will bow before His feet,
>   And He's a friend of mine.

It is unspeakable, it is unfathomable, it is unimaginable, the glory Christ Jesus brings to those who love Him. No wonder Paul quoted from Isaiah, "Eye hath not seen, nor ear heard, neither have entered into the heart of man, the things which God hath prepared for them that love him" (1 Cor. 2:9). He is able to save to the uttermost them who come to God by Him, seeing He ever liveth to make intercession for them. He is bowing down His ear to hear our prayers. He is giving us the dreams, the hopes, and the visions of our hearts. All things are ours, and He puts in our hearts to want, to covet, and to pray for the things that are right, good, and best.

The Riches of His Presence

Paul preached that not only there in heaven in His ascended grace and glory do we find His riches, but also we have His riches here in His presence with us in this earth. Like a veritable sea of grace and glory do the ocean waters of Christ's love flow around the shores of our common life. In everything that we do, there the Lord is. His presence is felt, loved, prayed for, and appreciated. Jesus is with us. The sweetest memory of all memories of my boyhood is something that was so unplanned and unthought for. I remember my mother singing as she worked in the house, singing as she washed the dishes, singing as she cooked at the stove, singing as she swept the house. She always sang the sweet songs of Zion, the hymns of the church, the songs about Jesus. The Lord's presence is like that in all of the common, everyday chores of our life, even in our sorrows, disappointments, and frustrations. They have God in them. Like the storm cloud with light streaming through, or like the showers in April that mix with the sunbeam, God's presence with us is rich in grace. It is our everlasting possession, comfort, and joy.

I remember a couple who had a little business. Both of them worked in it. They were a sweet, precious couple, On Christmas Day he had a sudden heart seizure and died. I made my way to the home so heavy hearted. Of all days the tragedy fell on Christmas Day and I had to go to that house to see if I could be of any comfort and encouragement to that poor young wife, her husband lying there dead before her. But One had been there before me, for she said to me: "When I was saved, I experienced God's saving grace. For the years of my life I have known His living grace. And now that my husband is gone, God has given me dying grace." Then she added: "It was God's Christmas present to my husband. For today, Christmas Day, God introduced him to the saints and to the angels in glory." When I left the house I left exalted and lifted up. Christmas Day brought death and separation to her, but in Christ it brought a Christmas present for him. "Today he was presented to the saints and the angels in glory." Oh, what God hath done for us!

The Riches of His Return

Paul preached the riches of Christ's return. He said, "When he ascended up on high, he led captivity captive, and gave gifts unto men" (Eph. 4:8). When the Lord shall come, captivity is captive, and death is no more. He gives this to men. Oh, our gifts are so feeble and faulty. But His gifts! Why, He will give eyes to the blind so they can see. He will give feet to the crippled so they can walk. He will give life to the dead so they shall live when the Lord comes in glory, in grace, in majesty, and in power. The riches of God in Christ Jesus!

Recently a young adult came to see me and said: "I am so troubled. I am afraid of the coming of the Lord. It strikes terror in my heart." I said: "Dear child, afraid? Afraid at the coming of Jesus? Tell me, had you lived in the days of His flesh, and had He knocked at your door, and had you gone to the door to open it and there stood the lovely Jesus, would you have been afraid? Had the Son of God in mortal flesh stood at the door, would you have been afraid? Would you not have been overcome with gladness and expectancy?"

When Jesus came into a house, one could not get near it because the blind, the lame, and the poor were brought that His hands might touch them and bless them. Mothers brought little babies that He might pray over them. Afraid? He may have cast aside His garments of poverty and now be robed in glory, but His heart is still the same. God's Book says so. "This same Jesus" shall soon come back "in like manner." It will be the Lord Himself "and He is a friend of mine." I am not to dread or be full of fear at His coming. It will be the same blessed face, the same gracious hands, and the same loving heart.

His Unending Riches

The redeemed millions never waste His abounding fullness. Though countless numbers have partaken, the table is still laden like a banquet. We need no preparation to come to the Lord. You may come just as you are. He has robes of righteousness, pure and white. You do not need to bring a crust of bread. He is the manna from heaven. You do not need to wash a single stain out of your soul — His blood cleanses us from all sin. You might as well take a candle to the sun as to bring your own righteousness to Jesus. Just come as you are. There is grace, forgiveness, and mercy enough and to spare. Oh, the unsearchable riches of God in Christ Jesus!

Chapter 15

WHEN ANGELS ATTEND CHURCH

> To the intent that now unto the principalities and powers in heavenly places might be known by the church the manifold wisdom of God. (Eph. 3:10)

Paul has written in the third chapter of Ephesians that there was a great secret in the heart of God. He kept it hidden from the world, from the angels, from the patriarchs, and from the prophets until the time came for Him to reveal it to His holy apostles. That secret was that there was to be a new creation, a new body, a new temple, and that Jew and Gentile alike were to belong to that new creation of God, the church. Then Paul wonders at the marvelous grace of God that He should be chosen to reveal and to preach that truth. After his exclamation of awesome wonder in verse 8 Paul says that he is to make known to all men the fellowship of this mystery, "To the intent that now unto the principalities and powers in the heavenly places might be known by the church the manifold wisdom of God."

Paul is describing by his words "principalities and powers" the families, the clans, the orders of the angels in heaven. He is saying in the text that by the church is made known to the angels and to the orders of celestial beings in heaven, the manifold, multicolored, multifaceted wisdom of God. Just the idea of it is astonishing, overwhelming, and almost unbelievable: that the angels in heaven, the orders of those heavenly beings, are taught the manifold wisdom of God by the church. They learn it here through us, these first-born, these elders of all God's created beings. In no other place in the Bible is it suggested that they learn the manifold wisdom of God except by the church. What an amazing discovery

Paul herein writes! Think of the angels' exalted position. They look with undimmed eyes upon the vision beatific. In awe and in reverence they worship before the throne of the Eternal where the Almighty reigns forever. They veil their faces, crying, "Holy, Holy, Holy." As it were, they stand in the sun. Yet the Bible does not say that by their exalted position they learn the manifold wisdom of God.

The Angels at the Creation of the World

Think of the angels' presence at the beginning of the creation. They were amazed and astonished at what God was doing when He made the firmament and the arches of the sky. Job says that the morning stars sang together and the sons of God rejoiced when God made the world. They looked upon each new creation with awe — the great milky way, the stars that were turned into flames by the light of deity, and the entire stellar creation of the Almighty. Yet the Book does not say that in this, as they beheld the creative genius of God, did they learn the manifold wisdom of the Almighty.

The angels were present when God's crowning creation was given life and breath. They were present when Adam was made, and when God created Eve, his fair consort, to walk by his side, both of them carefully and wonderfully made in body, mind, and soul. The last creative, highest, genius of the Almighty was in making the man in His own image and in His own likeness. The angels were there and looked upon it. Yet even in that, the most wondrous of all of God's creations, the Bible does not say that the angels learned the manifold wisdom of God.

Throughout the centuries and the millennia of God's providences apart from the church, throughout the geological ages, the billions and billions of years that the firmament has reflected the glory of its Maker, and throughout all of the providences of life, the Scriptures do not say that the angels learned the manifold wisdom of God. They learn God's wisdom in the church.

What an exalted conception and idea of the church this is! What the angelic beings did not learn in the presence of Deity, and what they have not learned in all of the providences of God through the centuries, they learn in how God saves men, and in how God's redemptive grace is building this new creation, the church, the body of the Lord. That is what Peter referred to in 1 Peter 1:12 when he said, "[And of these] things the angels desired to look into." He speaks of the marvelous, redemptive purpose of God as He works it out among fallen human beings in their regeneration and in their addition to the church. Let us look at what the angels learn as they look upon the church and see the grace of God add to the building up of the body of Christ.

THE ANGELS LEARN GOD'S PLAN OF SALVATION

First, the angels learn as they see how God saves fallen men, God's plan of salvation. Had there been a called parliament of all the celestial spirits of God's universe and had there been proposed to them the problem of how can God be just and justify the ungodly, they might have discussed and debated it for the unending ages. Yet could they never have come forward from that assembly of debate and forensics with an answer. How can God be just and still justify the ungodly? How can God be righteous and holy, upholding the laws of His universe, and at the same time abrogate that justice and those laws for a sinful, fallen man? Yet in this divine plan of redemption every virtue and every attribute of God shines forth in undiminished luster. Like the crown of an Oriental monarch with clusters of jewels all around, so is the corona of God. None of the attributes of God is soiled or diminished by the way God saves men. God is just. God is righteous. God upholds His righteousness. When there was sin found in Lucifer, God flung him headlong, flaming from the ethereal sky down to the abyss. When Samson, the strongest man in the world, sinned away his hour of grace, he bowed his head and said, "God, let me die with the Philistines," and he did. God is just. When David, the man after God's own heart, sinned, the Lord said to him, "The sword shall never leave thy house," and it did not. The story of David is written in blood. God is just. But at the same time, in His holiness and in His righteousness, in His upholding inexorable law which is grounded in His character and in His very being, the Lord is merciful, gracious, forgiving, and abounding in love. He is both of them: just and merciful.

God has kept that amazing and astonishing dualism of opposites without contradiction by the God-man, Christ Jesus. Christ upholds the righteousness of God, not one jot or tittle falling from it. At the same time He pays the penalty for our sin thus upholding the righteous judgments of God and yet showing mercy, dying in love for our fallen souls. How the angels, looking upon that, must have been astonished! What we lost in Eden in the sin of the first Adam, we have gained and more besides in the second Adam, Christ. The fellowship with God that was disrupted by the transgression in Eden is restored to us in the cross. All of the tragedy of our lost paradise is more than restored to us in the fellowship of the new Jerusalem. How the angels looking upon it must have been astonished!

In the wisdom of God, those who encompassed our destruction are destroying themselves. Satan is stung by his own venom. Goliath is slain by his own sword. Death is destroyed by its own captive. As in Adam all die, even so in Christ shall all be made alive. As by one man, Adam, sin came into this world, and death by sin, so by one man, the God-man Christ Jesus, is sin destroyed, and life and immortality brought to life. What an astonishing fact! What the angels learned in the redemptive purpose, program, and plan of God!

God's Book says that the angels rejoice in heaven when a lost sinner comes back to the Lord. Did you ever think upon that? Up there in glory watching over us, looking at us, the angels are attending the services of the church. When someone comes down the aisle and gives his heart to Jesus, there is rejoicing in heaven. The angels of heaven are learning in the church and rejoicing in the church.

In Acts 9 the story is told of the Apostle Paul breathing out threatening and slaughter against the church. But suddenly he was struck down by the brightness of the glory of the presence of Christ. As he approached Damascus, led by the hand now, this proud and bitter Pharisee has been blinded by the glory of God. Inside Damascus the Lord appeared to Ananias and said, "Go into the street which is called Straight, and inquire . . . for one Saul of Tarsus: for, behold, he prayeth." This proud, blaspheming man is now down on his knees praying, confessing, asking God to forgive the chief of sinners. It is a miracle. It is a glory and it happens every day. It is something that the angels are introduced to in the church, to the intent that "unto the principalities and powers in heavenly places might be known by the church the manifold wisdom of God."

THE ANGELS LEARN OF GOD'S PREPARATION FOR THE COMING OF CHRIST

The angels have watched the development and the progress in type and in story through all of the years as God prepared for the coming of the great Redeemer. It was Abraham who entertained those angels unawares. It was an angel who stopped the hands of Abraham when he raised it to plunge the knife into his son, Isaac. It was the angels who, when Jacob was asleep at Bethel, ascended and descended the ladder that leaned against the throne of heaven. It was the angels who welcomed Jacob back from Pandan-aram, back to the promised land. It was the angels, who all through the dispensation of the law, looked full upon the mercy-seat. One here, one there, their wings touching and their faces looking down upon the mercy-seat where the blood of expiation was poured. It was the angels who announced the coming of the Saviour at Bethlehem. It was the angels who followed and ministered to Him. It was the angels who comforted Him in His suffering. It was the angels who rolled away the stone and announced that He was not there, for He was risen. It was the angels who watched Him ascend into heaven and said to the apostles who followed Him upward that He would come again in the same manner He left. And it is the angels, the holy angels of God, who will accompany the Son of glory when He comes back at the consummation of the age.

THE ANGELS WATCH GOD'S BUILDING OF HIS CHURCH

The angels watch and see the building up of the body of Christ here in the earth, the temple made without hands. The great cornerstone is not Michael, nor Gabriel, nor a patriarch or prophet or apostle, but the God-man Himself, Christ Jesus. As the living stones are added to the building they all lean on the cornerstone, the God-man, our Saviour. What kind of a temple is it? Is it Romanesque? No. Gothic? No. Grecian? No. It is a temple rising after the pattern shown to Moses on the mount, like the sanctuary that is in heaven. It is both down here and up there.

122   *Ephesians: An Exposition*

Some of the living stones are up there in the pinnacle of paradise, above the clouds and stars. Some of the living stones are down here, we who are yet in the earth. But whether some of them are there in the glory of heaven or whether some of us are here in the pilgrimage of this earth, we are all together in the body of our Lord, they there and we here. In that glorious temple called the church, the house of God, the Lord Himself dwells, and He teaches us and the angels. We learn together. As the Lord discloses His heart to us and teaches us the manifold wisdom of God, the angels are present. They hear, they feel, they sense, and they come to know what God is teaching us.

One of the passages that is so astonishing to me is in 1 Corinthians 11 when Paul says to the women that they ought to dress a certain way because of the angels. I have read every possible commentary on that text that I can find and I still do not know exactly what it means. How ought a woman to dress because of the angels? Whatever it may ultimately mean, one thing is sure: Paul says our conduct, our deportment, our presence, and the presentation of ourselves should be circumspect because of the angels. When you come to church do you ever think that the angels are there also? They are there and they are listening and they are learning. What they could not know by looking at Deity and what they could not know by looking at God's creation, they come to know as we preach the grace and love of God in Christ Jesus. We teach the angels as we respond to the Gospel and as the Lord regenerates our hearts. What an astonishing revelation!

All of life is like that. The infidel scientist looks through a telescope. He looks, and he looks, and he looks, but all he sees is just more materialities. The same pseudo-scientist looks down as he dissects an insect, a frog, or maybe a human cadaver. All he sees is protoplasm, cells, nuclei, structure, and bone. It is only we who know God who see the divine wisdom of the shaping of life and of the universe. When we look through those telescopes up into the heavens we see the glory of God and look upon the lace work of His hands. When we look down into the minute, infinitesimal microcosm of God's universe, we see the hand of the Lord painting the wing of a butterfly, placing a song in a mockingbird's heart or revealing Himself in the innocence of a little child. I may be rude and harsh in what I say, but I do not think that any man comes to wisdom who does not know God. He may be learned in facts, he may be studied in scientific development and achievement, but he does not know the truth of the universe until he comes to know it in the Lord. That is what the angels see. That is what the angels learn, and we are learning it together as God reveals Himself in the church, in the Book, in the message of a true Godly preacher, and in our heart's response to the invitation of the Lord. To the intent that under the celestial orders in heaven might be known by the church the manifold wisdom of God.

THE ANGELS LEARN TO KNOW US

The angels learn in the church God's plan of salvation. They learn of God's preparation for the coming of the atoning grace in Christ, and the gathering together of those living stones that make up the temple of the Lord. But they also learn to know us through the providences of God's love in our pilgrimage through this life. The angels see us, watch us, and know us. In the fiery trials of life the true Christian magnifies, glorifies, and praises God, and God is with him in those fiery trials. When the three Jewish lads were thrown into the fiery furnace, the king looked and said, "But I see a fourth, and his face, his countenance, is like the Son of God." When we go through the fiery trials of this life God is with us. The angels look upon it and are astonished at the forbearance, patience, and comfort that God gives us. The Bible speaks of the angels that behold the face of God who watch over our little children — guardian angels. I have never seen why (although it is a human deduction), when we grow out of childhood, the angels should forsake us. If there was a guardian angel that represented me before the face of God when I was a little boy, I do not see why that guardian angel would forsake me now that I am a grown man and face all of the storms, tempests, and trials of life. So I keep my fancy still that there are guardian angels who know us, watch over us, precede us, help us, comfort us, and strengthen us.

Finally (and this is no deduction), the Bible says that the angels come for us when we lay down this mortal life. They bear our souls to glory. Like the old song:

> My latest sun is sinking fast,
> My race is nearly run;
> My strongest trials now are past,
> My triumph is begun.
> O come, angel band,
> Come and around me stand.
> Oh, bear me away on your snowy wings
> To my immortal home,
> Oh, bear me away on your snowy wings
> To my immortal home.

Do you believe that? God says it is so. He marks the place where we suffer. Angels look upon our sufferings, and they learn as we trust God through it all. When we finally lay the burden down, the angels are there to bear us up to heaven, to carry us into glory. Ah, Lord, how much we learn, and how much the angels learn through us. May that knowledge be sweet and precious and honor Thee through the years of our pilgrimage.

Chapter 16

THE ETERNAL PURPOSE OF GOD

According to the eternal purpose which he purposed in Christ Jesus our Lord. (Eph. 3:11)

In our study of the Book of Ephesians we have come to the middle part of the third chapter. Paul speaks of a *musterion*, a mystery, a secret hid in the heart of God from the beginning of time now revealed to His apostle; namely, that between the rejection of the King (His crucifixion) and His return in glory there is to be an interlude, an intermission, in which God will create a new thing, the church, the *ecclesia*, the body of Christ. In that *ecclesia* all may have a worthy and heavenly part, no one above another: the Jew, the Gentile, the bond, the free, the rich, the poor, the male, the female. All are alike in the kingdom of heaven in the fellowship of the church. Paul says in verse 8 something like this: Unto me, who am less than the least of all saints, is this grace given, that I should be God's messenger, apostle to the Gentiles, to declare to the nations of the world this great mystery, this new thing that God has chosen to do, to make all men see what is the *oikonomia*, the administration of this *musterion*, which from the foundation and beginning of the world was hid in God to the intent that now (and he names the orders of the heavenly hosts) the principalities and the powers in the heavenly places might know by the church, the manifold wisdom of God (and then the text) "according to the eternal purpose which he purposed in Christ Jesus our Lord."

The Meaning of Purpose

"According to the eternal purpose." The Greek word here for "purpose" is *prothesis*. It is also the Greek word for "shewbread."

In the Tabernacle and in the Temple, in the sanctuary, in the Holy Place before the veil was the golden altar of prayer, of intercession, of incense. On one side of the Holy Place was the seven-branch lampstand. On the other side was the table of shewbread. Every Sabbath there were twelve loaves of wheat bread that were placed there in two rows, six in one row, six in the other row. The twelve loaves represented the twelve tribes of Israel. When I look at the text I am attracted to that unusual word, "according to the *prothesis ton aionon*," "according to the *prothesis* of the ages."

The shewbread was called *prothesis* because it was exhibited, it was something expressed and seen. From that situation in the Tabernacle and in the Temple, the exhibition, the showing of the bread, the word came to apply to a pre-determination, a purpose, an election, and it is so used here in the Word of God. For example, Romans 8:28 says: "And we know that all things work together for good to them that love God, to them who are the called according to his *prothesis*," His pre-determined counsel, His elective and sovereign will.

In Romans 9 the apostle is speaking about the election of Jacob (Israel), and the rejection of Esau, his twin brother. And he writes, "For the children being not yet born, neither having done any good or evil, God chose Jacob that the *prothesis*, the pre-determined counsel and purpose of God according to the election might stand, not of works, but of Him that calls" (see v. 11).

In Ephesians 1 Paul writes about Christ "In whom also we have obtained an inheritance, being predestinated according to the *prothesis*, the purpose of him who worketh all things after the counsel of his own will" (Eph. 1:11). According to the eternal *prothesis*, the eternal, elective counsel and purpose of God. One might translate it "planned according to the eternal plan of God." If one were to translate *prothesis* exactly as it is written here in the Greek text, *prothesis ton aionon*, it would be "the plan of the ages."

When an architect or a contractor builds an edifice he will do it according to a blueprint, according to a plan. If a woman makes a dress she will do it according to a pattern. If a woman bakes a cake she will do it according to a recipe. So Almighty God in framing the ages did it according to a plan, a pre-determined purpose in His elective sovereignty.

The Eternal Purpose of God

Now that purpose is known to us in the use of the word that Paul has employed, *prothesis*. It is something laid out for view, something one can see. That *prothesis* concerns Christ Jesus. The whole plan of all the ages centers in Him.

Do you remember how the Book of Hebrews begins? "God, who at sundry times and in divers manners spake in time past unto the fathers by the prophets, hath in these last days spoken unto us by his Son, whom he hath appointed heir of all things" (1:1, 2). Now listen further: "And by whom he constructed the ages." In the King James Version it is translated, "By whom he made the worlds," but an exact translation is "by whom he constructed the ages." God's purpose through the ages has to do with Jesus Christ.

The use of the word *prothesis* refers to something exhibited, something we can see, something we can follow. By prophecy we can see its ultimate goal and consummation. There are two things in the *prothesis* of God that He has brought out to view in His elective purpose concerning Jesus Christ. One is the purpose of God in redemption, and the other is the purpose of God in exaltation. Both of them are centered, summed up in Jesus our Lord.

God's Purpose in Redemption

First, the purpose of God in Christ in redemption. Before time, before creation, the Son was in the bosom of the Father sharing the glory of God. In that faraway, unknown age of the ages before time was, God was opposed and Lucifer lifted himself up and sin was found in Satan. God foresaw the fall and the destruction of His created universe, but the purpose of God did not fail. In that unknown, distant age of the ages, according to Hebrews 10, Christ, the Son of God, offered Himself for the redemption of the fallen world. As Peter will refer to it in the first chapter of his first epistle, and as John will refer to it in Revelation 13, "Christ the Lord was the lamb slain from before the foundation of the world." This was the purpose of God in redemption before time. Now comes the purpose of God in redemption in time.

When our first parents were placed in paradise, outside the gate of the garden stood a sinister being, God's enemy. As he encompassed the fall of the universe, so he brought about the fall of our first parents and they disobeyed the mandate of God. But the purpose of God in redemption did not fail. There in the garden was the first sacrifice, the blood of an innocent animal poured out in crimson on the ground, and the skin of the innocent victim was used to cover over the nakedness of the man and his wife. When they were driven out of the Garden of Eden, at the East Gate of the Garden the Lord placed cherubim, always symbols and signs of mercy and of welcome. An altar was built and there the man was invited back to God to offer sacrifices in repentance and in faith to make atonement for the breach, the sin that separated them.

God's purpose of redemption continued as He unfolded it in Abraham and his seed. The Lord God said to Abraham, "And in thee and in thy seed all of the families of the earth will be blessed." That holy covenant was repeated to Isaac and to Israel (to Jacob) and to the nation.

In Exodus 20 God gave to Israel the Ten Commandments, the oracles of God, but in chapter 19 God said to Israel, "Ye shall be unto me a kingdom of priests and an holy nation." The prophet Isaiah in speaking of that assignment from heaven said: "But ye (Israel) shall be named Priests of the LORD: men shall call you the Ministers of our God" (Isa. 61:6). The great purpose of God in choosing Israel was for them to be the priests of the world, to represent men to God and God to men, and to teach the nations of the world the oracles of the Almighty.

But here again God was opposed and Israel fell into gross idolatry. As the centuries passed, Israel had this one thing in common with the Greeks and with the Romans: they all divided mankind into two divisions and each placed himself first. Israel said, "The Jew and the Gentile dog." The Greek said, "The Greek, the cultured Greek, and the uncultured hordes of the barbarians." The Romans said, "The Romans, and the provincials in slavery and subjugation."

But the purpose of God in redemption did not fail, for out of Israel came that promised Saviour of the world. Revelation 12 magnificently portrays that Promised One in symbol. "And there appeared a great wonder in heaven; a woman clothed with the sun, and the moon under her feet, and upon her head a crown of twelve stars: And she being with child cried, travailing in birth, and pained to be delivered . . . and she brought forth a man child, who was to rule all nations with a rod of iron" (vv. 12:1, 2, 5a).

The purpose of God did not fail. He came to the earth and in the days of His flesh His coming was announced by the angel. His ministry was filled with deeds of holiness and goodness. "But he came unto his own, and his own received him not" (John 1:11). They said, "He is not fit to walk on the earth," and they cried, "Away with Him! Crucify Him!" Israel crucified his own Son, and the Gift of God was handed back to heaven on the point of a Roman spear.

But the purpose of God in redemption did not fail, for Christ Jesus came into the world not to be a hero or to be a martyr or to be an example, but He came into the world to die for our sins. He is the Lamb of God who takes away the sin of the world, and the purpose of God in redemption continues on. In this day of grace He is presented and lifted up as the Saviour of the world. "For God sent not his Son into the world to condemn the world; but that the world through him might be saved" (John 3:17). This is salvation for the whole world. "God was in Christ, reconciling the world unto himself" (2 Cor. 5:19). "And he is the propitiation for our sins: and not for ours only, but also for the sins of the whole world" (1 John 2:2). There is one true religion, there is one true God, there is one true Saviour. There is one body, one Spirit, one Lord, one faith, one baptism, one Father, and one God and Father of all.

Christianity, the faith that is preached in this day of grace, is the one true religion of the world. In Portuguese East Africa a convert said to a missionary, "Missionary, missionary, you have opened to us a door great and wide to the whole world and we have learned that when we join the church of the Lord Jesus Christ we join a world thing." This is the purpose of God — the calling of the nations and the peoples of the whole earth to faith and trust in the Lord Jesus our Saviour.

But again God is opposed. There are false gods. As Paul walked through Athens and looked upon the idolatry of those cultured people, so a man can walk through the nations of the world today and see their gods. They bow down before gods of gold. They bow down before gods of science. They bow down before gods of materialism, gods of atheism, gods of communism, gods of fame and fortune, and gods of self and selfishness. There are as many gods seemingly as there are people in this earth and the earth is afflicted with religions. There are those who say each one should choose a religion for himself. A white man may choose Christianity or atheism. The brown man may choose Hinduism. The yellow man may choose Buddhism. The black man may choose animism. But for each one the religion will be best suited for him. If the white man is to be a Christian, the yellow man can be a Buddhist. The Arab can be a Mohammedan, and each one can have his own faith and his own religion.

That is a diametrical opposite of the purpose and plan of Almighty God, and it is of all things not Christian. There is no semblance of a Christian idea in that broad latitudinarianism. There is one Lord, one faith, one baptism, one body, the church, and there is one God. What should be our attitude toward these other religions of the world?

We have a magnificent example in Paul as he preached in the university city of Athens. He begins with a compliment, "Men of Athens, I see that in every respect you are (translated in the King James Version) very superstitious." The Greek word is *deisidaimon*. Is not that an unusual word? "Men of Athens, I see that in every respect you are *deisidaimon*, reverently religious." It was a compliment to them. There were gods everywhere. They were reverently religious, bowing down to gods all over the city. One could find more gods in Athens than he could find men. "And as I went by," Paul says, "I saw an altar inscribed to the unknown god." There might be one god whose name the Athenians did not know and they bowed in reverence before him.

Beginning there Paul preached to the Athenians the message of Christ. They interrupted his sermon; he never finished his address. Yet he preached Jesus. And that is the Christian attitude toward all of the faiths and religions of the world. It is preaching, a witnessing, a telling, a calling, a converting religion. This is a divine purpose of Almighty God, and God did not fail in that purpose.

In a relatively short time the gods of the Graeco-Roman world were forgotten, falling into disunion, despair, and disuse. The temples themselves fell away. The Coliseum, the Roman praetorium, the whole complex of civilization, were changed by the preaching of the Gospel of the grace of the Son of God. And as the centuries pass, if God delays His return, increasingly the world shall see that compared to the fullness, the glory, and the blessing of the faith of Christ, the atheist, the Hindu, and the Buddhist are as nothing. The truth revealed, spread out to view, can be seen in the purpose of God in Jesus Christ, which purpose He purposed from the eternal ages in Jesus our Lord. This is God's eternal purpose in redemption.

GOD'S PURPOSE IN EXALTATION

God's eternal purpose is Christ is found also in our Lord's exaltation. It is the purpose of God, predetermined before time was, that the kingdom, the rule, and the reign shall belong to Jesus our Lord. We read in Revelation 11, "The kingdoms of this world are become the kingdoms of our Lord, and of his Christ; and he shall reign for ever and ever" (v. 15). As Paul would write in Ephesians 1, "that in the *oikonomia*, in the dispensation of the fullness of time, God might gather together in one, that God might sum up all things in Christ, both which are in heaven and which are in earth"; everything shall be summed up in Him. It is the purpose of God through the ages that everything shall be summed up in Jesus Christ. He shall reign as Lord over all God's creation: men, women, institutions, the planets, the stars, the earth, the vast creation of God. This purpose is opposed; it is rejected and denied everywhere, but it shall surely come to pass.

Ask any school boy, "Which way does the Mississippi River flow?" He will say, "From north to south." If you have flown over the Mississippi there are times and places where the Mississippi River will flow due north. There are times and places where the Mississippi River will flow due west, but it ultimately and finally flows south. So the elective purpose of God in Christ Jesus is frustrated, turned, twisted, but it is God's purpose of the ages that the reign and the kingdom shall belong to Him.

There is to be another age following this era. Paul says in Romans 11, ". . . that blindness in part is happened to Israel until the *pleroma*, the fulness of the Gentiles be come in" (v. 25b). *Pleroma* can be translated only "the full number." We are in this present age of appeal, witnessing, evangelizing until the "full number" of the Gentiles be come in, and when that last one is saved and the last one comes in, we shall be introduced to another age, another dispensation. In that ultimate dispensation and era, the age that follows this one, we shall see the consummation of the purposes of God in Christ Jesus. He shall be exalted.

EXALTED AMONG THE JEWS

The purpose of God shall not fail in Israel. All Israel shall be converted. They shall turn; they shall accept their Lord and King, their Messiah. "And so all Israel shall be saved: as it is written, There shall come out of Sion the Deliverer, and shall turn away ungodliness (unbelief, rejection) from Jacob: For this is my covenant unto them, when I shall take away their sins. As concerning the gospel, they are enemies for your sakes: but as touching the election, they are beloved for the fathers' sakes. For the gifts and calling of God are without repentance" (Rom. 11:26-29). God does not change.

When God made a covenant with Abraham, He made it to keep it. When He made a covenant with Israel, He made it to keep it, and the purpose of God shall not fail. In the age which follows this one, Israel will be converted. They will accept their Lord Messiah, Christ their King, Paul writes in Romans 11 that the apostasy, the rejection of Israel, was only partial and temporary. Is that true? Yes, indeed. What race were Paul and the apostles? They were Jews. The first Christian message was delivered by the Jews. The rejection of that message has been only partial through the years.

Edersheim, the historian who wrote the incomparable work, *The Life and Times of the Messiah*, was a Christian Jew. Benjamin Disraeli, the Victorian statesman, was a Christian Jew. Today there live mighty men of God who are Christian Jews. Most Jews have rejected Christ, but that rejection according to the Apostle Paul is only partial and temporary. Some day we will see the whole nation of Israel turning to the Lord, and Paul remarks on the glory of that hour. He says, "If the rejection of them, if the taking out of that olive branch, was your salvation and your redemption, think what the acceptance of Israel will be."

My impression is that one genuinely-converted Jew has in him the power and unction of witnessing to equal a thousand Gentiles. The purpose of God shall not fail. It will not fail in Israel. The New Jerusalem, what is it like? The twelve gates are the twelve tribes of Israel, and the foundations are the twelve apostles. There are twenty-four elders, twelve for the patriarchs and twelve for the apostles. We shall be one — the Jews converted and the Gentiles converted. We shall all be one in the faith of the Lord, serving King Jesus.

Exalted Among the Gentiles

The purpose of God will not fail with the Gentiles. Philippians 2 has in it one of the most moving passages in the Bible. After Paul has described the condescension of the Lord Jesus, His crucifixion, and His redemption for our sins, he then adds, "Wherefore God also hath highly exalted him, and given him a name which is above every name: That at the name of Jesus every knee should bow" (vv. 9, 10). Some day in the purpose of God every knee shall bow and every tongue shall confess that Christ is Lord, to the glory of God the Father.

The purpose of God shall not fail with the nations of the earth. We all some day shall bow, confess, and give honor and glory to Jesus our Lord. The only difference is that if we bow now in contrition and in confession, in faith, in repentance, in belief, we are saved. God writes our names in the Book of Life. But if we bow by coercion and by judgment, we are cast out, separated from God and the everlasting kingdom forever. Oh, that we might bow now, accept now, believe now, and love the Lord Jesus now!

Chapter 17

THE ABLENESS OF GOD

> For this cause I bow my knees unto the Father of our Lord Jesus Christ,
> Of whom the whole family in heaven and earth is named,
> That he would grant you, according to the riches of his glory, to be strengthened with might by his Spirit in the inner man;
> That Christ may dwell in your hearts by faith; that ye, being rooted and grounded in love,
> May be able to comprehend with all saints what is the breadth, and length, and depth, and height;
> And to know the love of Christ, which passeth knowledge, that ye might be filled with all the fullness of God.
> Now unto him that is able to do exceeding abundantly above all that we ask or think, according to the power that worketh in us,
> Unto him be glory in the church by Christ Jesus throughout all ages, world without end. Amen. (Eph. 3:14-21)

This chapter is an exposition of one of the most meaningful prayers in Holy Scripture.

There are two prayers in the Book of Ephesians. The first one is found in 1:16 and continues to the end of the chapter. The second prayer begins at 3:14 and continues to the end of the chapter. The first prayer is for spiritual enlightenment. "Making mention of you in my prayers; That the God of our Lord Jesus Christ, the Father of glory, may give unto you the spirit of wisdom and revelation in the knowledge of him: The eyes of your understanding being enlightened" (1:16-18a).

There are things invisible and eternal in the Gospel of Christ that are beyond the frontiers of our common knowledge and understanding. There are depths, treasures, and riches in Christ and in the Gospel message beyond what ordinary understanding and comprehension could ever know or grasp. So the first prayer of the apostle is for spiritual enlightenment that we might understand, that we might grow into the knowledge that in itself is the fullness of the presence of God.

The second prayer is for spiritual strength. As we cannot enter into the glories of the divine Gospel of Christ without spiritual enlightenment, without God touching and opening the eyes of the soul, so we cannot implement the noble assignments of God for us unless God helps us and gives us strength for the task.

The apostle begins, "For this cause I bow my knees unto the Father of our Lord Jesus Christ, of whom the whole family in heaven and earth is named" (3:14, 15). There could hardly be a more magnificently impressive picture than the apostle down on his knees in that Roman prison. Next to the picture of our Lord down on His knees in Gethsemane is this picture of the Apostle Paul down on his knees in a Roman dungeon. There in supplication and prayer or in stocks and in chains, the manacles and the bonds fall from him and he is free.

> Stone walls do not a prison make,
> Nor iron bars a cage.

An how less so when this apostle kneels down to pray! He is free. His spirit soars. Paul thus triumphantly writes in the jail in Rome before he is executed. In the second letter to his son in the ministry, Timothy, he speaks of his own imprisonment, then he says, ". . . but the word of God is not bound" (2 Tim. 2:9b). God's Word could never be encased or imprisoned in stone or steel or iron jails. The Word of God is free. So is the spirit of the apostle even though incarcerated in manacles and in chains.

When he kneels to pray he is free. In this prayer he soars in spirit and includes all the hosts of heaven, the little company of saints in Ephesus, all the Lord's children, the family of God of all time. As he kneels he bows before the great hosts of the Lord God in heaven. He speaks of them — "Of whom the whole family in heaven and earth is named." He had just spoken in the verse above: "that unto the *arche* and *exousia*," — orders of the Lord in heaven, great companies of the angelic hosts. The *arche* and the *exousia* are translated here "principalities and powers." What they are we will not fully know until we see them when we meet them in heaven, but before them Paul bows and names them as the great hosts in heaven. In 1 Corinthians 4:9 the apostle says that we are a "spectacle" to the angels in heaven. The imagery is of a Graeco-Roman amphitheater. The arena is the earth, the great tiers and galleries are the angels, and the spectacle is the church, the saints of God. Paul bows and looks up to that great host of angels in glory. Day and night they are in the presence of God. They have their high and holy orders — the archangels with their mighty dominions, the cherubim in their dazzling glory and light, and the seraphim in their burning love. As Paul looks up to them from his knees, so they look down upon the apostle from their palisades, battlements, palaces, and glories of light, splendor, and iridescent beauty.

I wonder what they are really like. Let us ask them: "In what image were you made? What substance are you? When were you created and how? What did Gabriel say to you about us when he returned to heaven? What did the angels at the resurrection tomb say to you when they came back? What did the angels of the ascension report? What do they say about us in heaven? What does Jesus tell you about us? In what language are you addressed? Do you know anything about sin or death? If one of you is gloriously gifted, are the others of you ever filled with envy? Do you ever grow weary? What did you think when Lucifer fell and one third of your number fell with him?" Only a fragment of the garment are we barely able to touch of the invisible, eternal glories of heaven.

Four Petitions

As the apostle prayed in the presence of the angels for divine illumination and understanding, so he prays here for divine enablement, for strength. There are four petitions in the prayer. Each one begins with a "that": "I bow my knees unto the Father . . . that he would grant you, according to the riches of his glory, to be strengthened with might by his Spirit in the inner man" (3:14, 16). Externalities are nothing as such to the church. All of the embellishments and accouterments — the stained glass windows, the height of the steeple, the carpet on the floor, the cushioned pews, the pile of masonry — all externalities are nothing to the church. Its strength is never defined or delineated in brick, mortar, stained glass window, or steeple. We could have church just as well in a warehouse on a sawdust floor or sitting on a split log. What makes the church strong is the moving of the Spirit in the inner man. When our souls are empty, when our lives are sterile, when our ministries are unfruitful, the church, however it may pile up before our eyes, is itself weak and anemic. The strength and the power of the people of God is never in externalities. It is in the inner man, it is in the soul, it is in the Spirit. I have been in churches that froze my heart. If ever there was any Spirit of God there, I could not sense Him or feel Him. God had forsaken the church and yet it is a magnificent structure there before Him. The church is not these externalities, these physical, mundane descriptions. The church is the power and Spirit of God, moving in the hearts of God's people. That is the church. So Paul prays according to the riches of God in glory that we might be strengthened by the Spirit in the inner man in order to be a vibrant, glorious, triumphant witness for God.

The second petition: "that Christ may dwell in your hearts by faith" (v. 17). Not a day or an hour but He may dwell in our souls, live there, all the days of our lives as long as we have breath — "that Christ may dwell in your hearts by faith."

The third petition: ". . . that ye, being rooted and grounded in love, may be able to comprehend with all saints what is the breadth, and length, and depth, and height: and to know the love of Christ, which passeth knowledge, that ye might be filled with all the fulness of God" (vv. 17-19). He mixes his metaphors there, does he not? "Rooted," like a taproot of a big pecan tree that goes down into the earth. "Grounded," that is, an architectural figure describing the foundation. It would take all eternity to realize the meaning of "filled with the fulness of God." What is God full of? Filled with grace, mercy, power, glory, understanding, compassion, love and redemptive purpose. Oh, the fullness of God! No wonder Paul says we need a divine revelation. We have only touched the hem of the garment.

"Now unto him that is able to do exceeding abundantly above all that we ask or think . . ." (and this gave title to the chapter, "The

Ableness of God") to Him who is able to do *huper-ek-perissou*. There is no particular word like that in the Greek; Paul just concocted it. It is made out of three Greek words, *huper, ek,* and *perissou* — aboundingly abundant; *ek,* "out," *huper,* "over and beyond." He puts the word together, *huperekperissou*, "the abounding, over and above and beyond abundance of the ableness of God."

God Is Able

Just how able is the Lord? How would one describe it when it is beyond description? How would one imagine it when it is beyond imagination? How would one say it when there is no language to contain it? Thus Paul puts that word together, *huperekperissou*, "over and beyond and abounding." Just how able is God?

The sun, 93,000,000 miles away, is so vast in its flaming orb that all of the planets could fall into it and be as nothing, furiously burning. We could ask: "Could the sun lighten up a room? Is there enough fire and flame to lighten a room?"

Just how able is God? One might ask: "Is there enough water in a vast river to slake the thirst of a thristing man?"

Just how able is God? That is why Paul uses the word *huperekperissou*. God is so mighty in His ableness. He is beyond what words can describe or minds could imagine — the exceeding ableness of the Lord Almighty.

Therefore, when we face our tasks and our assignments, we are not to do it in our own strength, but we are to do it in the strength of God. Oh, how weak, anemic, and puny, how infinitesimal and Lilliputian we are. But how mighty the champion of our cause, God in heaven! When we face mountains that we cannot move, He can touch them and they go up in smoke as incense before His face. When we are coming up the hill to the big stone that is not rolled away, not only is it heavy and enormous, but it is also sealed with a seal. Not only is it sealed with a seal, but there are watchers there. We are not to fall into despair or frustration or live as though we were defeated. There is power from God to break the seal of the greatest empire that ever existed, to strike the watchers down as dead, and to roll the stone away. Oh, the ableness of Almighty God!

The Ableness of God

That is the spirit of victory and triumph in which we are to face our present world. We live in a world of increasing paganism and secularism, anti-Christianity and anti-Christ. I am not talking about Russia or Red China. I am talking about the United States of America. The institutions of our nation are becoming increasingly pagan and secular. They are avowedly and statedly so. Reaping the whirlwind is what we see in our daily newspapers. Yet we are called upon to confront these pagan institutions.

Here is an example of what we face in American life today. A pastor from Akron, Ohio was interviewed by twenty-six members of the Canadian government in the Parliament of Canada in Ottawa. One of the questions they asked him was, "What do you think about the recent violence at Kent State University?" His answer: "I live close to Kent State. In fact, I live between Kent State University and Akron University. Recently I took Rev. Bob Harrington, the chaplain of Bourbon Street, a man who can really communicate with youth, on a tour around the Akron area. He spoke at high schools, civic clubs, junior highs, and even at Akron University. When he was through speaking at each place he received a standing ovation. But they would not allow him to speak at Kent State. A religious speaker is not allowed on that campus. For many years, however, they have encouraged a radical political element to come speak. Only a week before the shootings at Kent State, Jerry Rubin, one of the most notorious activists of our day, came on the Kent State campus and advocated revolution. He spread the philosophy of revolution that says, 'kill your parents, burn down your churches, and do away with the Establishment.' He can do that; he can take the flag, throw it on the ground and trample it under foot. But I cannot go there and speak to those twenty-three thousand people about basic faith, principles, sex, or anything else. This is one of the tragedies of our day. These young people ought to have a balanced program. Let them hear both sides. That is what college is for. Then the student can make up his mind more intelligently because then he has a choice he can make. But when the student does not get a chance to hear both sides, then we are in trouble. The only side they are hearing is the side of these radical leftists — burning draft cards, spitting on the flag, scoffing at the church, denying God, making fun of the Bible — those are the pagan institutions that are molding the thought of the young people of America today."

God Is Exceeding Abundantly Able

Shall we quail and cower before such paganism? No. It is just another mountain to be removed, another heavy millstone around the neck of our nation to be rolled away. Not because we are able in ourselves, but because He is *huperekperissou* — "exceeding able abundantly above what we could ask or think."

Do you ever get down on your knees and say, "I have been presumptuous. I have entered in a petition that I ought not to lay before God. I have asked of God more than He has the power and ableness to give"? Could we ask too much of God? He is able to do "exceeding abundantly above all that we ask or think." Who would have dared to ask in redemption for the atonement of Jesus Christ — for God to come down in human flesh and die on the cross for our sins? Who would have dared to ask God to do that? Who would have dared in sanctification to have asked for the outpouring of the Holy Spirit, the presence of God that we feel in our souls? Who would have dared to ask in adoption that we be made sons of God? When the prodigal returned he said, "Make me one of your hired hands." Who would have dared to ask that we be sons and fellow-heirs with Jesus Christ? In the hour of our death, who would dare to ask for a resurrection? Think of the dissolution of these bodies as they are mingled with the dust of the ground and blown by the wind. And yet God says He marks the spot; He marks the dust; He marks the very atoms, particles, and molecules of our bodies, and some day God shall raise them up. In the renovation who would have dared ask for new heavens and a new earth? How we circumscribe and crimp our praying and our asking! But God says, "Ask, and it shall be given you; seek, and ye shall find; knock, and it shall be opened unto you."

"He is able to do exceeding abundantly above all that we ask or think." "Eye hath not seen, nor ear heard, neither have entered into the heart of man, the things which God hath prepared for them that love him" (1 Cor. 2:9). Now we think that verse in 1 Corinthians 2:9 means what God has prepared for us in heaven, and I am sure that is true, but it is also true down here. He never said, "That is over there." It is beyond what mind could imagine

The Ableness of God

what God will do for those who love Him down here. Who would have thought of water pouring out of the dry rock in the desert? Who would have thought for the manna, the angels' food, given to those who were famishing in the wilderness? Who would have thought for the mouths of lions being closed, or for the three men delivered out of the fiery furnace, or for the iron doors opening of their own accord? Who would have thought for the little shepherd boy being the king on whose throne a Son shall sit forever? Who would have thought about Amos, the gatherer of sycamore fruit, being the great, first writing-prophet? Who would have thought about Peter the fisherman preaching at Pentecost, or Saul of Tarsus who wasted the church being the apostle who kneels here in intercession? Dear brethren, "above all that we ask or think," God is able.

Lord, that we might lay ourselves in Thy hands, at Thy feet! Use us, Master. Feeble as we are and unable as we are, God, strengthen us and bless us because it is Thy cause; it is Thy work, blessed Jesus. We are Thy servants and glad to be, choose to be. He is able!

Chapter 18

THE FAMILY OF GOD

> For this cause I bow my knees unto the Father of our Lord Jesus Christ,
> Of whom the whole family in heaven and earth is named.
> (Eph. 3:14, 15)

This chapter is built upon the singular form of a substantive: *patria,* "family." *Pater* means "father," *patria* means "the family of the father." Here it is the family of God, "of whom the whole family in heaven and earth is named." We have the name, the family name of our Father in heaven and in earth. We are called "the family of God."

Bereavement, the sorrow of separation in death, is one of the most poignant griefs in human experience. God permits us to love these whom He has given to us and our hearts weave precious, loving tendrils around them. Then when they are taken away the empty void is filled with nothing but falling tears and daily, sorrowful remembrance. Death is an experience all of us sometime and in some way share. There is not a father but that could understand the lament of David when, even though his son was unworthy, cried: "O my son Absalom! Would God I had died for thee, O Absalom, my son, my son!" (2 Sam. 18:33).

In the Book of Chronicles it is stated that Jeremiah lamented over the death of good King Josiah. In Zechariah 12 it says that when the Lord Christ shall return Israel will mourn. And it says it will be like the mourning of Israel at Hadad-rimmon, a place located before the hill of Megiddo. It referred to a time lost to us in history when the whole nation mourned at Armageddon (the hill of Megiddo) over the death of good King Josiah. In Acts 8, at the death of Stephen, the first martyr, it says that devout men buried Stephen and made great lamentation over him. In chapter 9 it says that when Dorcas died, the poor widows that she had helped held up the garments that Dorcas had made, weeping. Simon Peter came and looked upon the sad and sorrowful scene. To be a stoic is no Christian. His spirit is a thousand times removed from that of the tender-hearted Jesus who wept over the death of Lazarus as the Saviour stood by the sisters, Mary and Martha.

This holy passage brings to us a comfort that is incomparably sweet and precious. "For this cause I bow my knees unto the *Pater,* the Father of whom the whole *patria* in heaven and earth is named." Death makes no breach in the family of God. Some of God's family are there in heaven, others of them are here on earth. But we are all the *patria*. We are all the family of God whether in heaven or in earth. God's family is not broken up by death. God's family is not separated by death. One would think that they belong to one order up there in heaven while we belong to another order down here. It is not so. The household of God is complete. Death does not divide it or separate it. Our Lord said expressly, speaking to Simon Peter, "On this rock I will build my church and the gates of hell, the gates of Hades, the gates of death, shall not hold it down" (Matt. 16:18). Death has no power to prevail or to break up or to separate God's family.

In Matthew 28 the angel said to the women, "Come, see the place where he lay; he is not here." Death has no power of termination or separation. The angel at the tomb continued to speak in these further words, "Tell the disciples He meets them at that appointed rendezvous in Galilee." "For I am persuaded that neither death, nor life, nor angels, nor principalities, nor powers, nor things present, nor things to come, nor height, nor depth, nor any other creature shall be able to separate us from the love of God" (Rom. 8:38, 39). We are always one in the family of the Lord whether there in heaven or whether here in earth. We are one *patria,* one inseparable family.

The Formation of the Family of God Is Not Artificial or Temporal

The formation of the family of God is both natural and eternal, not artificial and temporal. Here in this life there are many associations that draw us together. In the ancient day men were organized by guilds — the guild of silversmiths, the guild of weavers, the guild of dyers, the guild of stone masons. In this modern day men and women are associated together by many common affinities and predilections. There will be political groups, literary societies, and business organizations, but all of these associations are artificial and temporary. Tastes change, society moves on, the national life is recolored, and the combination is broken up. Whatever the association may be, the end is inexorable and inevitable; it ends in dissolution. If for no other reason, it is dissolved by death.

But it is not so in the family of God. The family of God is formed naturally and everlastingly. As I am born into my family, my mother is my mother forever; my father is my father forever; my sisters and brothers are my sisters and brothers forever; my child is my child forever. So it is when we are born into the family of God. Our relationship is not artificial. It belongs to the eternal order of things and is everlasting. The *patria* is both in heaven and in earth. Some are there and some here.

Also, the Scriptures emphasize that indivisible oneness in the family of God, whether there or whether here, whether on that side of Jordan or on this side. On the other side of Jordan was the Tribe of Gad, the Tribe of Reuben, and the half-tribe of Manasseh; but Israel was one even though the swollen stream ran between. So it is with us. Whether some are on that side of the Jordan River, having crossed over already, or whether some of us remain on this side, the family of God is one and indivisible.

We are all named in one register, the Lamb's Book of Life. The hand that wrote in that Book the name of the apostles and the prophets is the same Almighty, moving hand that writes your name and mine in that Book. On the same leaf and on the same page that God has listed the heroes of faith, the martyrs, and the Old Testament saints, on that same page God writes the name of the least of us who trust in His Son. We come in successive ages and generations and we cross over one after another at different times, but God saw us, named us, saved us, and chose us from before the foundation of the world. That is the way this Book of Ephesians begins, "According as he hath chosen us in him before the foundation of the world" (v. 4). We are all one in this register, in the Book of Life listing the children of God. Whether there or whether here, we are all born into the family. We all have been regenerated by the blood of Jesus Christ, washed clean and pure in His mercy and grace. All of us are members of the fallen family of Adam. We all know sin and the liability to death, but we also belong to the children of the second Adam, the family of Christ. They up there in heaven have found renewal and regeneration in the love of God in Jesus. We down here on earth have found a regeneration in that same blessed Lord. In fact, if we choose between those who are ungodly in this earth, and those who are translated to heaven, we feel far closer and more akin to our fellow citizens in heaven than we do to the ungodly here in the world. Down here we are strangers, pilgrims, foreigners, and sojourners. Our citizenship, our commonwealth, is in heaven, and whether here or whether there, we belong in the same family and kingdom of God. Whether there or whether here, we are all alike washed in the blood of the Lamb and we are one company.

One in Redemption

"And one of the elders answered, saying unto me, What are these which are arrayed in white robes? and whence came they? And I said unto him, Sir, thou knowest. And he said to me, These are they which *erkomenoi* [are coming out of the great tribulation], and have washed their robes, and made them white in the blood of the Lamb" (Rev. 7:13, 14). They are coming out. It is looked upon as one company — they who already arrived and we who are yet coming. "These are they who are coming." But whether there or whether here, we are looked upon as one throng, one family, one *patria* of God. The blood that washed them clean and white is the same blood that washes the stain of sin out of our souls. We are one whether there or here.

One in the Love of God

We are one, also, in the love and in the care of God. God does not love them any more than He loves us. The care of the Lord is not more manifested to them than it is to us. "The foundation of God standeth sure, having this seal, The Lord knoweth them that are his" (2 Tim. 2:19). God does not know them any more than He knows us down here. God does not love them any more up there in glory than He loves us down here in the earth. We are one in the loving care of our Lord.

One in Nature

We are one in nature whether there or here. The course of immortality floods through their spirits and the same floodtides of immortality flow through our souls. They have in them the incorruptible, undying seed of God and the same incorruptible seed of the precious Gospel has been sown in our hearts. We are the same in nature. They are the children of God and we are the children of God. They belong to the church of the firstborn and we belong to the church of the firstborn. Their life is hid with God in Christ and our life is hid with God in Christ. We are one. They have bodies that somewhere are buried in the earth but we still live in our mortal bodies. Yet that immortality of soul lives forever, regenerated by the Holy Spirit of God, and is theirs and ours alike. "Verily, verily I say unto you," said Jesus, "whosoever liveth and believeth in me shall never die" (John 11:26). They do not die in heaven, and we shall not die in earth. Their bodies have been buried, ours we still possess, but to both alike God has promised a resurrection change into glory (1 Cor. 15:51-57). The immortality that God promises us is ours, as it is theirs. We are *patria* in heaven and in earth.

One in Worship and Adoration

Our worship and adoration are the same. They sing in heaven about Jesus, we sing in earth about Jesus. They bow in worship in heaven before the blessed, Holy Lord Jesus; we bow in earth before the same, exalted Lord. Their delight is the blessed Jesus, our hope and happiness is the same living, exalted Lord. Who leads them to living fountains of water? The blessed Jesus. Who leads us? The blessed Lord. Who wipes the tears away from their eyes? Even Jesus. Who comforts us in our hearts of sorrow? The blessed Jesus. When we worship the Lord up there or down here we find ourselves in one company, singing and praising and loving and adoring the same Christ. "But ye are come unto mount Sion, and unto the city of the living God, the heavenly Jerusalem, and to an innumerable company of angels (myriads of them), To the general assembly and church of the firstborn, which are written in heaven, and to God the Judge of all, and to the spirits of just men made perfect, And to Jesus the mediator of the new covenant . . ." (Heb. 12:22-24).

One in Body

We belong to the same body. "For as we have many members in one body, and all members have not the same office: So we, being many, are one body in Christ, and every one members one of another" (Rom. 12:4, 5). The body of our Lord is not torn asunder, nor does death wrench it and waste it. But the body of Christ is complete as He has chosen us from before the foundation of the world. Some of the members of the body of Christ are in glory, some of the members of the body of Christ are in the earth. But whether in heaven or whether in earth, we all alike are members of the body of our Lord, members of one another in particular, and God needs us all. The Apostle Paul, Simon Peter, Elijah, and Moses are vital to the work of our Lord, but also, Dorcas, Martha, Mary, and the least of the saints that have trusted in Him. All are alike, chosen of the Lord, loved, died for. We belong to the *patria* of God. The little wren as well as the soaring eagle in the sky belongs to God. The little, retiring violet as well as the flaming orchid are His. We all alike are needed, adopted, and born into the kingdom of God.

One in Service

We all are fellow servants. Up there in heaven they serve Him. We down here in the earth are fellow servants of God. In the Apocalypse John says of the revealing angel: "And I fell at his feet to worship him. And he said unto me, See thou do it not: I am thy fellow-servant, and of thy brethren that have the testimony of Jesus: worship God: for the testimony of Jesus is the spirit of prophecy" (19:10). And again: "And I John saw these things and heard them. And when I had heard and seen, I fell down to worship before the feet of the angel which shewed me these things. Then saith he unto me, See thou do it not: for I am thy fellow-servant, and of thy brethren the prophets, and of them which keep the sayings of this book: worship God" (22:8, 9). They serve the Lord in heaven, and we serve the Lord in earth. We are fellow servants and brethren in the committed worship and service of the King in glory. The cherubim and the seraphim are my brothers, though they are angels in heaven. We all belong to the family of God. The prophet and the apostle are my fellow-servants: they are in heaven and we down here in the earth.

One in Joy

When people are saved they rejoice in heaven, and we rejoice in earth. In Luke 15 the Lord said, ". . . joy shall be in heaven over one sinner that repenteth" (v. 7). And again, "Likewise, I say unto you, there is joy in the presence of the angels of God over one sinner that repenteth" (v. 10). When someone comes down the aisle and takes the Lord as his Saviour, all of us thank God. The Lord has been so good. And while we rejoice in earth, God says that they rejoice in heaven. We are one *patria*, whether in glory or here in the earth.

One Deed to Glory

We all share alike the title deed to glory. The promise is not any more to them than it is to us. "And if children, then heirs; heirs of God, and joint-heirs with Christ . . ." (Rom. 8:17). All alike we inherit the glories of God, some of them there, some of them here.

We feel the influence of these who have gone on before — Martin Luther, John Knox, John Calvin, Jonathan Edwards, or George W. Truett; each one has left behind his bow and his arrow, but he has also left behind his victories. Some sow and others reap, but whether we sow or whether we reap, we are one in the great, marvelous, triumphant, victorious kingdom of God.

Their title deed to heaven is no more secure or assured than our title deed to heaven. We are all joint-heirs with Jesus Christ, fellow-heirs of the promises of God. Some of them are there like Peter and Paul, Elijah and John the Baptist. Some of us are here like you and me. Their security is no more sure than ours. The promise is no more to them than it is to us. We are all members of the same *patria* of God. We belong to the family of the Lord.

One in Destiny

Finally, our destiny is the same. We lift up our eyes and look forward to the same great consummation, for they are not complete without us. As the last verse in Hebrews 11 says (after the author calls the roll of the heroes of faith who are in glory), "that they without us should not be made perfect." Not until the last one of us comes into the kingdom and is resurrected and glorified are they complete. The family is not complete until all of us are in. They are waiting for the great Resurrection Day, to wit, the redemption of the body. Their bodies still lie in the dust of the ground, buried in the earth. Our bodies are still burdened with this present decaying carnality. But they are not complete until we also are complete. We are all alike, whether in heaven, or in earth. They are waiting for the great consummation of the redemption, the resurrection, the glorification of their bodies which sleep in the dust. They are looking forward to the second coming of Christ when the Lord shall join again body and soul. We also are looking forward to the glorious change in our bodies, to the rapture of the church, and to the return of our blessed Lord with all the holy angels. They cry, "O Lord, how long?" in heaven. And we cry, "O Lord, how long?" in earth. The consummation toward which their eyes are affixed is the same triumphant, glorious end of the age toward which our hearts are lifted up in eagerness and in anticipation.

Think what a day it shall be when all of God's *patria,* all of God's family are together! Some of us shall belong to the company of the resurrected, we shall be raised from the dead. But some of us shall belong to the rapture of the church, never seeing the decay of the body. "We shall all be changed, in a moment, in the twinkling of an eye, at the last trump" (1 Cor. 15:51b, 52a). But we shall all be changed alike. Those who are raised from the dead and we who are alive unto His coming, all shall be changed, in a moment, at the last trump. We shall rise together to meet the Lord in the air — God's one unbroken family.

That is what Paul meant when he wrote in the descriptive and dramatic resurrection chapter, 1 Corinthians 15: "Then shall be brought to pass the saying that is written, Death is swallowed up in victory. O death, where is thy sting? O grave, where is thy victory?" (vv. 54b, 55). The triumphant cry of us who are alive and remain unto the coming of the Lord will be, "O death, where is thy sting?" The victorious cry of those who are resurrected from the grave will be, "O grave, where is thy victory?" And both together, these who are resurrected and these who are changed at the rapture of the church, both together shall say, "Thanks be to God, who giveth us the victory through our Lord Jesus Christ." Whether there or whether here, whether we are resurrected or whether we are raptured, it is all one *patria*, one family of God.

Paul says, "Wherefore comfort one another with these words" (1 Thess. 4:18). We shall not fail in this blessed hope. Our Lord emphatically said: "And I give unto them eternal life; and they shall never perish, neither shall any man pluck them out of my hand. My Father, which gave them me, is greater than all; and no man is able to pluck them out of my Father's hand" (John 10:28, 29). Our names are written in the Book of Life, our souls are washed in the blood of the Lamb, and God's loving care is watching over us and guarding us. Whether in heaven or whether in earth, He loves us just the same. He cares for us just the same. The rich, incomparable inheritance that they enjoy in bliss today shall be ours tomorrow in our time and in our succession. For they and we alike belong to the one family of God, whether in heaven or in earth.

Chapter 19

GOD'S LOVE IN FOUR DIMENSIONS

> That Christ may dwell in your hearts by faith; that ye, being rooted and grounded in love,
> May be able to comprehend with all saints what is the breadth, and length, and depth, and height;
> And to know the love of Christ, which passeth knowledge, that ye might be filled with all the fulness of God.
> (Eph. 3:17-19)

The third chapter of Ephesians contains one of the sublimest prayers in the Bible. "For this cause I bow my knees unto the Father of our Lord Jesus Christ, Of whom the whole family in heaven and earth is named" (vv. 14, 15). There is one family. Some of us are in heaven, some of us are down here in the earth, but we all belong to one family. Death makes no breach in it. Death cannot separate us, not from God, and not from one another if we are in Christ. Paul continues to pray, "That he would grant you, according to the riches of his glory, to be strengthened with might by his Spirit in the inner man; That Christ may dwell in your heart by faith; that ye, being rooted and grounded in love, May be able to comprehend with all saints what is the breadth, and length, and depth, and height (the word for height is *platos*, and the word "plateau" comes from it meaning "a great, broad expanse"); And to know the love of Christ, which passeth knowledge, that ye might be filled with all the fulness of God" (vv. 16-19). This is the love of God in four dimensions. In the breadth and the length and the depth and the height, Paul says, it is immeasurable. It is so vast, extensive, high, deep, and broad. It passes knowledge. So great is this truth that it can hardly be conceived by a man.

Things That Seemingly Contradict the Love of God

There are many things that seemingly contradict the love of God. The world of nature itself seems to deny a place for God in it. The laws of nature are so impersonal and inexorable. Sometimes the behavior of nature is cruel and relentless. The waves drown us, the fires burn us, earthquakes destroy us, and the winds beat us. The path of the cyclone and the hurricane, and the entire world of law by which the universe is so meticulously controlled seem so often beyond the intervention and the providential care of God.

Not only does the world of nature seemingly deny the truth of the love of God, but the world of human history seems to contradict it. The world of humanity is filled with fears and heartaches. There is vice, crime, violence, and war, and when God from heaven looks down upon it, one wonders if He is moved by it or if He even sees it. There seems to be no evidence of God's care for man's inhumanity to man continues unabated, so vicious, so vile, so terribly heartbreaking.

But the apostle avows that he is not speaking philosophically or metaphysically. He is not speaking forensically, argumentatively. He is speaking empirically, experientially. This is a knowledge that we know with all the saints. It is something they have experienced and have come to know and it is something that we also have learned, even though by mere human approach it is unknowable. It is an unscalable mountain that the Christian climbs. It is an unfathomable secret that is revealed to the heart of the child of God. The love that passes knowledge is something that we share with all the saints. Its breadth, its length, its depth, and its height are experienced by those of us who know Jesus.

In this chapter I have taken that four-dimensional love of God and applied it to the golden text of the Bible, John 3:16. There are those same four revelations of the greatness, the broadness, the boundlessness, and immeasurableness of the affection of God for us. "For God so loved the world (the breadth of it), that he gave his only begotten Son (the length to which God did go in His love for us), that whosoever believeth in him should not perish (the depths to which God reached) but have everlasting life (the height to which God raises us)."

God's Love in Four Dimensions   153

THE BREADTH OF GOD'S LOVE

First, its breadth — the *platos*. God so loved the world — the whole world. There are three words that the Apostle John could have used in this text in John 3:16 to express "the world." He could have used the word *ge*. In the Greek language "geography" means the writing down of the *ge*. The earth, our planet with its soil, dirt, and ground — this is the *ge*, the planet earth. But he did not use that word. He could have used the word *oikoumene*. I would have thought he would have used it. *Oikoumene* refers to the world of humanity, culture and civilization. It would largely have referred to the then known civilized world around the Mediterranean Sea. *Oikoumene* means the world inhabited, the cultural, civilized world of humanity. But he used another word, one familiar to you, *cosmos*. The ancient Greek looked into the sky and saw the regularity of the movement of the stars in the heavens, the planets around the central sun, and the other ordered demeanor and deportment of the whole creation. He took the word to describe that which means "beautifully ordered," *cosmos*, and applied it to God's creation. The word "cosmetic," to make beautiful, comes from it. John took the word *cosmos* and applied it to God's vast universe. "For God so loved the whole creation."

What the apostle is saying is that God did not love our world in part, in parcel, in piece, or in section. Nor did God love just the elect or the few, the gracious and the adorable and the gifted, but God loved the whole creation. Some of the stars are burned out, some of the suns have turned to cinders. Some of the planets have great deserts on them, some of His humanity is afflicted in depravity, ignorance, superstition, disease, and finally death. But the whole creation of God is dear to Him. This is why in Romans 8 the Apostle Paul says that the whole creation shall share in the redemptive purpose in Christ Jesus. Oh, the breadth of the love of God! It includes all of God's handiwork and it includes all of God's humanity. The love of God for us is broad.

There has never been a preacher who has been the object of more stories than Dwight L. Moody. Out of all of them, one of the most meaningful and significant is this. Mr. Moody was in Birmingham, England, holding a revival meeting. When he had finished the revival, there came up to him a young Britisher who introduced himself and said, "Mr. Moody, I hope to go to America some day and when I do, I shall come to your church in Chicago and preach for you." Mr. Moody was gracious and said, "When you come to America, we shall be delighted to welcome you." Six months later Mr. Moody got a letter from New York signed by that young man. The young fellow said: "Dear Mr. Moody, I am in New York City. Wednesday I shall be in Chicago and I shall preach for you that Wednesday night." Well, Mr. Moody took the letter, amazed at it, and presented it to his deacons and said: "I have to be out of the city Wednesday. This young fellow from Birmingham, England, is coming, so we will let him preach for us. I have no idea how it will be, so you be prepared to take over the service if he stammers and stutters too much and thus you can close with a few remarks yourselves." With that, Moody left town. Wednesday night came and the young fellow, Harry Morehouse, was introduced. He stood up in the Moody church in Chicago and read his text, John 3:16. He poured out his heart in a marvelous message on the love of God. When he was finished (as they did in the latter part of the last century), he made appeal by saying, "All of you who are interested in the after-service, stay and we shall deal with you personally." Not a soul left. They all stayed. In the appeal during the after-service there were more than twenty who were saved that night. The deacons came up to him and asked, "Young man, could you be here tomorrow night?" He said: "I have nothing else to do. I am in the city." So they announced services for Thursday night. Thursday night the crowd had grown. He took his text again, John 3:16. When he had poured out his heart in appeal there were more than thirty that were saved Thursday night. The deacons were overwhelmed. They came to him and said, "Young man, will you be here tomorrow night, Friday night?" "Yes," he said, "I have nothing else to do." So they announced services for Friday night. Friday night the throng had grown still more. When he gave the appeal there were still scores of others who were saved. They said, "Can you be here Saturday night?" "Yes," said the young man, "I have nothing else to do." So they announced services for Saturday night.

Saturday afternoon Mr. Moody came back into town. Mrs. Moody said to him, "Mr. Moody, we are having a revival down at our church." Moody was amazed and said: "A revival? Why, the deacons said nothing to me about a revival, and I have planned

God's Love in Four Dimensions

no such thing. What do you mean?" She said: "Dear, that young man from Birmingham, England, who wrote you the note, is preaching at our services and we are having a God-sent revival. Mr. Moody, I want you to go down and listen to that young man and I want you to get converted." Well, Moody was dumbfounded and overwhelmed. "Converted?" he said. "Converted? Why, I have been a preacher over twenty years and I have been the pastor of this church for years. I get converted? What do you mean?" She said, "You go to the service tonight and you will understand what I mean."

Moody went to church and sat on the front row to listen to the young man. Quite critically, he looked at that young fellow. Once again the English preacher took the same text, John 3:16, and preached again Saturday night on the love of God in Christ Jesus. When he gave the appeal, once again, scores were saved. As Moody looked at it and watched it he said, "I never felt so like getting converted all over again in my life."

That went on for six weeks. For six weeks the young man preached on John 3:16! It was one of the greatest revivals in America. When it was finished Dwight L. Moody said: "It changed my preaching. Heretofore I had been preaching on the Sinai side of the cross, the judgment side of the cross, the wrath of God side of the cross, the perdition and damnation side of the cross, the penalty for sin side of the cross. But after that young man preached for six weeks on John 3:16, I began to preach on the other side, the Calvary side, the love of God side, the grace and mercy of God side. I began to preach on the outpouring of the Spirit of grace side of the cross."

Oh, that is what we need! We ought to preach wrath and judgment. No man declares the whole counsel of the Almighty without it. We ought to preach the fire of judgment and damnation. But it leaves us so helpless and so hopeless. There is no one but is conscious of his weakness, dereliction, sin, and shortcomings. Weakness and inability give way to old age and death. We are a dying people and we know it. But is there any word of encouragement? Has God said anything? Does God do anything? Does God see and care? Is it a matter to God? That is what we need to preach. That is what we need to emphasize. That is the good news of the evangel, the Gospel, the good news.

> The love of God is greater far
> Than tongue or pen could ever tell,
> It goes beyond the highest star
> And reaches to the lowest hell.

Wherever that song is published there is a little asterisk that points down to the bottom of the page which says that the third stanza of this poem was found on the wall of the cell of an inmate in an insane asylum:

> Could we with ink the oceans fill,
> And were the skies of parchment made,
> Were every stalk on earth a quill,
> And every man a scribe by trade;
> To write the love of God above
> Would drain the ocean dry;
> Nor could the scroll contain the whole,
> Though stretched from sky to sky.

Think of that! A wretched, miserable inmate died in a cell in an insane asylum. When the poor creature died and they took him out to bury him, they found that verse on the wall.

> For the love of God is broader than the measure of man's mind,
> And the heart of the eternal is most wonderfully kind.

The *platos*, the breadth of the love of God.

THE LENGTH OF GOD'S LOVE

God so loved the world, that He gave His only begotten Son. This is the length to which God did go in expressing His love for us. He gave His only begotten Son. What are the most meaningful and precious treasures in our lives? They are certainly not material, they are not monetary. They are always deeply personal. They are of the heart.

For example, did you ever notice the value that we place on things that have no particular intrinsic worth at all? Did you have a little baby who died, who fell asleep in Jesus? Do you have a picture of him? Ah, how treasured that little piece of paper! Do you have a lock of the baby's hair? It is worthless in itself. Do you have a wedding band? On the market it is worth very little. But how much value it holds for you because someone who loved you gave it to you! It represents life itself. If a man had the whole universe, if he owned it all, and he had a boy who died in Vietnam, I can easily imagine that father standing up and saying: "I own thirty million stars and I own ten thousand universes. I own forty continents and fifty oceans. But I would give every star I own, every planet that is mine, and all the continents and oceans if I could just have that boy back again." The priceless gifts are never monetary or material. They are of the soul and of the heart.

That is what the text says. God has given us the stars and the moon to shine at night and the sun to shine by day. He has given us the earth on which to walk. But all of these things are as nothing compared to the love of God in the gift of His Son, Christ Jesus. When God gave the Lord to us, He gave Himself. When Christ died for us, the God of heaven suffered. When the Lord bled, suffered, and died, it was God in His grace and mercy pouring out His love for us. Oh, the length to which God did go to express His love for us!

The Depth of God's Love

God gave His Son that whosoever believeth on Him should not perish. That is the depth of God's love. It reaches to the perishing. It is easy to love the adorable, the gracious, and these who return our affection. Likewise, by some token of neglect or thoughtlessness, the shallow pool of our affection is soon dried up. But the depth of love can always be defined in how we react if people mistreat us, speak mean of us, and if they do not do good by us. God loves them just as much. That is God's love. It reaches down to those who are perishing, to the flotsam and the jetsam of humanity. Some are so wretched in their disease, ignorance, and misery.

One time I went on rounds with a Christian doctor, one of our Baptist missionaries in the heart of Africa. We left at dawn and did not come back until after the sun had set, visiting his "clan settlements," his term for leper colonies. All day long we went from one clan settlement to another in a great arc through the country. In Africa if one is found leprous, even a child, the people shove him out to die of starvation, exposure, or to be killed by wild animals. As lepers they are not even allowed to approach the village. This Christian doctor had gathered all of the lepers in villages, called clan settlements. Then he regularly ministered to them. In a little English car I went along with him. Always when he would come to a place he would stop the little car in the middle of the village, get out all of his medicines, and all the lepers would come around him. Their fingers had fallen off, their toes had fallen off, and their faces, noses, and ears had large tumors, signs of the disease. There were lesions all over them.

At this particular settlement I called the doctor back after he had gotten in his car and was ready to go. I said, "Before you go, just look at one of those men." When he put his weight on his right foot there would be a squirt of blood that reached over his head. I said, "Doctor, I think you ought to come and look at him." One of those ulcers, unhealing on his foot, had decayed into an artery. As I stood by the car and watched the doctor, I thought: "That is God. That is God's love. That is the Christian faith. That is the Christian message." As I looked at it, I thought, "Who sent out that missionary?" We did. "Who bought that medicine?" We did. "Who is ministering to these people?" We are.

They are not only in ignorance, superstition, disease, poverty, and wretchedness, but they are bound in vice and in sin, living like the vermin of the earth, underneath, in the shadows of the night and in the dark. Oh, how depraved they are! The judgment of sin in their lives is seen in the spots on their arms, in the look in their eyes, and in the loss of mind and strength and body. Such jetsam! Such flotsam! Yet the Lord's love reaches down to them. No man has ever sunk beneath the reach of the love of God.

An infidel came up to a preacher and said, "I challenge you to debate the Christian faith." The preacher said: "I shall be delighted. You name the time and place. But when we come I want you to bring a hundred who have been in the wretchedness of iniquity, in the vice of sin. I want you to bring one hundred converts who have been lifted up and saved from the depths of sin by your preaching of infidelity. Then I shall bring a hundred who have been saved and delivered by the grace of God in Christ Jesus." The debate never came off. It would not! Where would one find a convert who had been lifted up out of the miry clay, his feet set on a rock, a new hope placed in his heart, and a new life found by the gospel of infidelity? Appoint me a place and a

God's Love in Four Dimensions

time any day, any night. I shall appear with one thousand, ten thousand who have been lifted up and saved by the Gospel of the grace of the Son of God.

> From sinking sand He lifted me,
> With tender hand He lifted me,
> From shades of night to plains of light,
> Oh, praise His name, He lifted me!

THE HEIGHT OF GOD'S LOVE

The height of the love of God is that "whosoever believeth in him should not perish, but have everlasting life." Everlasting life expresses the height of the love of God. There is a heaven for us. There is the announcement of the marriage supper of the Lamb. There is a new heaven and a new earth for us. Let us make it, let us be there.

> On Jordan's stormy bank, I stand,
> And cast a wistful eye
> To Canaan's fair and happy land,
> Where my possessions lie.
>
> I am bound for the promised land,
> I am bound for the promised land;
> O who will come and go with me?
> I am bound for the promised land.

Will you? Oh, who will come and go with me? I am bound for the promised land. This is the height to which God's love can lift you. Let Him do it now, believe in Him now, trust Jesus as your Saviour now. You, too, can experience the love of God in four dimensions. The breadth — He included you. The length — He sent Jesus to die in your place. The depth — He reaches down to you. The height — He wants to lift you up to heaven. He wants to save you, and He wants to do it now.

Chapter 20

TAKING HOLD OF THE ABOUNDING ABLENESS OF GOD

> Now unto him that is able to do exceeding abundantly above all that we ask or think, according to the power that worketh in us,
> Unto him be glory in the church by Christ Jesus throughout all ages, world without end. Amen. (Eph. 3:20, 21)

The title of this chapter is from the text, "Now unto him that is able to do exceeding abundantly above all that we ask or think." We are to take hold of the abounding ableness of God by daring to petition Him to do great things for us. He is able to answer those petitions no matter how great they may be. Out of the myriads of things we could ask God, I choose four.

ABLE TO FORGIVE

First, we can ask Him for the forgiveness for sin. He is able to do exceeding abundantly above all that we ask or think. The abounding ableness of God is great enough to bestow any gift, even the gift of the forgiveness of sin. How can we who are vile and evil come into the presence of God? How do we dare to call upon His name, covered as we are with transgression and iniquities on the outside and on the inside? Every part of our nature is fallen. Our thoughts, our emotions, our desires, every part of us shows us to be creatures of the dust. How do we appear before God laden with sin? The psalmist said: "Who shall ascend into the hill of the LORD? or who shall stand in his holy place? He that hath clean hands, and a pure heart . . ." (Ps. 24:3, 4). But whose hands are clean, and whose heart is pure? All of us are weighted down with carnal sin, outward sin like the prodigal son.

Taking Hold of the Abounding Ableness of God   161

All of us are laden with spiritual sin, inward sin, like the elder brother. Whether the prodigal son or whether the elder brother, we are like them both.

How do we pray? How do we come before God, sinful creatures that we are? How could I ever hope to enter into heaven, fallen as I am, for the Holy Scriptures say, "And there shall in no wise enter into it any thing that defileth . . ." (Rev. 21:27). If heaven is pure and perfect, and if I enter in, it is no longer pure and no longer perfect. Sometimes I will run across a fellow who will say, "I am looking for the perfect church." Then I say to him: "Do not join it. The very minute you join it, it will not be perfect any more." All of us are so much alike. How is it that we could enter heaven? How do we walk through those pearly gates and down those golden streets if nothing could ever enter in to defile it?

It is a strange thing about human nature. The further away we get from God, the finer we seem to be to ourselves, and the higher esteem we have of ourselves. But the nearer we get to God, the more unworthy and self-conscious of unrighteousness, sin, and guilt we feel. If I have any hope of entering heaven, of coming into the presence of the Lord, the closer I get, the more sinful I feel. How could I ever enter into God's presence? Isaiah, in the vision in the sixth chapter of his prophecy, said that he saw the Lord, high and lifted up. In the presence of that awesome majesty, the first reaction of the prophet was, "Woe is me! for I am undone; because . . . mine eyes have seen the King, the LORD of hosts" (v. 5). I am sinful and unworthy in His presence.

Simon Peter was like that. I presume he had been out on the seas for the years of his life fishing with no particular weight or burden of sin on his soul. But when he was in the presence of the Lord and saw the glory of God in Jesus, he fell at Christ's feet and said, "Depart from me; for I am a sinful man, O Lord" (Luke 5:8b). The nearer we get to God, the more laden with sin we become. We are sensitive to it. How then shall I ever call upon his name? How could I ever enter into heaven? Lord, is it too much to ask that I might be forgiven my sins, that I might be washed clean and pure? This is a part of the abounding ableness of God. He is able to forgive. First John 1:7b says, ". . . and the blood of Jesus Christ his Son cleanseth us from all sin."

When I was a boy I listened to the pastors in the little church where my family belonged. Some of the illustrations the preachers would use, I can remember so well. One of the pastors said that a girl dreamed she had entered heaven and God showed her the book of her life. Every page was stained with sin: wrong thoughts, wrong imaginations, wrong deeds. The pages were literally covered with wrong and sin. She cried out saying, "How could I be here with my life so stained with sin?" Then she had a vision of the blood of Christ, falling from His wounds. As it fell, it fell on those pages and washed those sin stains clean and white.

Another pastor illustrated it another way. He said that a little boy in London was with his father watching through the window of a building the British soldiers pass by in parade. They were dressed in brilliant red coats. The little boy exclaimed as he watched the soldiers pass by, "Ah, what beautiful white uniforms they have." The father said, "Son, they are not white; they are red, brilliant red." "Oh, no," said the little boy, "they are white, just as white as snow." The father with surprise looked down closer. Around the window (something he had not noticed) was a band of red glass. When one looks at anything red through a red glass, it looks perfectly white. And the little boy, looking through the red glass on the scarlet coat saw it pure white. The pastor said, "Thus does God look at our sins through the blood of the Crucified One and we look pure and white." All of those things made an indelible impression upon my heart. How God forgives our sins.

How does God forgive our sins? He does it as a kind friend would redeem a slave who has been sold into slavery. Someone comes and redeems the slave and sets him free. That is what Peter referred to when he said, "... ye were not redeemed with corruptible things, as silver and gold ... But with the precious blood of Christ" (1 Peter 1:18, 19). We have been bought back from slavery by the redemptive grace of our Lord.

Another way to say it is that we have been sold for a debt that we could never repay, but a kind and generous friend paid the debt for us, opened the door, and set us free. He paid it all. All to Him I owe. It is like someone diseased and leprous. Suddenly he is healed, he is cleansed, as Naaman was cleansed. The Lord heals us of the leprosy of sin and the disease of iniquity. It is like the resurrection from the dead. We are dead, the Scrip-

Taking Hold of the Abounding Ableness of God

tures say, in trespasses and in sins. We are dead and helpless, but the great Giver of Life quickens us and raises us to a glorious, triumphant life in the Lord. This is a gift that only God can bestow.

So emphatically does God speak of that absolute and eternal forgiveness that He says He buries our sins in the depths of the sea. He remembers them against us no more. He blots them out as a thick cloud. We come before the Lord and we say: "Lord, that sin I committed back there, do You remember, Lord? That evil that I did back there, do You remember, Lord?" And the Lord says: "I do not know what you are talking about. I have no remembrance. I have blotted it out. It is gone forever." Ah, the abounding grace, the overflowing love of our Lord! He is able to do exceeding abundantly above all we could ask or think. He is able even to forgive our sin.

HE IS ABLE TO COMFORT

Second, what will I ask of the Lord? In His abounding ableness to bestow upon us above all that we could ask or think, I would ask for strength and comfort in time of sorrow and soul needs. Down the street from us in Muskogee, Oklahoma, there lived a banker who had an only son, fifteen years of age. The teenager went swimming at Point of the Pines on the Illinois River in the Cookson Hills, and the boy drowned. It broke the heart and the life of his father. He brooded over it, and one day he took his own life.

In the city of Dallas a few months ago there was the story of two neighbors, two friends who lived side by side. One of them had a little girl who was playing in the driveway of his friend. The friend, not knowing that the little girl was there, backed out his car over the little girl and killed her. After the passing of weeks, the man who accidentally killed the little girl was in a restaurant when the broken-hearted father whose child had been run over took a long butcher knife and plunged it into the back of his neighbor — and friend.

Sorrow has such deep repercussions in human life. They are as deep as the soul is deep. When the only son of Sir Harry Lauder, the great Scot singer and entertainer, was killed in World War I, he said: "I had three choices. One, I could drown my sorrow in drink. Two, I could drown my sorrow in the grave; I could take my own life. Or three, I could find hope and comfort in God." And the famous singer said, "I turned to the Lord." Sorrow can warp, like nothing else in the world your soul, your mind, and your life. Or it can bring you close to God. It can bind you with golden chains to the very presence of the altar of the Lord. God is able to do exceeding abundantly above all that we ask or think. Oh, God, that sorrow might bind my soul closer to Thee!

HE IS ABLE TO OVERCOME BITTERNESS

Of Him who is able to do exceeding abundantly above all that we ask or think, could I ask that in age I not grow bitter and cynical? Could I ask that as I grow older I might be sweeter and finer, that I might learn to smile more, trust more, love more, and be more of what God would have me to be? It is so easy to grow bitter in age.

My first pastorage after seminary was at Chickasha, Oklahoma. One day I went to see a woman there who lived by herself in a dilapidated house. I knocked at the door. There came to the door a woman who looked more like wretchedness than any countenance or figure I had ever seen. I introduced myself and said, "I have come to see you." "Well," she replied, "what do you want?" I said, "I am a pastor and I have come to visit you." She answered, "There is no need for anybody here like you." I said, "But I have come to see you and visit with you, and I want to come in." She finally invited me in and I sat down. She asked, "Where do you preach?" I told her. "You say you believe in God?" she asked gruffly. "Yes," I said, "I believe in the Lord." "Well, I do not believe in God," said she, and she cursed Him. As I visited with her the terrible, tragic story of her life came out. Ever since she and her husband had moved to Oklahoma it was one wretchedness after another. Her husband had died and her children had left her. She was in want and her eyesight had gone. She was almost blind. As I continued visiting with her she said: "I write poetry. Would you like to hear some of my poetry?" I said, "Yes, let me hear it." The poem she repeated made such an impression upon me that when I was through with my visit I went out in the car and wrote it down. This is it:

Taking Hold of the Abounding Ableness of God 165

> I hate Oklahoma!
> Not the land of my native birth
> Put a land by all the gods that be
> A scourge on the face of the earth.
> I hate Oklahoma!
>
> I hate Oklahoma!
> Where the centipede crawls in your bed at night,
> And the rattlesnake lifts its fangs to bite,
> Where the lizard and the scorpion play on the sly,
> And the lonesome vultures sail high in the sky.
> Where water and food are an eternal lack,
> And a man's best friend sticks a dagger in your back.
> I hate Oklahoma!

All her poetry was like that, like the bitterness of old age. I talked to her and asked to pray. She said, "I do not believe in God and it does not do any good." But I wanted to pray and I knelt down by her chair and prayed. I did what I could to encourage her. I went again to see her, talked to her, prayed with her. She died not long after that and I buried her. When she was dead they found a little note. In that note was an expressed written appreciation for me. She said in the note: "There is nothing of value in the house but the rug on the living room floor. I give that to the pastor for the First Baptist Church in Chickasha." I took it and put it on the floor where our primary children met. When I had her service I had a congregation of only one. There was just one somebody there, a daughter-in-law who came from I do not know where.

Ah, Lord, as I grow older, may I not become cynical or bitter. But may my love for God and for You be deeper and wider. May my faith in the things of glory be clearer the nearer I approach them. He is able to do exceeding abundantly above all that we ask or think. Lord, let it be that I may be sweet and kind, full of faith and full of hope in the Lord.

HE IS ABLE TO TRIUMPH OVER DEATH

A fourth request I have to ask; namely, that in death I may be triumphant. What an unspeakable, inexpressible tragedy to define life in terms of its ultimate end! Is this all? Is there no meaning, no purpose, no future? Oh, Lord, is there not more to life than just decay, corruption, and death? Is there not great meaning, purpose, and goal? Is there not a consummation to it? Lord, give that to me. Oh, that I might find a resurrection from among the dead! That I might live in thy sight! That the end of life might be its greatest triumph! Let me not face ultimate defeat and decay but have assured victory and entrance into glory. Lord, give that to me. He is able to do exceeding abundantly above all that we ask or think. Lord, I ask that from Thee. Help me to see that to be born, to live, and to die is but a part of the eternal will and purpose of God. Help me to believe that, if this body is planted in corruption, it shall be raised in incorruption. If it is planted in dishonor, it shall be raised in glory. If it is planted in weakness, in decay, it shall be raised in strength and power. If it is planted a natural body, it shall be raised a spiritual body.

Help me, Lord, to see that it is only in death that I can enter into manifest eternal life. As long as I am in this house of clay, I cannot see God face to face. I cannot enter that beautiful city. I cannot mingle with God's redeemed glory. This body must be changed. Oh, Lord, give me the triumphant promise that this body will be made, some day, like the glorious body of the Lord Jesus. We have the promise by divine inspiration from the Apostle Paul:

> Now this I say, brethren, that flesh and blood cannot inherit the kingdom of God; neither doth corruption inherit incorruption.
> Behold, I shew you a mystery; We shall not all sleep, but we shall all be changed,
> In a moment, in the twinkling of an eye, at the last trump: for the trumpet shall sound, and the dead shall be raised incorruptible, and we shall be changed.
> For this corruptible must put on incorruption, and this mortal must put on immortality. . . . Death is swallowed in victory" (1 Cor. 15:50-54).

Ah, Lord, that the victory, the triumph, and the glory might be ours when we face the crossing of that swollen river. As our forefathers used to sing:

> My latest sun is sinking fast,
> My race is nearly run,
> My strongest trials now are past,
> My triumph is begun.
>
> Oh, come angel band,
> Come and around me stand.
> O bear me away on your snowy wings,
> To my immortal home.
> O bear me away on your snowy wings
> To my immortal home.

"O death, where is thy sting? O grave, where is thy victory?" (1 Cor. 15:55). It is not for us who find refuge in Christ to avow defeat in death. For us Christ is able to make us triumph over death.

Will you take hold of the abounding ableness of God? Will you ask Him to save you? He is able to forgive your sin. He is able to comfort you in your need. He is able to give sweetness instead of bitterness as youth and maturity give way to old age. When you finally stand at the mouth of the dark and lonesome vale of death, He is able to lead you through to the other side in triumph. "Now unto him who is able to do exceeding abundantly above all that we ask or think." He is able.

Chapter 21

THE GLORY OF GOD IN THE CHURCH

> Now unto him that is able to do exceeding abundantly above all that we ask or think, according to the power that worketh in us,
> Unto him be glory in the church by Christ Jesus throughout all ages, world without end. Amen. (Eph. 3:20, 21)

There are two words used in the Bible that are translated "glory." In the Hebrew Old Testament it is *kabod*. In the New Testament it is *doxa*. Our word "doxology" comes from it. Those two words, *kabod* and *doxa*, are translated in the King James Version, "glory." "Unto him be glory in the church." But what does it mean when we translate it into English? What is "the glory"? As I pore through these Scriptures it seems to me that there are five distinct meanings used in the Bible for the word "glory." We are going to learn those five meanings, then we shall apply them to the church.

THE GLORY OF BEAUTY

First, the word "glory" is used to refer to "beauty" and "symmetry," an impressive, gorgeous appearance. For example, David said: "I cannot build God's house for I am a man of war. But my son Solomon will build it, and I will gather materials and prepare for that building." He also said, ". . . and the house that is to be builded for the LORD must be exceeding magnifical, of fame and of glory throughout all countries" (1 Chron. 22:5). There is an instance of the use of the word *kabod* in the sense of beauty and symmetry, an impressive appearance.

The Glory of God in the Church

THE GLORY OF POWER

The word is used again to refer to the power, majesty, and dominion of God. In Psalm 19:1 we read, "The heavens declare the glory of God." In Matthew 4 Satan, in the third temptation, causes to pass before the Lord Jesus all the kingdoms of the earth and the "glory" of them. In the Sermon on the Mount the Lord says, ". . . even Solomon in all his glory was not arrayed like one of these (beautiful lilies)" (Matt. 6:29). Majesty, dominion, and power are included in the meaning of the word "glory." In Revelation 21 the Apostle John says of that beautiful city, ". . . the kings of the earth do bring their honour and glory into it" (v. 24). The Lord spoke of Himself in Matthew 16 saying, "For the Son of man shall come in the glory of his Father with his angels . . ." (v. 27). In majesty, in power, in great dominion Jesus is coming in glory. The two disciples James and John came to the Lord and said, ". . . Grant unto us that we may sit, one on thy right hand, and the other on thy left hand, in thy glory" (Mark 10:37). In John 17 the Lord spoke of ". . . the glory which I had with thee (the Father) before the world was" (John 17:5). So the word refers to majesty, dominion, and power.

THE GLORY OF GOD

Again the word "glory" refers to the essential character and being of Almighty God. The first historical use of the word in the Bible is in Exodus 33. When Moses came before the Lord he said, "I beseech thee, shew me thy glory" (v. 18). The Lord replied, "Thou canst not see my face: for there shall no man see me, and live . . . I will put thee in a clift of the rock, and will cover thee with my hand while I pass by: And I will take away mind hand, and thou shalt see my back parts . . ." (vv. 20-23). Moses was able to see only the after-glow of God's great glory. There the word "glory" refers to the being, the presence, the character, the existence, the person of Almighty God. In Isaiah, 40:3-5 is found the marvelous prophecy that is sung in *The Messiah:*

> The voice of him that crieth in the wilderness, Prepare ye the way of the LORD, make straight in the desert a highway for our God.

> Every valley shall be exalted, and every mountain and hill shall be made low: and the crooked shall be made straight, and the rough places plain:
> And the glory of the LORD shall be revealed, and all flesh shall see it together: for the mouth of the LORD hath spoken it.

That is a prophecy of the personal coming of Jehovah, God in Christ, the Messiah. "And the glory of the LORD shall be revealed." This is none other than the coming of Christ, both in the first and in the second coming of His glorious appearing. That is why the Apostle John wrote in John 1:14, "And the Word was made flesh, and dwelt among us, (and we beheld his glory, the glory as of the only begotten of the Father,) full of grace and truth." There the word "glory" refers to the presence, the character, and the being of Almighty God.

GLORY AS GOD'S GARMENT

Then sometimes the word "glory" is used to refer to the splendor, the brightness, the shining of God. I think of it as the garment of the Lord, the "shekinah" glory of God, the garments with which God dresses Himself.

In Deuteronomy 5 there is reiterated from Exodus 20 the Ten Commandments. When the law-giver Moses reviews the Ten Commandments, he recalls to the children of Israel that at Mount Sinai which burned with fire they saw the greatness and the glory of God. They saw how God dresses Himself in light, in fire.

In the journey through the wilderness the Lord appeared in a cloud by day and a pillar of fire by night. The Scriptures refer to that as "the glory of God." When the Tabernacle was finished, the priest could not enter because of "the glory of the presence of the Lord." To them it looked like burning smoke. In the dedication of the Temple of Solomon the priests could not enter in to minister because the house was filled with "the glory of God." And again, to them it looked like burning smoke. Glory is the garment of God.

In the recounting of the call of young Isaiah to be a prophet, he says: "In the year that king Uzziah died I saw also the Lord . . ., high and lifted up, and his train filled the temple. Above it stood the seraphims . . . one cried unto another . . . Holy, holy,

holy . . . the whole earth is full of his glory" (Isa. 6:1-3). To the young prophet it seemed that the entire earth was bathed in the light of the presence of God and the overflowing garments of the Almighty filled the whole earth with glory, with splendor, with brightness.

In Luke 2 we are given the story of the angelic announcement of the nativity of our Lord. The Book says an angel came down to announce the wondrous birth to the shepherds and then the narrative adds, "and the glory of the Lord shone round about them" (Luke 2:9). The presence of the angels was so bright and God's garments so marvelously splendid that when He came to announce the birth of the Lord, the whole earth around the shepherds was bathed in dazzling light.

In Acts 22, Paul recounts his conversion on the road to Damascus when Jesus met him in the way. Paul says that he was blinded by the glory of that light. When the Lord Jesus appeared, Christ's countenance was like the sun shining in its strength. In the presence of that glory, the physical eyes of Paul were blinded. That is why we could never see God in this mortal flesh. The dazzling, iridescent splendor of the beautiful vision would be blinding.

Revelation 18:1 begins like this, "And after these things I saw another angel come down from heaven . . . and the earth was lightened with his glory." The shining, the splendor, the dazzling iridescence of God — these are garments of the Almighty, His glory.

THE GLORY OF PRAISE

Then the word "glory" is used to refer to the praise and the honor, the thanksgiving, and the reverence that we bring in a sacrifice or a tribute to our great and living Lord. Glory, thanksgiving, and praise belong to God, as in the announcement of the angelic host from heaven when the Lord was born. "Glory to God in the highest and on earth peace, good will toward men." Glory, praise, honor, and thanksgiving be to God for His unsearchable, unspeakable gift.

When the Lord healed the ten lepers, only one, a Samaritan stranger, came back to thank the Lord. When Christ saw him return in thanksgiving for his cleansing, the Lord asked where the other nine were. The Lord asked, "Is there but this stranger who returns to give glory to God?" Praising God brings glory to God. In the Book of Galatians, Paul, in recounting his conversion, says that he was unknown by face to the churches of Judaea. They had only heard that he who had wasted the church now preached the faith that once he destroyed. The Paul adds, "And they glorified God in me" (Gal. 1:24). Thanksgiving, honor, and praise bring glory to the Lord.

It seems to me that those five categories and definitions mostly include what God means by the word *kabod* in Hebrew and *doxa* in Greek. We shall now apply their meaning to the church. "Unto him be the glory in the church by Jesus Christ." What is the glory of God in the church?

BEAUTY IN THE CHURCH

First, the word refers to beauty, to symmetry, and to beautiful appearance. As a young pastor, having two half-time churches, I had some brethren come from a community that was isolated and neglected. They said to me: "Our church has died, but we have so many young people who need the Lord. Could you come and preach for us on a Sunday afternoon once a month?" I first asked God if He would help me and bless me, and I had an impression from the Lord that He would. So I told the brethren that I would come. The church was in disrepair. Mischievous boys had broken all the window panes. The weeds were higher than my head, and the church was full of dirt.

Having prayed and believed that God would bless me as I tried to bring the message of Christ to the community and to the young people, the first thing I did was to call all the men together. I said: "Bring your scythes and your hoes. Get some putty and some window panes. Bring a brush and some paint. The first thing we are going to do is to cut down the weeds. Then we are going to put in the glass that is broken out. Then we shall sweep out the house of the Lord. Then we shall paint it on the inside and the outside." I think that glorifies God. The disrepair, the weeds, the broken light, the neglect, dishonors God. God's house ought to be as fine and as beautiful as we can make it. This is the glory of God in the church.

I do not mean that God does not meet with us when possibly we are unable to present before Him a beautiful place of a meet-

The Glory of God in the Church

ing house: In the heart of Africa I preached one time in a leper settlement, in a clan settlement, where lepers had made their church house out of mud. The pews were mud, the pulpit was mud, the pulpit stand was mud, and the two little benches in the choir were made out of mud. Everything in the church was made out of mud. But it was pretty mud! It was the best mud that they could contrive, and God honored the attempt of those poverty-stricken, sad lepers as they sought to build God a house. They did no less than their best. If we do less than we can for God in His house, we dishonor our Lord. Let us make it beautiful, let us make it fine, let us make it the best we can. That is glorifying God in the church.

POWER IN THE CHURCH

Second, the word "glory" is used of power and dominion. This we pray for in the house of God. The glory of God in the church is found in its power. Power to regenerate, to renew, and to save is the greatest demonstration of the miraculous ableness of God experienced in human heart and life.

See the stars up there? God made them by fiat. He spoke the word and they came into existence. That is miraculous, indeed. But far more miraculous, dynamic, and powerful is the wonder-working miracle of God when He recreates a man, when He saves him. God spoke the world into existence, but when He saves a man, Christ has to die, and the Holy Spirit has to be poured out, and the man has to be regenerated in his soul. This is the power of God in the church.

In how many churches do you see the power, the glory of God missing? "Ichabod" is written on the door. "The glory is departed." For the glory in power in the church is seen in the conversion of people, the saving of the lost, the response to God's blessed and precious invitation. The power of God in the church is one of conversion, one of salvation, one of regeneration. When people come to the Lord, the power of God is present to remake them. For the Lord is able, and the Lord is mighty. That is the glory of God in the church. I can be a better man and we can be better people. We have deep weaknesses that plague us and drag us down, but God can help us overcome them. For defeat, He can give us victory. For the ashes of mourning, He can give us joy celestial. That is the glory of God in the church. It is the power of the Lord to remake us.

God's Presence in the Church

Third, the presence of God, the essential nature of God, is the glory of God. As His people we share the divine nature of the Lord. In 1 Corinthians 11 Paul says that the men are not to wear hats on their heads in church. The reason for it is that man was made in the image and in the glory of God. When we are regenerated, we become fellow heirs with Jesus Christ our Lord. We share His glory.

There is no more meaningful verse in the Bible than this that Paul wrote in 2 Corinthians, "But we all, with open face beholding as in a glass (a mirror) the glory of the Lord, are changed into the same image from glory to glory, even as by the Spirit of the Lord" (v. 18). That is, as we look at Christ, as we focus our heart's attention upon the Lord, as we pray to Him, talk to Him, love Him, give our lives to Him, our homes, our children, our families, our business, our work, and our hands, as we come before the Lord, look at Him, and serve Him we are transformed into the same image from glory to glory, that is, from one degree of glory to a higher degree of glory until finally we come to the perfection of glory in heaven. When we see Him as He is, we shall have a body like His, a heart like His, a mind like His, a soul like His, and a life like His. We are going to be like the Lord some glorious day. That is what the psalmist meant when he said, "Thou shalt guide me with thy counsel, and afterward receive me to glory" (Ps. 73:24).

God Clothes the Church With Glory

In 2 Corinthians 3, Paul writes of the glory of God that shined in the face of Moses when he came down from the mountain. The Apostle Paul calls that shining the glory of God. Moses was up on the mountain forty days and forty nights with the Lord. When he came back down the mountain, the skin of his face shone.

Is it not a loss that there is a chapter heading in 2 Corinthians at the close of chapter 3? For in the next chapter, after Paul has described the glory of God in the face of Moses (and that glory faded away), he speaks about that glory in our face. He says,

The Glory of God in the Church

"For God, who commanded the light to shine out of darkness, hath shined in our hearts, to give the light of the knowledge of the glory of God, in the face of Jesus Christ" (2 Cor. 4:6). That is the glory of God in His church. Our faces are to portray it. The very tone of our voices is to exhibit it. The glory of God is in His people. When you look mule-like, and you are down, you are just that much away from the Lord. But when your face shines, and your eyes shine, and your voice sparkles, you are close to God. That is the glory, the shekinah glory of God. God's people ought to look different from the people of the world. There ought to be a joy, a gladness, a triumph, and a glory in us that the world knows nothing about. This is the glory of God in the church, the glory of God in the church triumphant. Oh, what God hath promised to us who love Him!

Moses and Elijah appeared to the Lord on the Mount of Transfiguration and the face of Christ shone above the brightness of the sun. As Jesus glowed in glory, so did Moses and Elijah. We are going to be that way. God shall give us that glory, that shining, that splendor. In triumphant 1 Corinthians 15, the Apostle Paul says that the glory of the celestial is one, and the glory of the terrestrial is another. There is a glory of the sun, a glory of the moon, a glory of the stars, and one star differs from another in glory. So it shall be in the resurrection of the dead. This body, planted in corruption, shall be raised in incorruption. This body, planted in dishonor, shall be raised in glory. This body, planted in weakness, shall be raised in power. Planted a natural body, it shall be raised a spiritual body.

What does he mean, planted in dishonor? You have been to memorial services as I. Death does something to the body. Death leaves it as food for the worms. Death leaves it like decaying dust. Buried out of our sight but for a while, it shall be raised some day in glory, in effulgence, in iridescence, in brightness, in immortality. Triumph over death is the glory God has promised to His church. We shall be raised in glory out of death.

Praise in the Church

And last, the glory of God in the church is the praise, the adoration, the worship, the singing, the sacrifice of thanksgiving and gratitude. The services of Christ in His church ought always to have an overtone of glory, thanksgiving, praise, and blessing. In the Book of 2 Chronicles David took the 38,000 Levites and divided them into courses. To some he gave an assignment of singing, to others he gave an assignment of playing musical instruments, which David had invented himself. When the people came to worship God in the Temple, there were the Levites praising God. The instrumentalists were praising the Lord. When we come to church, always there ought to be a feeling in our souls that we have been to church, not to a lecture, to a discussion, to a book review. We ought not to feel that we have just been to hear an essay on economics or political life. But when we go to church and go home, there ought to be the feeling in our souls that today we were in the presence of the Lord. We felt God in our souls. We are praising the Lord, loving the Lord.

The people of the world give thanks when they are up, rich, affluent, happy, and on top. But the Christian says we give thanks even when we are saddened, hurt, sick, aged, dying, and poor. Job said: "The LORD gave and the LORD hath taken away; blessed be the name of the LORD."

There ought plainly to be the sacrifice of thanksgiving in the communion service. Lord, the body of Jesus was so cruelly mutilated for us. Thank You, Lord. And that blood, coursing through His veins, God poured out. Lord, my sins were washed clean and white. Thank You, Lord, for the blood of Jesus, the sacrifice of our Lord.

And then, Lord, thank You for the trials that I know and the discouragements that I experience. Thank You, Lord, for those days when I have been so humbled and so down. May I glorify God in suffering, in trial, in age, and finally in death. That is the Christian faith.

And what of the glory of God in your life? Let Christ come in and make life beautiful and glorious. Let Jesus come in and clothe you with the glorious garment of His righteousness. He will make you shine for God. Let your life be one of thanking and praising Jesus for what He has done for you. Let His power regenerate you, give new life to you, convert you, and change you. Let God come into your life. What glory that will be!

Chapter 22

THE TRUE ECUMENISM

I therefore, the prisoner of the Lord, beseech you that ye walk worthy of the vocation wherewith ye are called,
With all lowliness and meekness, with long-suffering, forbearing one another in love;
Endeavouring to keep the unity of the Spirit in the bond of peace.
There is one body, and one Spirit, even as ye are called in one hope of your calling;
One Lord, one faith, one baptism,
One God and Father of all, who is above all, and through all, and in you all. (Eph. 4:1-6)

THE SEVENFOLD UNITY OF THE CHURCH

This chapter especially emphasizes verses 5 and 6. They speak of the sevenfold, true unity of the church. The true ecumenism is wrapped up in that unity: one body, one Spirit, one hope, one Lord, one faith, one baptism, and one God and Father of all. I speak on this subject because in the last several years the whole world of Christendom has been colored by the ecumenical movement.

There is a Greek word, *oikoumene*, which means the inhabited earth. From that word *oikoumene* comes the word ecumenical, universal. Usage has shortened the word to "ecumenism," a term referring to the movement in the theological world toward one organized church. All of this would be fine were it done in the truth and in the revelation of God. The problem lies in the compromise required and in the willingness on the part of the men who further that ecumenical movement to throw beliefs away in order to find some kind of a lower denominator upon which everyone could agree. All of this means that for the most part, ecumenism is a rejection and a denial of some of the tremendous truths and doctrines revealed in God's Holy Word.

That longed-for, looked-for goal of a universal religion has characterized the political world from the beginning of history. About 165 B. C. Antiochus Ephiphanes (Antiochus the Illustrious) was the gifted, cruel, and merciless king of the Syrian empire. In order to strenghthen his kingdom he thought that he should have one religion, so he coerced a common worship of pagan gods. Now it happened to be that in the Syrian empire was little Judaea. In those days when he was forcing the Jew to call upon the name of Jupiter and to do sacrifice before all the gods of the Greeks, Mattathias stood up against Antiochus with his sons, one of whom was Judas Maccabeus. The marvelous story of that resistance is written in the apocryphal books of 1 and 2 Maccabees. I wonder what the worshipers of the true Jehovah who spilled their blood rather than desert the tenets of their religion would think of today's ecumenical movement? I wonder what the Christian martyrs of yesteryear would think of this modern ecumenical movement that seeks to wash out the conviction of the people of the Lord? Ignatius, the martyred pastor of the church at Antioch; Polycarp, the martyred pastor of the church at Ephesus; John Bunyan in Bedford prison; or Roger Williams, who left the Massachusetts colony in order to find freedom for worship in Providence and Rhode Island — what would they think of a movement that seeks to erase the doctrines for which they suffered or died?

But there is a true ecumenical movement and there is a genuine ecumenism. It pleases God to set it forth in His Holy Word. There are seven unities in the true church and in the true Christian faith.

ONE BODY

There is one body, the church of Jesus Christ. Here in the text the word is used in the generic sense. Most of the time in the New Testament the word "church" is used in a local sense. For instance, there are the churches (plural) of Galatia, the churches (plural) of Macedonia, the churches (plural) of Achaia, or of Judaea. But there is also in the Bible the use of the word in a general sense, in a universal sense. We use a like general idea in saying "the school," "the state," "the court," "the family," "the home"; so also one says "the church" in a generic sense.

For example, Hebrews 12:23, refers to our coming to the "general assembly and church of the firstborn, which are written in heaven." There is a universal church in the family of God. In this universal church is found the community of those who love God and seek to do His will. The author of the church is God. The leader and head is Jesus. The moving, quickening Spirit is the Holy Ghost. The rule and the standard of faith and practice is the Holy Scriptures. It is the universal church of Jesus Christ. Wherever a born-again believer finds his fellow believers in Christ, there is a community of love, friendship, and devotion that is felt in the deepest soul. For our unity is not so much man-made as it is God-made. The golden chains that bind us together are held in the hands of our Lord Himself in heaven.

In 1947 I went to Germany. I made a like journey in 1950 and again in 1955. When I first went through the war-torn and ravaged country in 1947, the cities were rubble, the nation was prostrate, and the people defeated. I went to the Baptist church in Munich. The building was destroyed, the people had been scattered, and the little group that gathered together was composed mostly of refugees. They met in a dark place underground and our light was a coal-oil lamp. When I preached the sermon had to be translated into three different languages so that the differing refugees could understand. Yet I felt the Spirit of God in that war-ravaged, defeated, and ragged little band. When I went back in 1950, they had built the church. That was the first time where, having observed the Lord's Supper that morning, I saw God's people join hands and sing, "Blest Be the Tie That Binds." I came back to Dallas and began that beautiful and lovely practice at the end of our Lord's Supper.

> We share our mutual woes,
> Our mutual burdens bear;
> And often for each other flows
> The sympathizing tear.

As I joined hands with that band of Baptists in Munich I felt the quickening, living Spirit and the unity of the church of God. There is one body.

ONE SPIRIT

There is one Spirit. The quickening power that makes us one is the Holy Spirit of God. Without His presence we are as dead, as lifeless, and as incapable as a corpse. By His Spirit we are quickened. We are made alive. We live unto God. Ezekiel was commanded at the valley of dry bones to speak to the wind, the breath, the Spirit of God. When he did, those corpses stood up and lived. In the synoptic gospels the church is congregated, it is organized. It has the ordinances, the discipline, and the commission, but it must wait for the outpouring of the quickening Spirit of God at Pentecost.

When we are together in the Spirit, we are all with one accord. When people are scattered like a covey of birds and there are a thousand wills among us, we see but an emphatic sign that we are not listening, we are not following the leadership of the Holy Spirit of God. There is one body. There is one Spirit. And He has but one mind, the mind of God.

ONE HOPE

There is one hope, and only one that is ultimate and final. That hope is bound up in Jesus our Lord. All other prospects and promises ultimately pass away. The eloquent author of the Book of Hebrews writes in his sixth chapter of us who are Christians "who have fled for refuge to lay hold upon the hope set before us: Which hope we have an an anchor of the soul, both sure and stedfast, and which entereth into that within the veil" (vv. 18, 19). There is heaven beyond the veil, "Whither the forerunner is for us entered, even Jesus, made an high priest for ever after the order of Mechisedec" (v. 20). Our hope is in Jesus, and He is beyond the veil. He is there interceding for us, mediating for us. He is our great Advocate and Pleader. He assures to us our inheritance, incorruptible, undefiled, that shall never pass away. He is there to see to it that we finally make glory, that we finally arrive in heaven. He is beyond the veil. He is our hope. But is He going to stay there forever? Will we never see Him? Will the Great High Priest never come out?

In the Book of Titus Paul refers to that "blessed hope" as being the appearing of our God and Saviour Jesus Christ. Some day He is coming outside the veil and we shall see Him personally, bodily, in glory, descending in the shekinah garments of God. That shall be at the end of the world, the consummation of the age, when all of the wrongs are righted. That shall be the day when the earth shall be filled with knowledge and righteousness as the waters cover the sea. That shall be the day when the dead shall be resurrected, and all of us shall be changed. We shall meet God face to face when our hope comes to pass and our Lord comes without the veil.

One Lord

There is one Lord, our blessed Lord Jesus. He is the One who purchased us with His own blood. He is the One who reigns and rules over the church. He is the One whom some day we shall see again. There is one Lord, our blessed Jesus. He is exalted and raised, not because of the suffrage of man, but because of the decree and edict of Almighty God. As Paul wrote in Philippians 2, "Wherefore God also hath highly exalted him, and given him a name which is above every name: That at the name of Jesus every knee should bow, of things in heaven, and things in earth, and things under the earth" (vv. 9, 10). There will be no unbowed knee in that day. There will be no unbelievers when God exhibits Christ to the whole created world.

Christ is to be exalted by the hand of God. Thus it is written in Revelation 5: "And I saw in the right hand of him that sat upon the throne a book written within and on the backside, sealed with seven seals. And I saw a strong angel proclaiming with a loud voice, Who is worthy to open the book, and to loose the seals thereof? And no man in heaven (not even the angels), nor in earth (not even the apostles and the prophets), neither under the earth, was able to open the book, neither to look thereon" (vv. 1-3). And John writes: "And I wept much, because no man was found worthy to open and to read the book, neither to look thereon. And one of the elders saith unto me, Weep not: behold, the Lion of the tribe of Juda, the Root of David, hath prevailed to open the book, and to loose the seals thereof. And I beheld, and, lo, in the midst of the throne . . . stood a Lamb as it had been slain . . . . And they sung a new song . . . Thou art worthy to take the book, and to open the seals thereof . . . . Worthy is the Lamb . . . . Blessing, and honour, and glory, and power, be unto him . . ." (vv. 4-13). That is the exaltation of God.

There is one Lord, our blessed Jesus. He is all and all to us in the church. If the church could be likened to a household, He is our Master. If the church could be likened to a school of faith, He is our teacher. If the church could be likened to a great army, He is our captain. If the church could be likened to a bride, He is our Bridegroom. There is none else besides. There is none other name under heaven given among men whereby we must be saved.

Do you ever wonder why it is that the Roman Empire persecuted the Christians? There never was a government, there never was a kingdom so liberal in matters of religion as the Roman Empire. Whenever they conquered a land (and they conquered the entire civilized world) the religion of the land that was conquered was accepted by the Romans. Hadrian built in the city of Rome a marvelous structure he called "The Pantheon," literally, "the all gods." It is one of the most beautiful buildings of antiquity and the most perfectly preserved. It can be seen today, a magnificent structure. Whenever Rome conquered a kingdom, a nation, or a principality, Rome accepted their gods and they put images of them in niches all around the Pantheon. There is a niche for Jupiter, a niche for Juno, a niche for Artemis, a niche for Osirus, a niche for Venus, and a niche for Neptune. There are niches all around the Pantheon showing the gamut of the religious life of the Roman Empire that was acceptable to the people. Well then, why did the Roman Empire persecute the Christians to death? The answer is simple. Rome said to the Christians, "See, here is a niche for Jupiter, here is a niche for Juno, and here is a magnificent niche for Jesus." But the Christians said: "No! There is no way our Jesus can be named in the same breath with a Jupiter, a Juno, or any other god. There is one Lord, and His name is Christ Jesus." So the Christians were put to death.

Every time I see a book on "Comparative Religions," and on the jacket there is a picture of Buddha, Confucius, Mohammed, Moses, and Jesus, my blood boils. To add insult to injury, the book usually equates all those religions in the world. Here is Islam, here is Buddhism, here is Confucianism, here is Shintoism. Take your pick. One is as good as the other. Not so! There is one Lord, separate and apart from all of the other so-called gods of the world. There is one true religion and that is the first-century Christian religion. That is what Paul means when he says that there is one body, there is one Spirit, there is one hope, and there is one Lord.

ONE FAITH

There is one faith, one body of objective truth, the truth that I hold here in my hand. All of us who are Christians believe this objective body of truth. We find in this Biblical revelation of the truth of God the saving of our souls, the forgiveness of our sins, and our hope of heaven. Just as there is an objective body of truth in chemistry, in medicine, in physics, in astronomy, in anatomy, or in any other science, so there is also an objective body of truth in the Christian faith. One man's idea of God and one man's idea of religion is not as good as another man's idea of religion. One might as well say one man's idea of smallpox and how to cure it is as good as any other man's idea.

In Africa one time I saw an entire section of the nation that had been wiped out by smallpox. Driving down the road the missionary said to me: "Do you see that broom in the yard? Do you see the broom on the roof of that thatched hut? That means there is smallpox there, and they are driving the demon of smallpox away. They do it by putting a broom on the roof and a broom in the yard." That is one idea of smallpox. But Pasteur had another when he said that smallpox was caused by bacteria and was a disease against which one could be vaccinated. One man's idea of the disease and the cure is not as good as another man's idea of the disease and the cure.

Just as there is objective truth in the world of chemistry, in the world of physics, in the world of medicine, in the world of disease, and in the world of anatomy, so there is also objective truth in the world of religion. That objective truth I hold in my hand is the Bible. This is the revelation of Almighty God. Here is where I learn the name of Christ. This is the way mapped out for me if ever I hope to see God and enter heaven. This objective truth I am to receive by study and by committal. Sometimes there will be a college student who comes back home and says: "Oh, that Bible fantasy, it is idiocy, it is myth and fable, it is a psychological aberration, it is illusion — there is no truth in it. There is no truth in religion and there is no truth in God." I would be very happy to agree with that person who comes back from school and tells me that, if I could believe that all I am is a conglomerate of anatomical particles. But the Book says that when the Lord God made the man, He breathed into his nostrils the breath of life and the man became a living soul, a quickened spirit. There is more to man than molecules, protons and electrons. There is more to truth than the agregate of anatomy or any other physical science. Aristotle, when he had put together in his philosophical works all of the things of physics, biology, astronomy, and chemistry, had another work beyond that which he called "metaphysics." "Metaphysics" means "things over and beyond the physical." That is why I say there is objective truth in things beyond the physical. It is the soul that makes a man a man, that separates him from the animals. There is one faith, an objective religion, and it is found in this blessed Book.

One Baptism

There is one baptism, not two. The meaning of baptism is found in the presented, biblical idea. There is an idea back of baptism. So many things are like that; their meaning is found in the idea, so the meaning of baptism is in the idea of it. It is a burial and a resurrection. We are buried with Christ and are dead to sin. We are raised with the Lord in the likeness of His own glorious life. The Sanhedrin said to John the Baptist: "Where did you get that ordinance? Where did you get that baptism?" (cf. John 1:14-28). The Jews had many washings and ablutions, but they did it themselves. They washed their feet, they bathed their hands, at times they ceremonially bathed themselves all over. They even ceremonially washed their pots and pans. But the first time a man ever took another man and washed him was when John did it. So unusual was the ordinance that they called him "John, the one who baptizes." The leaders of the nation asked him: "Where did you find that ordinance? Who told you to do that?" And John said, "He that sent me to baptize told me how to do it. God did it." The idea of the pattern of baptism is in heaven. Baptism means a burial and a resurrection.

In Spirit baptism we are taken out of the world and placed in the body of our Lord. The Holy Spirit takes us out of our sins and death and puts us into the living body of Christ. There is one baptism, and the baptism in water symbolizes this glorious spiritual resurrection.

ONE GOD AND FATHER

There is one God and Father of all. There are not ten gods, there are not innumerable gods, there are not even two gods or three. There is no such thing as dualism, tritheism, or polytheism in the Holy Scriptures. There is one God. In the Bible there is monotheism and that alone.

The true God has revealed Himself to us in the person of Jesus Christ. In the Old Testament, preincarnate, His name is Jehovah. In the New Testament, incarnate, His name is Jesus the Lord. And in the world that is to come, He is our reigning and glorious King. To come to Jesus is to come to God. To love the Lord Jesus is to love God. To accept the Lord Christ is to accept God. To give your heart to the Lord Jesus is to give your heart to God. To do the will of Jesus is to do the will of God. There is one God, the God revealed in Jesus. Accept the Lord as your Saviour. Put your life in the fellowship of His church. Join yourself to the company of God's people.

Chapter 23

THE ONE BAPTISM

> One Lord, one faith, one baptism. (Eph. 4:5)

A commentary may state this "one baptism" in the verse refers to baptism in water. Another commentary will say that the verse refers to Spirit baptism, the one baptism by the Holy Spirit wherein we are added to the body of Christ (1 Cor. 12:13). As I read the Book and as I study it the best I can, I think it refers to both. There is one baptism. Initially, introductively, it is the baptism in water, burial and resurrection. Symbolically it came to be used to depict the baptism by the Holy Spirit. We are taken out of death and we are added in life to the body of our Lord, thus buried and raised. My persuasion is, however, that whether the baptism is in water or whether it is by the Spirit, there is one baptism. There are not two, there are not three, there are not half a dozen, but there is one baptism as there is one body, one Spirit, one hope, one Lord, one faith, one God and Father of us all.

In this chapter we are going to take baptism initially — what it actually is. Symbolically, the baptism refers to the work of the Holy Spirit, but actually, initially, and originally it is an ordinance which is used to symbolize something else. It is like the Lord's Supper. The bread and the fruit of the vine in the Lord's Supper symbolize something else, but the supper actually is bread and fruit of the vine which we eat and drink. So the "one baptism" actually is an ordinance, it is an action although it symbolizes something else.

Let us look at the unique position on the ordinance of baptism held in the New Testament.

BAPTISM RECEIVES THE HIGHEST HONOR

First, baptism receives the highest honor. Look at its unique position in this verse. "One body, one spirit . . . one hope . . . one Lord, one faith, one baptism." It is unusual that the apostle should place that one baptism in the company of things which he names in the unity of the revelation of God in Christ Jesus. When I turn to Matthew 3 I am impressed again with baptism's honored and unique position. In this passage all three persons of the Godhead are present and active in the baptism of the Lord Jesus. The Son comes to be baptized in the Jordan River, the Holy Spirit descends upon Him, and the voice of the Father is heard saying, "This is my beloved Son, in whom I am well pleased" (Matt. 3: 17). The Son submitted, the Holy Spirit descended, and the voice of the Father commended. The only time and place in the entire Word of God where all three persons of the Godhead are present and active is here in the baptism of the Lord Jesus.

Note also that in His first public utterance our Lord establishes the ordinance. The first time we hear the voice of Jesus in His public ministry is when He says, "Thus it becometh us to fulfil all righteousness" (Matt. 3:15). Then John baptized Him. In the Book of Matthew, the last public utterance of our Lord established the ordinance in perpetuity. We are to make disciples of all the nations, baptizing them in the name of the Father, the Son, and the Holy Spirit (28:18-20). From first to last in the utterances of our Lord, baptism receives the highest honor.

BAPTISM COMMANDED IN THE GREATEST NAME

Second, baptism is commanded in the greatest name. The only commandment which is made in the name of the triune God is the commandment to baptize. "Go ye therefore, and teach all nations, baptizing them in the name of the Father, and of the Son, and of the Holy Ghost" (Matt. 28:19, 20). Why are those three persons of the Godhead named in that baptismal formula and one commandment? The reason is found in this. In 1 Corinthians 15: 1-4, the Apostle Paul writes, "Brethren, I make known to you, I define for you the Gospel." What is the Gospel? Paul sets it forth plainly. "Brethren, I define for you, I make known unto you the Gospel, wherein ye stand, wherein ye are saved." What is that

Gospel that saves us? "How that Christ died for our sins according to the Scriptures. Then He was buried and the third day He was raised according to the Scripture." And that gospel message is portrayed in the ordinance of baptism. The Lord died, He was buried, and He was raised from the dead. In baptism we are buried and we are raised (Col. 2:12). Salvation involves all three persons of the Godhead.

First, God the Father looked down from heaven on the lost and depraved children of old man Adam, and in His mercy, grace, and love He planned the way of salvation. It was born in the heart of God. Second, Jesus, the divine and only-begotten Son of God, worked out that salvation for us. He came down into this world to die for our sins, to suffer, to be crucified, and to be buried. Third, the Holy Spirit effected that salvation in our hearts. God loved us and planned it. The divine Son worked it out in His life, ministry, death, and resurrection. The Holy Spirit effected it, used it for the regeneration of our souls. That is the way we are saved, and the way in which salvation in the Gospel is portrayed in the ordinance of baptism. When I am baptized I am publicly announcing to the world that I am a disciple of the Lord and that I have received grace and mercy from His loving hands.

BAPTISM SYMBOLIZES THE GREATEST DOCTRINES

Third, baptism symbolizes the greatest doctrines. Paul wrote in Romans 6: "Know ye not, that so many of us as were baptized into Jesus Christ were baptized into his death? Therefore we are buried with him by baptism into death: that like as Christ was raised up from the dead by the glory of the Father, even so we also should walk in newness of life. For if we have been planted together in the likeness of his death, we shall also be in the likeness of his resurrection" (vv. 3-5). Baptism illustrates, symbolizes, presents the greatest doctrines.

Baptism refers to a past redemption, one worked out for us by the triune God. Baptism presents a present regeneration. We have been born anew. We have been raised in Christ. And baptism presents the most glorious hope that we have: that of glorification, resurrection, the visitation of God, the gathering of God's people at the end time. Those three doctrines are presented symbolically in the ordinance of baptism.

Baptism Symbolizes the Greatest Facts

Fourth, baptism symbolizes the greatest facts. Paul says in Romans that baptism is a symbol of the greatest fact of the Christian faith which is that Christ died for our sins and was raised for our justification. He died, He was buried, He was raised, and that resurrection of our Lord demonstrates His deity, manifests His power, and proclaims our redemption.

Of His resurrection Paul says, "He was raised again for our justification" (Rom. 4:25). What he means by that is that Christ was raised from the dead to declare us righteous. He would ascend into glory after His resurrection in order to see to it that before God's judgment throne we were accepted as righteous. We are not actually righteous, we are not holy; rather, we are full of sin, all of us. We are all either saved sinners or unsaved sinners. But the Lord justifies those who accept Him; He declares us righteous. He was raised for that justification; namely, to see us through, to see that we get to heaven. You will always find this note of preaching in the apostolic message. They preached with triumph the resurrection of Jesus. And that great and glorious fact of our faith is proclaimed, manifested in this holy ordinance of baptism. He who died for our sins and was buried is raised from the dead. That is why to us a crucifix could never be a symbol of the Christian faith. On a crucifix there is a dead Christ who has been nailed to a cross. But we have a living Christ. So the sign of the Christian faith is a cross with a Saviour gone from it. Where has He gone? He is raised from the dead and He is in heaven. He lives! Baptism symbolizes this greatest fact of our faith.

And it symbolizes the greatest fact of our experience: our death to the world, our death to sin, and our resurrection to a new life in Christ. One of the most eloquent passages in Paul is Galatians 2:20: "I am crucified with Christ, nevertheless I live: yet not I, but Christ liveth in me: and the life which I now live in the flesh I live by the faith of the Son of God, who loved me, and gave himself for me." Here, again, is death and resurrection. Baptism, therefore, symbolizes our regeneration. We were born in trespasses and sin, dead in them, and the Lord resurrected us. He made us sensitive to the cause of Christ, to the Spirit of the Lord, and to the will of our God. He quickened us. As Paul said: "If any man be in Christ he is a new [creation]: old things are passed away;

behold, all things are become new" (2 Cor. 5:17). New! It is a new day, a new life, a new hope, a new love, and a new dedication. It is a new thing. And that is symbolized in our baptism. We are raised to a new life in the Lord. If the Lord delays His coming and we die, if we are planted together in the likeness of His death, then some day we believe God will raise us out of the dust of the ground, out of the heart of the earth, and that we shall live in His sight.

Baptism truly symbolizes the greatest hope of the Christian. We are going to live even though we die. We are going to be raised. Flesh and blood cannot inherit the kingdom of God but God has shown us the mystery of resurrection and rapture. We may not all sleep, but we shall all be changed in a moment, in the twinkling of an eye, at the last trump, when the trumpet shall sound and the dead shall be raised incorruptible. If we die and are buried we shall be raised from the dead. Now that is what it is to be a Christian. That is the faith. That is the hope. That is the glory, and it is symbolized in this glorious, unique, honored ordinance of baptism.

What if you change the mode of the ordinance? One of the unusual passages that Hebrews 8 quotes from Exodus says, "As Moses was admonished of God when he was about to make the Tabernacle: for See, saith he, that thou make all things according to the pattern shewed to thee in the mount" (v. 5). And in the Book of Exodus it is carefully recorded that Moses did exactly that. He made the Tabernacle exactly according to the pattern that God had showed him on the mount. Now we are to do the same thing with the ordinance of baptism. We are to do it exactly as God gave it to John the Baptist. We are not to change the pattern. If we do, we ruin it. It is baptism no longer. There is one baptism that God gave to John the Baptist. God said that baptism is burial and resurrection. One has to be buried and one has to be raised. That is what baptism is according to the pattern which God gave to John the Baptist.

Another thing, when one breaks that pattern and one baptizes unregenerated, unconverted people, then he lays the church open to all kinds of heresies. The tragedy written on the pages of Christendom arising from the baptizing of unregenerate people is one of the darkest pages in human history. When one baptizes people

The One Baptism

who are not regenerated, such as infants, he loses a regenerated church. God says, first, one must be a disciple. Second, on that confession of faith, one is to be baptized (Matt. 28:19,20). When people are baptized into the church who are not saved, a regenerated membership is lost.

Baptizing infants was the way they made the church synonymous with the state. When a child was born his name was registered in a book as a citizen of the state. When a child was born they christened the child into the church. The church and the state were synonymous. The Spirit had nothing to do with it. All this was made possible when they changed God's pattern of baptism. Then what happened? The church used the state to persecute those who dissented. There is no darker page in human history than the page of the church using the state to burn heretics at the stake, to see them rot in dungeons. Sometimes entire little nations would be wiped out by the power and direction of the church. How could such a thing be? It came about by changing the ordinance of baptism and making the church and the state congruent. This is what happens and this is what tragedy follows when we break the pattern of God.

BAPTISM IS IN KEEPING WITH THE MOST BLESSED EXAMPLE

Fifth, baptism is in keeping with the most blessed of examples. Not only does baptism receive the highest honor, not only is it commanded in the greatest name, and not only does it exhibit, symbolize, the greatest doctrine, but also the ordinance of baptism is in keeping with the most blessed of all examples. In John 1 the Baptist preacher is on the banks of the Jordan River preaching his message, announcing the kingdom. His converts he baptized in the river. It was an astonishing sight. The world had never seen that kind of baptism before. There were many ablutions, many washings, many baptisms, among the Jews, but a man always did it to himself. He baptized his feet, he washed his feet. The word in Greek means "immerse." Sometimes he baptized his pots and pans. But the first time in the history of the world that anyone ever saw any man take another man and wash him, baptize him, was when John did it on the banks of the Jordan River. Now there were as many men named John in that day as there are today, so they called this one "John the Baptist," "John the one who baptizes." Immediately the whole world knew who he was, because no one ever did such a thing before John did it.

A committee from the Sanhedrin went down to the Jordan River and asked: "Who are you? Are you Elijah?" John replied, "No." "Are you the prophet Moses spoke about?" "No." "Are you the Messiah?" "No." Then they said, "Who are you?" And John replied: "I am the voice of one crying in the wilderness, 'Make straight the way of the Lord'." Then they said, "If you are not the Messiah, by what right, by what prerogative, do you come with this new ordinance?" And John replied, "God in heaven sent me to baptize, thus to announce that the Messiah is at hand. He is standing among you now (and you do not know Him), but that He might be made manifest to Israel and to the world, God has sent me with this new ordinance." And it was upon that, that Jesus came and was baptized. And John bear record saying, "I saw the Holy Spirit descending upon Him in body like a dove. This is He! The Son of God!" God gave the ordinance of baptism to John for the manifestation of the Messiah to Israel and to the world.

Sometimes I try to relive that scene. It was sixty miles from Nazareth down to the Jordan River where John was baptizing. The Jordan River is a muddy river. It starts up on Mount Hermon which is 12,000 feet high and in just a comparatively short distance it runs down to the Dead Sea which is 1,200 feet below sea level. Jordan means "descend." It rapidly rushes down and consequently is a muddy river.

It has been said that one should never baptize where the water is muddy. All the years of my beginning ministry I would not have had any place to baptize if I had followed that idea. The only place I baptized was in creeks and in stock ponds, and they were all muddy. I think of Naaman when the prophet Elijah said to him: "You go down and wash yourself, baptize yourself (as the Septuagint Greek translation reads) seven times in the Jordan River and your flesh shall come again like unto that of a little child. You will be clean." And Naaman said: "In the Jordan? Oh, no! Let me go baptize myself in the Abana or Pharpar." Have you seen the Abana and Pharpar Rivers of Damascus? They are not large but they are as clear as crystal. Naaman said: "Are not the

The One Baptism 193

Abana and Pharpar, rivers of Damascus, better than all the waters of Israel? May I not wash in them and be clean?" Thus Naaman turned and went away in a rage. It was then that his servant said: "My father, had the prophet bid you do some mighty and great thing, wouldst thou not have done it? How much better, then, to go down to that muddy Jordan and be baptized." "Baptized" — that is what the Septuagint Greek translation said. And upon that saying the mighty General Naaman pulled up his horses, swung them around, and went down to the Jordan River and dipped himself. The Greek says he "baptized" himself seven times. When he came up the seventh time he looked at his flesh and it had come again like the flesh of a little child. He was clean! Wash and be clean. This is symbolized in our baptism — washing and cleansing.

BAPTISM IS IN KEEPING WITH THE HOLIEST URGE IN OUR HEARTS

Sixth, baptism is in keeping with the holiest urge in our hearts. Not only is baptism of highest honor, commanded in the greatest name, sets forth the greatest doctrines, follows the most blessed of all examples, but also our response in being baptized is in keeping with the holiest urge in our hearts. Whenever a man is saved, the first thing he will want to do is to be baptized. The Spirit of the Lord said to Philip, "Go down on a mission for Jesus." As Philip obediently stood by the side of a desert road, the treasurer of Ethiopia came by in his chariot, reading Isaiah 53. And the Spirit said, "Go near." When the eunuch invited Philip to come up into the chariot, he asked: "Of whom speaketh the prophet this: 'All we like sheep have gone astray, and the Lord laid on Him the iniquity of us all.' Of whom speaketh the prophet this?" Philip began at the same Scripture and preached to him Jesus. And as they went on their way they came to a certain water and the eunuch said: "Look! Here is water. What hinders me from being baptized? I want to be baptized just as the Lord commanded." Philip answered and said, "If you believe with all your heart you may." And the eunuch answered and said, "I believe that Jesus is the Son of God, God manifest in the flesh for our salvation." The treasurer commanded the chariot to stand still and they went down both into the water, both Philip and the eunuch, and he baptized him, symbolizing burial and resurrection. And when they came up out of the waters the Lord took away Philip, that the eunuch saw him no more, and he went his way rejoicing.

Says the new-born Christian: "Here is water, what hinders me from being baptized? I want to be baptized." That holy urge will be in your heart when you are saved. "I want to be baptized."

For the first ten years of my life as a young preacher, I preached out in the country where we had no baptistry, just holes of water, ponds, and wherever we could find a place. The people would be gathered all the way around a stock pond, or on the bank of the river, or on both sides of a creek. I would wade out into the middle of the water with my Bible in hand, open the Book, and preach to the people. The occasion was always on a Sunday afternoon. The whole countryside would gather around to see the beautiful and meaningful sight.

In South Central Texas there is a river called the Leon River. I was out in the middle of that river with an open Bible preaching before I was to baptize my candidates. One Sunday afternnon when I got through preaching, I came back to the bank, and extended the invitation. Down the side of the bank of the river came a man named Will Burt. He was the patriarch in Burt Hollow. Down he came with his wife, his teenage children, his brother, his brother's wife, and his brother's children. The whole hollow came, all of them. The whole patriarchal family from Burt Hollow came. They all came and said, "Today we give our hearts to Jesus and we want to be baptized." "Why," I said, "you are not prepared. You have not brought any extra clothes. You are not prepared to be baptized," And Will Burt said to me: "We do not have to bring extra clothes. We have been saved and we want to be baptized right here and right now." So when I went out into the middle of the river, I not only had my candidates, twenty, thirty, thirty-five of them, but also I had that whole patriarchal family from Burt Hollow. I baptized them, one after another. They went home with their clothes wet from the baptismal waters.

Truly, the cry of the new convert is: "I want to be baptized now. See, here is water. What hinders me from being baptized? I have it in my soul. I have found the Lord. I want to be baptized." That is God. That is the Spirit of the Lord. There is one body.

There is one Spirit. There is one Hope. There is one Lord. There is one faith. There is one God. And there also is one baptism. God bless us as we follow the sweet and humble example of our Saviour down through the waters of the Jordan.

Chapter 24

THE HEAVENLY ASCENSION

> Wherefore he saith, (then Paul quotes Psalm 68:18) When he ascended up on high, he led captivity captive, and gave gifts unto men. (Now that he ascended, what is it but that he also descended first into the lower parts of the earth?
>
> He that descended is the same also that ascended up far above all heavens, that he might fill all things.) (Eph. 4:8-10)

This is a passage depicting the ascension of our Lord and His triumphal entry into glory, leading captivity captive and bestowing gifts, heavenly gifts, charismatic gifts, upon men. He ascended up, far above all heavens, above the first heaven where the birds fly and the clouds pass by; above the second heaven, the Milky Way, the sidereal spheres and the innumerable, immeasurable stars; finally into the heaven of heavens where God has His throne and where the Lord is preparing the Holy City, the New Jerusalem that shall come down at the consummation of the age out of heaven perfected, glorious from the hands of God.

In this message we speak of that ascension of our Lord. There are five extraordinary events in the life of Christ:
1. His virgin birth.
2. His death for our sins.
3. His resurrection for our justification.
4. His ascension into glory.
5. His glorious and incomparable Second Coming.

Our Lord, who was born of a virgin, died for our sins according to the Scriptures. This is the plan and purpose of God through the ages, that Christ should die for our sins. Without the shedding of blood there is no remission of sin. The manger and the cross are the two meaningful, heavenly signs and seals of God's loving purpose toward us. The virgin-born Christ Jesus was also raised for our justification. He is the first-fruits of those who shall be raised from the dead and presented as trophies of grace to lay at His precious feet. He is the morning star of the glory which shall yet be revealed in us. After His resurrection, our Lord ascended into heaven. The apostle then writes that He ascended, "leading captivity captive," standing at the head of the glorious train, and "giving gifts unto men." How eloquently beautiful! Some day this same Lord Christ shall return to earth. Each one of these five events in the life of our Lord points to the next event and all of them to the final denouement and consummation of the age.

"He that descended is the same also that ascended up far above all heavens, that he might fill all things." This is a reference to the passage which closes the gospel of Luke and the story that begins the Book of the Acts. The little band of apostles was walking with their risen Lord up the slopes of the Mount of Olives. There so hushed, so quiet, so awe-stricken, they were filled with intensive joy as they walked by the side of their risen Lord. When they came to the brow of the hill they stopped. While they conversed with the Saviour, He lifted up His nail-pierced hands in blessing upon them. As He blessed them, He began to rise up and up and up, to the regions of the clouds. Then a chariot of light, the shekinah glory of God, the garments of the Almighty enclothed Him, engulfed Him. He was swept out of their sight. The disciples, wonder-struck, awe-stricken, stood riveted on the brow of the mount looking up into heaven whence the Lord disappeared.

They could not help it, standing there steadfastly looking upward. Many times our hearts lead us to do things that are hard to explain logically, such as going to a grave and weeping. What is the benefit, what is the good? It is just that our heart dictated the action. So it was with the disciples, just standing there, transfixed, looking up into heaven. But they must not tarry too long. So the Lord sent an interrupting angel, not with a sword or with a rod, but clothed in garments of light. He turned the disciples back to their work.

We cannot help but ask: "Lord, why this separation from us? We need You and Your presence is so infinitely valuable. Why leave us, Lord? Why be taken away from us?" Like the disciples at Emmaus who would constrain the Lord to tarry, we say, "Stay with us, Lord, stay here." Ah, we think, His one presence would be worth ten thousand apostles. Just think what it would mean if our Lord were here and He stayed with us! Why, we could ask Him anything, take before Him every problem and every decision, and the answered word would be the word of heavenly wisdom. Think of the miracles of His gracious hands! Think of His voice that could raise the dead! Think how He would confuse and confound His enemies! He, the leader, marching at the head of a triumphant army — think of the conquest if He were here! Think of the conversion of this vile and villainous world! We say: "Oh, if the Lord had just stayed here! If He were still present!"

In His Upper Room talk to His disciples one of those sentences He said was, "It is expedient for you that I go away." I want to point out five reasons why the Lord was ascended. Why did He say, "It is expedient for you that I go away"?

ASCENDED TO HIS THRONE TO DIRECT THE ADVENT OF HIS KINGDOM

First, we are not to think that the Lord has forsaken us, or that He has lost a battle, or that He has quit the field, or that He has injured or hurt His flock. Our Lord has arisen into heaven, ascended to the throne, that from that high and holy place He might direct the advent of His kingdom in the earth. It is the despisers who say: "His cause is done for, Christianity is spun out, the battle is lost, the Saviour is gone. There is no trace of His miracle-working hand." It is they who say that, but not we, for our Lord still lives. He has just gone up to the top of the hills. He has just ascended the throne of glory, there to survey the whole circumference of the field of conflict and there to direct His people in their war against our darkening and spiritual enemies. Our Lord still is at the head of His people. He still directs us in our work. There in glory He is mustering those omnipotent powers and forces by which He shall some day return to this earth. He is mounting the white horse of the Apocalypse and it may be in a moment, in the twinkling of an eye, that He will return and with Him the hopes of glory (cf. Rev. 19). Our Lord has not met defeat nor has He forsaken us or forgotten us, but He is ascended, that from the throne of glory and grace, He might direct His kingdom work in the earth.

Ascended to Become the Object on High of Our Prayers, Dreams, and Hopes

Second, He has ascended that we might lift up our hearts and our souls, our prayers and our dreams, our hopes and our visions upward, always heavenward, Christward, and Godward. The Apostle Paul wrote to the church at Philippi, "For our conversation is in heaven; from whence also we look for the Saviour, the Lord Jesus Christ" (Phil. 3:20). Our citizenship, our home, our commonwealth is not here; it is in heaven. Our home, our fatherland, our country is in glory. It is again as the Apostle Paul wrote to the little church at Colosse, "Set your affection on things above, not on things on the earth" (Col. 3:2). Our hearts are ever to be Godward. The windows of our souls are ever to be opened heavenward, up there in glory. Our Head and Sovereign has gone to the land of the sky and we are hid with Christ in God. Where He is, our life is always upward. Our treasure is there, our inheritance is there, our reward is there, our crown is there. By and by our friends are there. Our family is there.

Sometimes, when I am conducting a memorial service, I think how tragic it would be were it the other way around. What if Christ remained here and we were forced to go yonder? Ah, the sadness of it! If our Lord were in this earth and had remained on this planet, then in death, one by one, we would all leave. What a horrifying, dismal, and unhappy prospect! But God never did it that way. He did it the other way. Our Lord is there, our home is there, our inheritance is there, our citizenship is there. Our commonwealth, our country is there. By and by everyone whom we love will be there. That is why our Lord lifts up our hearts and our souls heavenward and Godward.

Ascended to Give Us Faith, Not Sight

Third, our Lord ascended into heaven in order that we might learn to walk by faith and not by sight. If our Lord were here in this earth, the whole earth would be shoving, elbowing, and pushing, trying to get to the Master. Faith concerns itself with what we do not see. It is the substance of things not seen. For if we have what we can see, why would we yet hope for it? Faith endures as seeing the invisible. Faith is looking, seeing with the eyes of the soul. Materiality and temporality have no part in it. God wishes that they who worship Him worship Him in spirit and in truth, not in materiality and corporality, by sight. We walk by faith and not by sight.

One of the most meaningful verses that Paul ever wrote was to the church at Corinth. "While we look not at the things which are seen, but at the things which are not seen: for the things which are seen are temporal; but the things which are not seen are eternal" (2 Cor. 4:18). He ascended into glory that we might learn to walk by faith and not by sight. The more material a religion is, the more unspiritual it is. We have no priest that we can see with our naked eye. We have no material altar. We have no sanctuary of gold or silver. We have no temple of monumental stone. We have no rites or rituals that are efficacious in mediating to us the grace of God. Our Great High Priest is in heaven, our altar is in heaven, our sacrifice is in glory, our sanctuary is in the sky. Our temple is the temple of God in heaven. And these we see by the eyes of faith. It is a poor faith that must put its finger into the nail prints in His hand and thrust the hand in the scar in His side. One of the most devastating observations that one could make in reading the Old Testament is that when Israel had their sanctuary and their altar and their feasts, they were most prone to idolatry. The same is true today. The more the church makes its religious body one of materiality, one of sight, the less spiritual it becomes. For God wishes His people to worship in spirit and in truth, seeing the invisible with the eyes of the soul.

One of the tragedies of the Christian religion, it seems to me, is that even our two ordinances (baptism and the Lord's Supper) have been fraught with all kinds of religious superstitions. There are some who say that the ordinance of baptism carries with it regeneration. One is actually washed from sin in the cleansing water. Others will say that in the Lord's Supper there are mediated to us the efficacies of God's grace. No! No! A thousand times no. By the Word of God an everlasting no, for the religion of God is always spiritual, invisible, and by faith. The soul lifts upward above the temporal world, upward and upward.

We worship God in spirit and in truth, bowing at the sanctuary of heaven. That is why a kitchen corner is as good as a cathedral from which to call on the name of the Lord. That is why walking down the road, or working at a counter, or in the middle of the night, or out in a desert place, there is the sanctuary of heaven. There can a man call on the name of the Lord and there can he have true fellowship and communion with God. In heaven is our altar and throne. In heaven is our sanctuary and priest.

Ascended to Secure Our Inheritance

Fourth, our Lord ascended in order that He might secure for us our inheritance. Here I am in a dark world, in a body made out of clay and dirt. Lord, how is it I can ever be assured that I will make it to heaven? Lord, how could it be? That is why the Lord ascended into heaven: to assure unto us our inheritance. He is there to keep it for us and to see us through and to bestow it upon us.

In the Book of Acts look how Luke the beloved physician begins the work, "The former treatise (speaking of Luke's gospel) have I made, O Theophilus, of all that Jesus began both to do and teach" (1:1). In the account in the gospel, Luke is telling the story of the life of our Lord in the days of His flesh on earth. In the Book of Acts Luke continues with the next verse, "Until the day in which he was taken up" (v. 2). He began His work of redemption down here in the days of His flesh, but He continues it and consummates it and brings it to that glorious conclusion and triumph in His work in glory. There He completes our redemption. There He ultimately and finally presents us faultless before the throne of God. The author of Hebrews says, "Wherefore he is able also to save them to the uttermost that come unto God by him, seeing he ever liveth to make intercession for them" (Heb. 7:25). Christ is there to secure for us our inheritance.

If I could choose a legal representative and send him to secure my eternal inheritance, he might fail, but not the Lord. He cannot fail. He said, "I give unto them eternal life; and they shall never perish" (John 10:28). I cannot miss it, I cannot fail it. He has given it to me and He assures it for me because He is up there to see me through and to keep it for me. What of me? I may die before the Lord comes, I may fall into the dust of the ground. Lord, what of my inheritance then? Why, bless God, He died. Bless the Lord, He was buried. But praise the Lord again, He was raised from the dead. We may know what it is to die and be wrapped in a winding sheet and be placed in a sepulcher. But if we die with

Christ we shall also know what it is to be raised with Him. O Lord, our life is hid with Christ in God and we cannot fail. We cannot miss it. If we die God will raise us from the dead even as the Holy Spirit did our Lord.

> But I would not have you to be ignorant, brethren, concerning them which are asleep, that ye sorrow not, even as others which have no hope.
> For if we believe that Jesus died and rose again, even so them also which sleep in Jesus will God bring with him. (1 Thess. 4:13, 14)

O Lord, what an incomparable promise and what a glorious gladness to know that God will see me through! It is not a matter of my clinging to the Lord. I might lose my grip in death and might not even know when I lost it. But my inheritance is a matter of God holding fast to me, which is while I am awake, while I am strong, and which is also when I am weak, when I am in a coma, when I die.

Once a family called me in tears, saying: "Our mother is dying. The doctor says it is just a little while. Will you come and pray with us." I went to the hospital and gathered the little family around and prayed with them while the mother was in a coma. She did not even know we were there. Lord, I might not even be awake, I might not even know, how could I cling to my inheritance then? That is why the Lord is in glory. He is the one who holds my hand. He is the one who sees me through. He is the one who keeps the inheritance for us who have placed our trust in Him. He is there to do it. He is on the other side of the river, there to receive us to Himself and to give us our golden crown.

ASCENDED TO INTERCEDE FOR US

Fifth, our Lord ascended in order that we might have an intercessor, a mediator who understands us and sympathizes with us. He has a human body. Is not that the most astonishing doctrine in time or history, that God who reigns over the universe is a man? What became of the body of our Lord? Did it just dissolve away, turn back into dust? As He ascended into heaven, was it an apparition that the apostles saw disappear? Did they look steadfastly upward at a myth or at a dream? No! In life He was the man-God. In His resurrection and ascension He is the God-man, forever and ever man.

It is as Paul writes to Timothy, "And without controversy (without doubt) great is the mystery (the *musterion*) of godliness: (Without controversy, without argument, great is the mystery of Godliness." What is that mystery? "God was manifest in the flesh, justified in the Spirit, seen of angels, preached unto the Gentiles, believed on in the world, received up into glory" (1 Tim. 3:16). Is not that unusual? Paul apparently quotes a song the first Christian church sang about the mystery of godliness — God made flesh.

Let us pause at one stanza in the song, "seen of angels." They had known Him through all the aeons, before the world was made. They were there at the incarnation in Bethlehem. They ministered to Him in the days of His flesh. They were there at the tomb when He was raised from the dead. They were there to speak to the disciples when He ascended into heaven, and they were there in glory when He entered in. His condition had changed, but not His nature and not His heart. He is the same Lord Jesus. Paul met Him on the Damascus road. The Saviour was radiant above the brightness of the Syrian sun, so much so that the blinded Saul struck down, cried, "Who art thou, Lord?" The Saviour replied, "I am Jesus whom thou persecutest" (Acts 9:5). There in glory, He was the same blessed Jesus.

The human body that Christ Jesus took upon Him at Bethlehem, He never laid aside. When the disciples looked and watched as our Lord ascended into the highest heavens, they watched a human body, a glorified body that was raised upward. Our Lord is one of us. He suffered in all points as we suffer. He was tried in all points as we are tried. He is able to sympathize with us in all of our sorrows and triumphs. Our great Mediator and High Priest is one of us — our flesh, body, life, and experience. He knows all about us.

Ascended to Give Gifts

Finally, our Lord ascended in order that He might bestow upon us those grace gifts of the Spirit. "Leading captivity captive." Oh, what an entree, what an entrance when the Lord went back up into glory! It is described in Revelation 5 when the whole creation — the four cherubim, all of the saints, the four and twenty elders, the angels numbering the ten thousand times ten thousand — bowed down and welcomed the Son of God in glory. He ascended into heaven that He might pour out upon us the grace gifts, the Spirit gifts.

One of Christ's ascension gifts was the Holy Spirit Himself, the Spirit who was poured out upon the world and upon us without measure. There is no limit to the abounding presence of the Holy Spirit in our hearts. Just as much as we will let Him possess us will the Holy Spirit of God live in us. He is our Lord's first ascension gift, the promise of the Father fulfilled at Pentecost. After the pouring out of the Holy Spirit come the grace gifts.

There is a difference between a natural gift and a grace gift. A natural gift is as when a man has astuteness in business, can trade, and make money. Or as when a man has great success in a line of endeavor. He is a pugilist, or a player, or an effective orator, and is knowledgeable with a magnificent vocabulary. These are natural gifts. But there are also grace gifts, gifts that God gives to His people by which He blesses the household of faith to His own honor and glory. Each one of us has a grace gift, a different gift. Some of us have several gifts. But all of us have gifts when we gather together in the church, each one bringing his grace gift. What God can do through you makes the whole church complete.

God gives each one a gift. There is a plan, a purpose, and a program for your life. There is something to which God has called you. When you give yourself to Him and are happy in your gift then you are happy in the Lord. But when you covet some other gift, have false, egotistic self-ambition, then you live miserably. When you receive from God what the Lord gives you, you are quiet and happy in His grace gift. The church is blessed and you are sweet in the presence of Jesus. The church needs all of you. The eye cannot say to the foot, "I do not need you." The foot cannot say to the hand, "I do not need you." The hand cannot say to the head, "I do not need you." All of us are needed, each in his separate gift. The endowment is something God bestows upon us.

When I began to preach as a teen-ager (seventeen years of age) in my little country church, I would stand up in the pulpit with that little congregation of eighteen and try my best at the morning hour to deliver the message of Jesus and fail so miserably. I could not preach. I could not frame the word to pronounce it. I could not put the sentence together. I would just try and fail. I would just bow my head and weep and weep every Sunday afternoon. But the Lord had called me and God soon gave me the ability to do it. And the Lord blessed the services. It is God who helps with the message; it is the Lord who fills the church; it is God who sanctifies the appeal. It is a grace gift. It is something God does. For each one of us there is a plan, a place, a purpose, and a program. When we give ourselves to it, yielding to God's call for us, He blesses us. He blesses the church and through us He honors His name in the earth.

Chapter 25

LEADING CAPTIVITY CAPTIVE

> Wherefore he saith, When he ascended up on high, he led captivity captive, and gave gifts unto men.
> (Now that he ascended, what is it but that he also descended first into the lower parts of the earth?
> He that descended is the same also that ascended up far above all heavens, that he might fill all things.) (Eph. 4:8-10)

This text is surely one of the most unusual and most significant revelations in all the Bible. As scholars study it, as interpreters write of it, and as I read what they write, I am both enlightened and disturbed in their elucidations. Scholars who study the passage make it refer to such unusually different things. In this message I am going to take two of the interpretations of the text suggested by devout, reverent scholars, then I am going to write in the third place of what I think it means. When I speak of what I think it means, I do it humbly and reverently, not as though other men were incorrect or that they did not understand the passage or that they misinterpreted it. As I study Scripture a meaning comes to me whether I am correct in its interpretation or not. Humbly, devoutly it speaks this to me. When it means something different, however, to some other man and some other preacher, I pray God's blessing upon him as he presents the truth of God as he sees and understands it.

One Interpretation

The first interpretation of the passage is by those reverent, devout, and scholarly men who believe it refers to the liberation of the Old Testament saints from Sheol or Hades up to glory. These scholars believe that Old Testament believers were captive in a waiting place called Sheol until the Atonement of Christ. Then upon the resurrection and ascension of our Lord, He took them with Him up to heaven. When He ascended up on high, He took captivity captive. These men understand the word "captivity" to refer to a great host of Old Testament captives.

The verse actually is a quotation from Psalm 68:18, "Thou hast ascended on high, thou hast led captivity captive." They say that this Psalm refers to an unknown victory that David was given by the Lord in which he liberated a number of captives who had been taken out of Israel. David brought them back in triumph and in victory to reunite them to their people and their homeland. In this interpretation the word "captivity" refers to that number of captives.

Another passage is used to substantiate that interpretation. Judges 5 is a record of the song of Deborah and Barak over the Canaanites. Verse 12 reads, "Arise, Barak, and lead thy captivity captive." The interpreters say it refers to all the captives (Israelites) who were subject to the Canaanites and were liberated by Barak. He overcame the Canaanites and brought those captives back. Based on the above verses they make the word "captivity" in Ephesians refer to a host of captives, a number of captives whom the Lord liberated and took up with Him into glory. They say the captives are Old Testament saints, God's people who died before Jesus' atonement. At death they went down to Sheol and waited for their liberation by the Lord, waited until their sins were atoned for, after which date the Lord took them up to glory.

There is no doubt but that now and since the atonement of Christ, the soul that believes in Jesus at death goes directly to God, to paradise, to heaven. That is most explicitly presented and explained in the New Testament. For example, when the Lord was dying He turned to the malefactor who was dying with Him and said, "To-day shalt thou be with me in paradise" (Luke 23:43). In 2 Corinthians 12 the Apostle Paul says that he was lifted up, whether in the body or out of the body he did not know, but he was raised up even to the third heaven, a place he called paradise. There God revealed to him things that he was not even allowed to reveal to us. You see, Paul did not go to Sheol.

He did not go to the grave. He did not go to Hades. He went to paradise. He went to the third heaven. He went where God is and to the throne of the Lord where Jesus is, where the saints now go when they die. Another passage would be 2 Corinthians 5, where Paul says, "Absent from the body . . . present with the Lord" (v. 8).

There is no doubt but that now, this minute, and in the whole Christian era in which we live, when a soul dies, that soul goes directly to God. But these interpreters say that in the Old Testament when one of the Old Testament saints died, he went to Sheol. He went to Hades. He went to a waiting place until the Lord made atonement for his sins. They quote many passages to sustain that contention. I point out just a few.

When Joseph apparently had been slain by a wild beast, his brothers took the coat of many colors, dipped it in blood, and brought it to Israel and said, "Your son is apparently slain." Jacob in his lamentation said, "I will go down into the grave (Sheol) unto my son mourning" (Gen. 37:35). The Hebrew word for "grave" is *Sheol*. Israel was saying, "I will go to Sheol mourning for my son Joseph."

Another instance is found in the Book of Job. When Job was so afflicted, he said to God, "O that thou wouldest hide me in the grave" (Job 14:13). There is the word *Sheol* again. Then can be found those endless passages like this: when Abraham died, he was "gathered to his people." When Ishmael died he was "gathered to his people," etc. When an Old Testament saint died he went to the grave, to Sheol. He went to be with his people, with his fathers, there to wait until the great translation up to heaven.

These interpreters ask, When did that occur? When were all of the Old Testament saints lifted out of Sheol, out of their waiting place, and transferred to glory? These interpreters say that was done as indicated in the passage here in Ephesians. When the Lord ascended up on high, when He went up to heaven, He took with Him all those captives and carried them up to heaven. They would say that when the Lord was transfigured and Moses and Elijah were talking with Him, they were talking to Him about His death which He should accomplish in Jerusalem. That is, Moses and Elijah were saying to Jesus: "You must die for the sins of all of us who have died before You, because our hope of heaven, our liberation, the end of our waiting in our captivity, lies in Your atonement for our sins and in Your ascension into glory. When You ascend, we will rise into heaven with You." I notice that the first Scofield Bible presented that view. I notice, also, that the new, revised Scofield Bible does not present it. The editors have hesitated before it. But in any event, that is a view that many devout scholars have of the interpretation of the passage. When Jesus went up into glory, when He ascended up on high, He took these captives, this multitude of Old Testament saints with Him, and they entered into paradise.

A Second Interpretation

There are those who believe that this passage presents the triumph of our Lord over Satan and the kingdom of darkness. "When he ascended up on high, he led captivity captive, and gave gifts unto men." These interpreters say that the "captivity" mentioned is the attempt of those who sought to make Jesus and us captives. Jesus captured demons, the kingdom of Satan, and they were a part of His triumphant train. They were tied to His chariot wheels when the Lord entered the glory of heaven.

They remind us that the high priest on the Day of Atonement went into the Holy of Holies to offer blood for the expiation of our sins. On the Day of Atonement each year an innocent animal was brought before the high priest. He laid his hands on the head of the innocent animal and confessed all the sins of the people. After the animal was slain, its blood was caught in a basin. Then the high priest on this Day of Atonement, Yom Kippur, went through the court of the Temple, through the holy place, into the Holy of Holies. There on the mercy seat he sprinkled blood of expiation, the blood of atonement. The interpreters say (and they say it correctly according to Hebrews 9): "Our Lord did just that. Our Lord is our great and faithful High Priest. He died for our sins on the cross and He was raised for our justification. He ascended up into heaven. There in the sanctuary of God He offered Himself, His blood in token of the fact that He had paid our debt. Our High Priest consummated the great atonement when He died and when He was raised. Then when He ascended up into heaven into the sanctuary of God, into the Holy of Holies, He offered blood of expiation for the sins of His people."

What these interpreters point out to us is this: that when the Lord ascended into heaven, He was impeded by this kingdom of darkness and demons. Satan tried to keep the Lord from being our Saviour. He tried to kill Him in Bethlehem. He tried to kill Him in Nazareth. He tried to slay Him in Gethsemane. And when the Lord finally died for our sins on the cross and His blood was spilled out on the ground, then Satan tried to keep Him in the tomb. He put a great stone over the sepulcher and sealed it with a Roman seal. He set a guard there to watch it to see that He did not rise. Thus Satan and his demons in the kingdom of darkness have always thought to impede the high priestly work of our Saviour. So also they did it here. As our Lord was raised from the dead, the kingdom of Satan (which is this fallen creation) sought to keep Jesus from ascending into heaven.

Satan is the lord over this fallen creation. That is his dominion. He claims it. He offered Christ the glory of it, all of it. When the Lord tried to ascend back up into heaven to complete the offering of His blood for expiation of our sins, to enter the Holy of Holies, as He left the earth and sought to go through the lesser heavens, the dominion of Satan and his demons sought to impede His progress. That contest, that confrontation, these interpreters find in this passage in Ephesians and in a like passage in Colossians 2:15, "And having spoiled principalities and powers, he made a shew of them openly, triumphing over them in it."

Principalities and powers, *archas* and *exousias*, refer to orders of demons. There are orders of demonic spirits just as there are orders of angels. There are cherubim, seraphim, and archangels in the angelic world. Also there are ranks in the demonic world. Two of those orders are named here in Colossians, the *archas* and the *exousias* which Paul lists as orders of demons. Paul says in this passage in Colossians that when Jesus was raised from the dead He *apekdusamenos,* that is, if I could translate that participle as a passive participle, He wholly, completely stripped Himself of them. The *archas* and the *exousias,* these orders of demons the Lord Jesus Christ "spoiled," He *apekdusamenos* them. He stripped Himself of them.

Then the next word in Colossians 2:15 is *deigmatizo*, translated here "He made a show of them openly." *Deigmatizo* is also in the first chapter of Matthew. When Joseph was going to marry

Leading Captivity Captive

the Virgin Mary in Nazareth, she was pregnant. His promised bride was with child. Knowing it was not his child, he thought upon it and he decided not to *deigmatizo*, to make a show of her publicly. He planned, instead, to put her away privately. The word *deigmatizo* means publicly to display, to exhibit (usually) in a disgraceful way. So with these *archai* and *exousiai*, these orders of demons, Jesus *apekdusamenos*, He stripped Himself of them, openly, publicly.

The final word we shall look at in Colossians 2:15 is "triumphing," *thriambeuo*. That is the Greek word for the name of the exalted festal hymn when Roman soldiers had their victory procession. The *thriambeuo* was begun and the Romans caught the spirit of victory. They called it "the triumph." When the Roman general came back laden with spoils from his conquered enemies, he was accorded a procession through the eternal city. This was a *thriambeuo* (Latin, *triumphus*), a victory procession. The slaves captured were tied to the general's chariot wheels as spoils of the triumph. These interpreters say that that is what happened with the Lord Jesus. When He ascended up into heaven, He was opposed by these *archai* and *exousiai*, the kingdom of Satan. But He stripped Himself of them. They were unable to bind Him and to make Him captive. Rather, He bound them to His chariot wheels. When He entered into heaven He came with these *archai* and *exousiai*, the whole kingdom of Satan chained to His chariot wheels as He entered heaven in triumph. When He ascended upon high He carried captivity captive. He took all that kingdom of darkness, Satan and the demons, and chained them to His chariot wheels, and in triumph entered into glory. That is the second interpretation.

MY INTERPRETATION

There is no doubt but that when Paul says, "He ascended up on high," it refers to our Lord's ascension into heaven. Paul explains it very carefully. He that ascended is He that descended into the lower parts of the earth. He came down and died and was buried and went into Sheol. He that descended is also He that ascended far above all heavens, the heavenly clouds, the birds, the heavenly stars, into the third heaven, where God is. There is no doubt but that the passage refers to the ascension of our Lord into heaven.

In the Bible is presented the most glorious depiction of the marvelous entry when the Lord in triumph returned to heaven, having died for our sins and having been raised for our justification. For example, let us look more closely at the passage that the apostle quotes, Psalm 68:18. First, look at the verse above it, verse 17, "The chariots of God are twenty thousand, even thousands of angels: the Lord is among them." Then verse 18 continues, "Thou hast ascended high, thou hast led captivity captive: thou hast received gifts for men." There is a picture of our Lord ascending up into heaven welcomed by the angels. The Book of Revelation says that there are myriads times myriads, ten thousands times ten thousands, and thousands and thousands of angelic hosts in heaven. When the Lord returned to heaven, the thousands and thousands of angels lined old glory road to welcome Him back home.

There is no doubt, also, but that the glorious passage in Psalm 24 refers to the same thing. "Lift up your heads, O ye gates; and be ye lift up, ye everlasting doors; and the King of glory shall come in. Who is this King of glory? The LORD strong and mighty, the LORD mighty in battle" (vv. 7, 8). The psalm refers to none other than Jesus. He is the King of glory. That passage refers to the triumphant entry of our Lord into heaven.

Ah, to have the eloquence of an angel, the tongue of a Demosthenes, or of a Spurgeon, or of a George Whitefield, that I might describe the glorious entrance, the triumphant entrance of our Lord into glory when He ascended from this earth, having died for us and having been raised for our salvation. Can you imagine it? Can you imagine the throngs of angels? Can you imagine the host of saints and all the heavens astir with the return of the Prince of Glory? Think of it! And to think, also, that this conquering Lord is my Saviour and my friend!

How the angels must have rejoiced when Christ returned to the exaltation and the praise of the blessed Lord. He did not come just alone. When He had ascended up on high, He led captivity captive. He led captivity captive and gave gifts to men. What is that?

VICTOR OVER SIN

To me that means that He took captive what had tried to make Him captive. He led captivity captive. What had tried to capture Him and hold Him and bind Him, He took captive. When He went up to glory He went a victor, triumphant. What tried to hold Him captive? Sin and the world. Sin tried to defile Him. In the person of evil men He was cursed, reviled, and blasphemed. They spat upon Him, they pulled out His beard, they beat Him, and finally, they nailed Him to a tree. But He was still undefilable. He was pure, sinless, and spotless when He went back into glory, just as He was when He was incarnated in Bethlehem. In His death all the sins of the world, your sins and mine, were carried into the tomb, but when He arose, He arose triumphant. He left our sins there in the grave. Our sins are still buried but He arose triumphant, pure, the victor over sin. He then returned to glory, victorious.

VICTOR OVER DEATH

Who are these that have tried to capture Christ? What is this captivity that He took captive? Death and the grave. Death tried to hold Him and to bind Him. The grave tried to keep Him and to seal Him. So certainly was He dead they did not break His bones. They just took a Roman spear and thrust it into His heart, and the blood followed it out to the ground. His grave was sealed with a great stone, and a guard was set to watch, but like Samson of old who broke the chains and the ropes, Jesus broke the bonds of death. He destroyed the grave and arose triumphant.

> Low in the grave He lay —
> Jesus, my Saviour;
> Waiting the coming day —
> Jesus, my Lord.
> Up from the grave He arose,
> With a mighty triumph o'er His foes.
> He arose a Victor from the dark domain,
> And He lives forever with His saints to reign.
> He arose! He arose! Hallelujah! Christ arose!

He ascended into heaven carrying captivity captive.

VICTOR OVER SATAN

Who are those who would have captured Him? Satan and the kingdom of darkness. Look at us. All of us are partakers of flesh and blood. Jesus also took part of the same that through death He might destroy Him who had the power of death. Through all our lives we are subject to, held in bondage to, the fear of death. This is the fear that Satan holds over us. The Lord took Satan and chained him to His chariot wheels and entered heaven triumphant and victorious. Carrying, leading captivity captive, He is victor over the devil.

Let me now bind all this together. Christ ascended up on high. He led captivity captive. That refers to everything: heaven above and earth beneath. All things that are against us, He has taken away and forever we are free. We are liberated. Our Great Conqueror has won the victory for us. There is a law and He has fulfilled it. There is a curse and He has taken it away. There are ordinances contrary to us. He has nailed them to the cross. Our foes are utterly defeated. Christ is triumphant and to His great triumphal train are added these He has conquered. Ah, what a glory! We are free, we have been liberated, we are saved. All things are ours in Christ. That is the *thriambeuo*. That is our song and hymn of praise. This is our "triumphus." That is why I love songs that praise the Lord. We are saved! We are redeemed! We are washed! We are free!

That is what it is to be a Christian — to exalt, to glorify, to praise God. That is the Book, that is the Lord, that is the glory, that is the shekinah, that is the life, that is the presence, that is the Spirit, that is God among us. Oh, that we would learn more and more to be happy in the Lord, to be encouraged in the faith, to love Jesus more and thank Him more, to rejoice in His triumph as He leads His people into heaven.

Chapter 26

THE GRACE GIFTS OF CHRIST

And he gave gifts unto men . . . .
And he gave some, apostles; and some, prophets; and some, evangelists; and some, pastors and teachers;
For the perfecting of the saints, for the work of the ministry, for the edifying of the body of Christ:
Till we all come in the unity of the faith, and of the knowledge of the Son of God, unto a perfect man, unto the measure of the stature of the fulness of Christ. (Eph. 4:8, 11-13)

This chapter concerns the grace gifts of our Lord. When our Saviour went back up into heaven, He poured out rich gifts upon His church. He enriched His church with His grace gifts.

In 1 Corinthian 12:1, Paul calls these gifts *pneumatika,* "spiritual gifts," literally, "the spirituals." In verse 4 he calls them charismata, "grace gifts," "charismatic gifts." But here in this passage he calls them presents, *domata.* When He ascended upon high, He led captivity captive and gave gifts, *domata,* unto men. The idea that lies back of the passage is that of a victorious general. After the battle is done and the war is won, the general distributes the spoils to his army. Each man is given a victor's gift, a part of the spoils. When the Lord ascended into heaven leading captivity captive, the Scriptures present the Master in the same language and imagery of a Roman general who is accorded triumph through the streets of the eternal city while the people shout the "triumphus," the Roman shout of victory. That is what the Lord did when He went back to glory. He entered with all the spoils of victory and the people shouted the *triumphus,* as the Latin called it, the *thriambeuo,* as the Greeks called it. Then the Lord in heaven bestowed gifts to His people, grace gifts upon His church.

God's Ministers Presented As Gifts to the Church

Usually when the Bible speaks of grace gifts, it will do it in a way as though the Holy Spirit were bestowing them. Usually they are spiritual gifts, charismatic gifts. But here it is the Lord doing it; *He* poured out these gifts. When Paul speaks of charismatic gifts, he usually speaks of them in terms of endowments. A man has a grace gift. Perhaps he has the spirit of wisdom, or the spirit of discerning, or the spirit of understanding. Each gift is an endowment. But here the apostle speaks of the gifts of Christ in personal terminology. The gifts are the ministers themselves. The Lord gives ministers to His church and He names them. Some of these gifts to the church were apostles, some prophets, some evangelists, some pastors and teachers. Here Paul presents the grace gifts as being the men themselves who have enriched the churches through the centuries.

Apostles

Some of them are apostles, *apostolos*. *Apostello* is an ordinary Greek word meaning "to send forth." An *apostolos* is one who is sent forth. It is used in two ways in the New Testament. Technically the word *apostolos*, "apostle," will refer to an office. As such there would be only twelve apostles. The Lord said in Matthew 19 that the twelve apostles would sit on twelve thrones judging the twelve tribes of Israel. In Revelation 21 the Lord says that the beautiful city, the new Jerusalem, is on twelve foundations which are the twelve apostles. In that sense there are only twelve. In Acts 1 when the apostles elected Matthias to take the place of Judas, I think they were going ahead of the Lord. He was not leading them in that lot-casting manner. In Acts 9 the Lord chose Paul to take that place. In any event, in the technical use of the word *apostolos*, there are only twelve.

But there is, also, a general sense in which the same word *apostolos* is used in the New Testament. In that sense the word refers to a missionary who is out on the frontier, preaching the Gospel, and founding churches where no Christians and no churches are. In the New Testament, Barnabas is called an *apostolos*, Andronicus and Junia are called *apostoloi*, and Epaphroditus is called an *apostolos*. The word is used technically for the twelve but generally for any frontier missionary.

PROPHETS

God sets others called prophets also in the church. The Greek word is *prophetes,* from the verb *propheteuo,* an ordinary word which means "to speak forth." A *prophetes* is a man who speaks forth, he forth-tells. He stands up and by inspiration of the Spirit of God delivers God's message. It was comparatively recently that the word in the English language came to mean prediction, prophecy, to foretell. It has no connotation like that as such in the Bible. The idea of prediction in the word "prophecy" is secondary and remote. The meaning of the word *propheteuo* in the Bible is "to proclaim," "to speak out," "to speak forth." It carries the picture of a man who stands up and delivers God's message.

The word is used two ways in the New Testament. It is used technically for an office, the office of a prophet. In Acts 21 the Bible speaks of a certain prophet named Agabus. He had the office of prophet as did Moses, Jeremiah, Isaiah, Malachi, and John the Baptist. They were all prophets. In the New Testament church the office of prophet was to tell the church what to do. They did not have any written New Testament until A.D. 100 or later. When problems and decisions came up the prophet told the church what to do. Now that we have the written New Testament, the technical office ceased, just as the apostolic office ceased.

But there is, also, a general use of the word "prophet" that still abides with us. It is a great gift from God. In this same Acts 21, in two verses side by side, Paul designates the technical and the general uses of the word. He will use the word "prophet" in the sense of an office for Agabus. Then he will speak of the four daughters of Philip, the evangelist, who prophesied. That is, they spoke under the inspiration of the divine, indwelling Spirit of Jesus. In that sense we have the inspired messengers of God who endow and enrich the Lord's church today. They who stand up and deliver God's message are God's prophets today.

PASTORS

Then there are some who are pastors, *poimen,* shepherds. There are three words used in the New Testament to describe the office of a pastor, and they are used interchangeably. Sometimes he is called an *episkopos,* translated "bishop," literally "an overseer." The word refers to the work of his office. Sometimes the same man is called a *presbuteros* or "elder." That refers to the dignity of his office. And sometimes he is called a *poimen,* a pastor, a shepherd. That refers to his relationship with his people.

Teachers

Then God has set in the church teachers, *didaskalos,* didactically gifted people. They can open God's Word and can teach in a way that the people understand and grasp what God has said in His revelation.

The Real Riches of the Church Through the Centuries

The apostle says that when the Lord went back up into heaven He poured out these grace gifts upon His church: apostles, missionaries; prophets, men who speak under the unction and in the divine burning of the Lord; evangelists, men who seek the lost, who conduct revivals; pastors, the undershepherds of our Lord; and teachers, gifted souls who make known the Word of the Lord. These gifts, these ministers of Christ, have been the riches of the church through all the centuries and are so today. The enrichment of the church is by no means piles of brick and stone, however ornate or impressive they may be. The actual riches of the church of Christ always is found in the grace gifts, the men, the ministers, the leaders that God has given. Through all of the centuries the Lord has endowed His church with those grace gifts. There has never been a generation without an outpouring of the graciousness of these charismatic gifts from God. There never will be until the Lord comes again.

In the apostolic days there were the Twelve Apostles, and Timothy, Titus, Tychicus, Epaphroditus; and the deacons, Stephen, and Philip, who became known as evangelists. Then Ante-Nicene, Nicene, and Post-Nicene fathers were given to the church. Polycarp was the pastor of the church at Smyrna, Ignatius was the pastor of the church at Antioch, Justin Martyr was the defender of the faith in Samaria. There were Athanasius, Augustine, and Chrysostom, the golden-mouthed pastor to the church at Antioch and Constantinople. How richly did Jesus endow the people of God through centuries!

Then came the ministers of the pre-Reformation. Peter Waldo, Savanarola, John Huss, Cranmer, Ridley, Hugh Latimer, Samuel Rutherford, William Guthrie — all were flaming ministers of Christ. Then came the days of the Reformation. Martin Luther, John Calvin, John Knox, Melanchthon, Balthasar Hubmaier, and Felix Mainz were just a few. The whole constellation of God's grace gifts may be seen in the history of the church. In the seventeenth century John Bunyan, George Fox, Roger Williams, and William Penn graced both sides of the Atlantic as God's shining stars. Then came the eighteenth century, the days of the far-reaching Wesleyan revivals and the Great Awakening. John and Charles Wesley moved two continents toward God. Jonathan Edwards, George Whitefield, David Brainerd, William Carey, and Adoniram Judson were God's grace gifts upon His church. Then followed the nineteenth century which swells in volume and in glory. There was Dwight L. Moody, Charles Spurgeon, Charles Finney, Sam Jones, John A. Broadus, and David Livingstone. In the twentieth century were Billy Sunday, George Truett, Lee Scarbrough, and Billy Graham. Paul says that this is our Lord's ascension gift to His church: the building up of the faith, the enrichment of the people of God through God's flaming ministers. Nor shall that gift ever end until the Lord comes again in glory. Every generation shall have its grace gifts, men of God, the ministers of Christ who shine and burn for Him.

Grace Gifts Continue

Sometimes I think of the gift of God in the Old Testament story when Elijah was carried up to heaven in a whirlwind. When he ascended up into glory, the mantle fell from his shoulders to the ground and Elisha, who poured water on the hands of Elijah, picked the mantle up and went to the swollen Jordan River and said, "Where is the Lord God of Elijah?" He then struck the waters of the swollen stream with Elijah's mantle, whereupon the waters parted and Elisha went over on dry ground. When the school of the prophets at Jericho saw what happened, they looked upon the face of Elisha and said, "The spirit of Elijah doth rest upon Elisha." This is God's true gift through the centuries. When one man lays a mantle down, there is another man to pick it up and carry it on.

One time I stood in Westminster Abbey looking at the monument to John Wesley. He is not buried there, but there is a large plaque in his honor. On the plaque are some of the sayings of John Wesley. One of them is "The world is my parish." The Anglican church would not open its doors to him, so he became pastor and preacher to the world outside. Another inscribed saying is, "God buries the workman but carries on the work." One man finishes his task and lays the burden down, but a younger man picks up the torch, holds it high, and carries it on. The grace gifts of Christ are in every generation. They are the gifts of the Lord, charismatic gifts. They are *pneumatika,* spiritual gifts. They are not natural but they are endowments from heaven.

Effective today are the works of God's *apostolos,* God's missionaries on the frontier. As I have visited for several years the mission fields of our world I am astonished at some abounding gifts. In Guatemala there is a missionary, an *apostolos,* and wherever he goes all over that nation, he establishes thriving churches. He is a grace gift of God to the churches of Guatemala. When I was in Rhodesia I met another man like that. He is a grace gift. Oh, the thriving and flourishing churches he has established in Rhodesia in the heart of Southern Africa!

To be an evangelist is a grace gift. No man can be an evangelist by simply saying, "I am going to be an evangelist." I was riding on a plane with one of my dearest friends who is a marvelously successful pastor. He had just held a meeting in a stadium. Seated there by my side he said: "Criswell, I have learned one thing from this stadium meeting. I am no Billy Graham. I am going back to my church." The office of an evangelist is a grace gift, it is something God bestows. One does not just decide to be an evangelist.

So it is with all of these grace gifts of *apostolos, evangelistes, poimen, didaskalos,* and *prophetes.* All of them are grace gifts. They have nothing to do with a man's looks, his endowments, or any natural riches that he might have inherited.

How God Endows Men

When I was in college and seminary I looked at some of my fellow students and thought, "I do believe God makes mistakes."

The Grace Gifts of Christ

I never saw such unpromising, unprepossessing students for the ministry and the work of the Lord in my life. Some of them just could not learn. But as time has gone on and these years have passed, I review sometimes in memory those fellow students. Some of those men I thought were the most unpromising are some of the greatest chaplains in the United States Army, the Air Corps, and the rest of the branches of our armed service. Others of them are magnificent professors and teachers. Some of them are the finest denominational leaders and missionaries, strategists, and statesmen that walk the face of the earth. When we equate God's gift with a natural endowment, we have missed it. It is not how a man looks. It is not his stature. It is not his physical form or presence, whether majestic or menial. It is God! It is God who makes him shine and flame and burn. It is God who makes him resplendent and incandescent. It is a gift of the Lord, a grace gift.

Thomas Chalmers had a sterile and barren ministry in a little place in Scotland called Kilmeny. But then he had an experience with the Lord. When the people went to church expecting those dull, dry, services, all of a sudden they had a burning flame in front of them. The people were amazed and overwhelmed by the miraculous transformation of Thomas Chalmers. It was a grace gift.

John Wesley came to America to win people to Christ, especially the American Indian in Georgia. He finally got on a boat and went back to England discouraged, defeated. He had failed miserably. Then he describes in his journal his Aldersgate experience in London. He writes: "I once called and they did not come. But I call now and they come." It is a grace gift.

Dwight L. Moody was a businessman. When God called him to testify for Him, he had an ordinary ministry. But one day walking down Wall Street in New York City, he had an electrifying experience. He rushed to the room of a friend and finally after hours said, "God, stay Your hand or I will die." Afterward Moody said: "I preached the same sermons, I used the same words, and I gave the same invitation. But before, where there were ones and twos that came, afterward there were thousands and thousands that came." It is a grace gift. It is something God does. It is an enrichment of His church.

In Whitewright, a town in North Central Texas, lived a young fellow barely twenty who was studying to be a lawyer. The congregation of a church met and said, "God called you to preach, young man, and we are going to ordain you." He said: "Ordain me? Why, I am studying to be a lawyer. I am not going to be a preacher." "Ah," but they said, "God has His hand upon you and we are going to ordain you." He went to his mother who said: "Son, these are God's people. If they believe God has called you to the ministry, that is the voice of the Lord." And they set him aside for that holy purpose. His name? George W. Truett. That is a grace gift.

How wonderful to see God take weakness and make it into strength. He takes nothing and makes it shine and grow into something for the Lord. It is something God does, it is a gift from heaven. Moses said, "Lord, I cannot speak." The Lord said, "Who made your mouth and your tongue?" God made him fire and flame like the bush that burned unconsumed. Jeremiah said: "Lord, I am a child, I am afraid of their faces. They frighten me." God said, "I will make you strong for Me." Simon Peter said: "Lord, I am a sinful man. I am unworthy, Lord." God said, "I will make you a fisher of men." God did it.

Saul of Tarsus, who became Paul the apostle, said, "Lord, take away this thorn in my flesh." We do not know what that was. Any man who has a burden, a handicap, or an affliction is a brother to the Apostle Paul. "Lord, this thorn in my flesh: take it away." But the Lord said: "Not so. My strength is made perfect in weakness." When I am crushed, when I am down, and when I am defeated, then is God magnified and glorified. It is something God does, not something we do.

John Wesley was barely four feet ten or eleven inches tall. Not only that, but he had a wretched marriage in later life. One day a friend came to see him and did not knock on the door. Instead the friend just walked into the house and there was the wife of John Wesley dragging him all over the house by the hair of the head. Yet that man flamed and shined for Jesus.

An English professor went up to Dwight L. Moody once and said: "Mr. Moody, I listened to your sermon today. There were seventeen grammatical errors that you made. Seventeen of them I have written here." If one were to read one of Moody's sermons uncorrected he would not think a man could speak that poorly. Dwight L. Moody replied: "Sir, I do the best I can for Jesus. Do you?" It is a grace gift.

The man who made the greatest impression upon me in four years of going to chapel at Baylor was a crippled and deformed man. I can still see him. He stood in that chapel pulpit with his head so bent that he could not raise it. He was deformed and he was crippled, but God made his ministry to shine and burn like fire. It is a gift from heaven.

The most moving, eloquent man who ever lived was George Whitefield. Benjamin Franklin said, "I want to hear him but I am going to leave all my money at home because he will get it all, they tell me, if I come with anything in my pockets." So Benjamin Franklin went to hear George Whitefield and left all of his money at home. While George Whitefield was preaching, Benjamin Franklin turned to a neighbor and said, "Sir, will you loan me some money that I can give to George Whitefield?" Another man that I read about said, "George Whitefield could pronounce the name "Mesopotamia" and bring a vast throng to tears, just by pronouncing the word. George Whitefield all of his life was an asthmatic. When he preached he gasped for breath. Yet he became God's eloquent preacher. When he came to Newberryport in Connecticut the villagers came and knocked on the door in the middle of the night and said to the host, "Would you ask Mr. Whitefield to come and preach for us?" So he got George Whitefield out of bed. The preacher came down the stairway and stood on the bottom step. There he preached the message of Christ to the people in the hall, on the porch, and out in the yard. George Whitefield had a candle in his hand in a little candle holder. When the candle burned down and went out, George Whitefield led a benedictory prayer, went back up to the room, lay down, and died with an attack of asthma. How could an asthmatic be such a preacher? It is God who does it.

It is not a man's education, though I not deprecate it. Nor is it a man's polished style and I do not deprecate that. Nor is it a man's chaste language or human wisdom. But by the Word of the Lord I am avowing to you what I read in the Bible and what I see in human history. Power from heaven is a grace gift. It is something God does. That, the apostle says, is the enrichment of the church. Not our building, not our vast mausoleum-like cathedrals, but God's grace gifts are our riches.

Unto everyone of us is given a *charis,* a grace according to the measure of the gift of Christ. Some of you can make money for Jesus — that is your gift. Some of you know how to guide an organization. Some of you know how to be a superintendent — that is your gift. Some of you are teachers. Some of you are personal soul winners. Some of you can sing. Each one of you has a gift. When you dedicate your life to Jesus, when you give your life to the Lord, oh, how He sanctifies the soul, the home, the life, the church! We are enriched and blessed through you.

Chapter 27

GRIEVING THE HOLY SPIRIT

And grieve not the holy Spirit of God, whereby ye are sealed unto the day of redemption. (Eph. 4:30)

This verse is one of the most moving of all of the texts in the Bible. The fullness of the revelation in the text is found mostly in the word "grieved." The word for sorrow, for grief in the New Testament is *lupe*. In John 16 the Lord said to His disciples, "But because I have said these things unto you (His coming passion and His going away), *lupe*, sorrow hath filled your heart" (v. 6). In Luke 22:45, when the Lord agonized in Gethsemane, He came back and saw the disciples "sleeping for sorrow." The verbal form of the substantive used here is *lupeo*, "to make sorrowful," "to grieve." When the rich young ruler came to the Lord Jesus, the Master said to Him: "Your riches come between you and God. Get rid of them and come." It was written in his face, the war in his heart, and he lost the battle. The narrative uses that word *lupeo*; he went away sorrowful, grieved, sad. No wonder the Lord loved that young man. "The Lord looking upon him, loved him." He was one of the finest young Jewish men of that day, but he lost that battle. He did not leave the Lord flippantly or lightly. He left Him *lupeo*, grieving, sorrowing.

Another instance of the use of the word is when the Lord said to Simon Peter, "Simon, do you love me?" When the Lord asked him that three times, the last time Peter was *lupeo*, grieved, hurt, because the Lord asked him the third time, "Lovest thou me." That word *lupeo* is the word used here, "Grieve not the Holy Spirit."

The Holy Spirit Is a Person

There is a veritable flood of revelation in this verse. For one thing, it shows that the Holy Spirit is someone. He is a person. He can be grieved. He can be hurt. The Holy Spirit is not a force, a law, or a motion. One could not grieve a law, a force, or a motion. To grieve one that one must be a someone. He would have to be a person with a heart. This is a revelation of the Holy Scripture, the Holy Spirit of God is someone. He is a "He" and not an "it."

I can easily understand why people would sometimes be led into the aberration that the Holy Spirit is an "it." For example, in the King James version out of which I always preach, in Romans 8 is the translation, "The Spirit itself beareth witness with our spirit, that we are the children of God" (v. 16). Then again verse 26, "but the Spirit itself maketh intercession for us with groanings which cannot be uttered." There the Spirit is referred to as an "it." What would be wrong in referring to the Spirit as an "it"? The Holy Spirit is a person, a member of the Godhead, and third person of the Trinity. To refer to God as an "it" is unthinkable. Why is this translation in the Bible? The reason for it is simple. In English we always use natural gender. A girl is always a "she." A boy is always a "he." A something, a desk, a microphone, is always an "it." But some of the great languages of the world do not use natural gender, they use grammatical gender. The language is built not in a natural gender referring to the sex of the one referred to, but in a grammatical manner. German is one of those languages. The word for "girl" in German is neuter. A girl in German is an "it," not a "she." It is not *"der madchen"* (masculine) or *"die madchen"* (feminine). It is *"das madchen"* (neuter). She is an "it" in the German language. The Greek has that grammatical gender, just as the German has. In Greek *pneuma* is not *ho pneuma* (masculine) or *he pneuma* (feminine) but it is *to pneuma,* (neuter). When translators translated the Bible they found *to pneuma* as neuter, so they translated it "the Spirit itself," neuter. But that is a grievous mistake. The Spirit of God is someone. He is a person and that is seen in this text: "grieve not the Holy Spirit."

There is a tenderness in the word of the text that is used. Had Paul written "anger not the Spirit," immediately you are in another world. For anger breeds anger. It is conducive to retaliation. When someone is in a fit of anger, filled with all kinds of flaming wrath, clamor, and evil, immediately there is in us a reaction just like that. But Paul did not say, "anger not the Holy Spirit." He said, "grieve not." Grief has in it a tenderness, a love. One cannot be grieved by someone he does not love. One cannot be hurt by someone he does not love. There is not repercussion in them of hurt and grief unless they love you. That is why whenever one loves someone, he lays himself open for hurt as wide as the sky. That relationship exists between the Holy Spirit and us. It is personal. It is full of heart and tenderness. There is an apothecary in heaven and He compounds that feeling. He puts in it some of the bitterness of myrrh. He places in it some of the sweetness of frankincense. That is grief, sorrow. He can be hurt, such as people whom you love can be hurt.

GRIEF PRESUPPOSES LOVE

Let me name some of the attributes of the Holy Spirit that would lay Him open to grief. One I have already mentioned. He loves us. When one speaks of the love of the Father and the love of the Son, he is also speaking of the love of the Spirit. He broods over us. We are in His heart, His mind, His care, His keeping, and His love, all of our lives. When you were a child, He quickened you. He touched your heart. He spoke to your conscience. When you were a little child, He presented to you the blessed Jesus, and you became conscious of sin. All of us as little children become conscious of sin, not because we have done so vilely and wickedly, but because in the presence of Jesus we see our unworthiness and lack.

Sin is not nearly so much doing this and doing that and doing the other, as it is our nature. We are just lost, imperfect sinners. The Holy Spirit quickens us so that we become sensitive to right and wrong. When we are thus quickened, the Spirit of God also will show us Jesus, our Saviour on the cross. The Holy Spirit will open our eyes and we see. The Holy Spirit will open our ears and we hear. The Holy Spirit will open our palsied, frozen, impotent hands and we can receive the blessedness of the preciousness of the love of God. All of this is the work of the Holy Spirit.

GRIEF PRESUPPOSES CARE

Another attribute of the Holy Spirit that would lay Him open to grief is that He helps us in our infirmities. He is a "comforter," so named from the Greek *parakaleo*, "the one called alongside," "the paraclete." The Holy Spirit looks down from heaven and binds up our broken hearts. He is our ever-present strength and refuge in our illnesses, infirmities, and sicknesses. He is with us in our trials and in our discouragements. Always the Spirit is present to encourage us and to help us.

Not only that, but the Holy Spirit is the One who shares our prayers with us when they are unsayable. Sometimes our prayers cannot be verbalized, they are unphraseable. We do not have the vocabulary or the language. We do not have the ability to pronounce the word or put the sentence together to lay before God's throne of grace our deepest need. Have you ever been like that? The agony of heart by which you came before the Lord was just too deep for words. All you could do was just weep, just feel. This Holy Spirit Himself makes intercession for us with groanings which cannot be uttered. You could not place the request to God in language so deep was the intercession, so consuming was the appeal for God. You just do not know the language of heaven. But the Holy Spirit knows. He feels with us. When you feel that way, He feels that way. When you are in agony, He is in agony. When you are bowed down, He is bowed down. He is moved by the feeling of our infirmities — He cares. When we cannot speak the language of prayer, the language of heaven, the Holy Spirit speaks it for us.

GRIEF PRESUPPOSES NEARNESS

Another attribute of the Holy Spirit is that "He dwells in you." Paul, writing in Romans 8, says, "If the Spirit . . . dwell in you, he . . . shall also quicken your mortal bodies by his Spirit that dwelleth in you" (v. 11). That is exactly what happened to the Lord Jesus. Evil men slew Him. Other men buried Him. But the Lord Jesus was filled with the Holy Spirit from His birth and doubly baptized by the Spirit. When He was baptized in water the Holy Spirit came upon Him preparing Him for His public and Messianic ministry. He was filled with the Holy Spirit. When He

Grieving the Holy Spirit

died and was buried, it was by the Holy Spirit of God that He was raised from the dead. And Paul avows the same thing will happen to us. We are the temple, the house in which He lives. This body has God in it, and one does not bury God. Put a seal on the tomb, put a guard there to watch it, but the Holy Spirit raised that body of Jesus from the dead and He will raise us. The apostle is saying to us: "This body is the house of God, the temple of the Lord. When it is buried, the Holy Ghost who dwells in this temple will raise it up." That is why in 2 Corinthians 5, Paul begins the chapter, "We have . . . a house not made with hands, eternal in the heavens." A common interpretation is that he is talking about that mansion in the sky, but He is not talking about a mansion. Paul is referring to this house, this tabernacle. Renewed, resurrected, it is made and fashioned without hands by the Holy Spirit of God. When the Lord raises it up it shall be an eternal dwelling place for our souls. The power of the resurrection lies in the Holy Spirit who dwells in us.

THE SEALING OF THE HOLY SPIRIT

Let us look again at these attributes of the Holy Spirit that could be grieved. "Grieve not the holy Spirit of God, whereby ye are sealed unto the day of redemption." A *sphragis* such as the word used in Revelation 7:2, is a signet ring. The king wore his seal on that ring. In matters of state a document was closed with soft wax and the king sealed it with his own seal. In matters of property and estates, papers were sealed with a signet ring. When Jeremiah bought back the inheritance from his fathers in Anathoth, he sealed it in two copies, in two ways. One copy Jeremiah sealed in an open document where everyone could read it, with the seal down at the bottom like a document, like an instrument of state. The other was sealed and placed in the archives for the future generations to know.

The same double sealing is done by the Holy Spirit with us. First, He seals openly and publicly where all can see. One cannot hide that seal. If you are not a child of God, it is very apparent. You cannot hide it. There is a worldliness about you, an unspirituality about you, an undiscipleship of God around you that is just apparent. But if you are sealed by the Holy Spirit of God you cannot hide that either. You are just different. You have the seal of God upon you. And then there is a secret sealing upon a document up in the archives of heaven. It has your name on it. That is what the Holy Spirit does for you. Here publicly He seals us and there secretly He seals us. Is that document in heaven authentic? How do you know but it is counterfeit? How do you know but that the scribe from hell itself, master of presumption and carnal security, has not written that document? How do you know? Because the seal of the Spirit is on the document. And as I say, it is publicly seen in you. You cannot hide it. It is also written up there in the archives of God's heaven. The sealing unto the day of redemption is a sign that God owns us. We are His property.

Out in the west where men have cattle on the ranges, they put their brand on each of the cattle. That is a sign it belongs to the owner. God has His brand, His trademark, His seal upon us. The Holy Spirit, evident in our lives, is a sign, a seal, that we belong to Him.

The Bible also says that we are sealed until the day of redemption, until the Lord comes again, and the complete, purchased possession is presented before God. How does one know he will make it? Do not worry. That is the doctrine of predestination. That is the doctrine of election. That is the doctrine of the perseverence of the saints. And that is the doctrine in the Bible. The saints of God are going to make it. We are sealed with the Holy Spirit of God and the Lord knows those who are His. Their names are written in heaven, and their lives are open books here in the earth.

Who Can Grieve the Spirit?

Who is it that grieves the Holy Spirit? After the Holy Spirit has loved us, after He has helped us, encouraged us, and has been moved by our tears and our infirmities; and after He seals us and is the guardian guide to present us some day in the very presence of God, how do we grieve Him? Who is it that grieves the Lord? There are three.

The Backslidden Christian

The backslidden Christian grieves the Holy Spirit. He does not pray anymore. The leaves of His Bible are stuck together. His witness is as a man would take a candle and hide it under a bushel.

He does not have any joy in his soul. There is no gladness in his religion. He gets bored going to church and He would like to be out there with the crowd in the world. The worldly Christian grieves the Holy Spirit. Well, how do you know he is saved? I will tell you exactly how you can know he is saved. Whenever a child of God is out there in the world he is one of the most miserable creatures alive. He is totally unhappy. He may present the finest picture of joy, gladness, and happiness as he drinks, and as he curses, and as he desecrates the Lord's Day, and as he uses his money for worldly purposes. One might think: "Is not he just like one of them? Is not he having a worldly time?" But if he is a born-again child of God, when he starts living in the world it becomes obvious that the peace and joy from his life is gone. An unsaved man may like all the world has to offer, but the Christian will not.

The concomitant to that condition of the backslidden Christian is if one is ever a born-again Christian he will come back home. One may be a prodigal in the hogpen, but the day will come when he sits on that top rail watching the hogs eat and the tears will start flowing down his face. People have come to me recounting how it was in the days when the Lord saved them. They cry out: "I want to come back. I want to come back." They feel in their own souls the grieving of the Holy Spirit.

And when the Holy Spirit is grieved, we are grieved as well. When the child of God finds no understanding in the Bible, no enlightenment, no answer to prayer, when the heavens turn to brass and the services of the church are just interminable wearinesses, that grieves the Holy Spirit of God and it grieves the Christian, too.

A Dead Church

What grieves the Holy Spirit of God? A dead church. When the Spirit leaves a dead church, the prayer meeting dwindles away and no one is saved. For a life to be born the womb has to be warm and bathed in blood, sometimes in tears, and sometimes in labor. Is not that right? It is the same way in spiritual life. There is no spiritual life in a dead church. The womb is not warm, there is no blood to nourish, and there are no tears of labor. To have life there must be the presence of the warm Spirit of God.

People say to me: "Pastor, why are you trying to enlarge the Sunday school? Why do you try to reach other people? Is not the church large enough?" As long as there is one who is lost, we are still down on our knees asking God for help, methods, and approaches to reach him. As long as there is someone lost on the mission field, we have a tremendous assignment. We are still praying, we are still hoping, we are still interceding, we are still asking God for help, we are still knocking at the door. The task is never finished. It will never be finished until Jesus comes again. If we had forty thousand people registered in Sunday school every Sunday and there were still families and children outside the reach of the Word of God, we would still be at it, trying to reach more. Such a church is a church full of love, intercession, and the Spirit of Christ. When we get away from that we become dead in our hearts and we grieve the Holy Spirit.

An Unrepentant Sinner

Who grieves the Spirit of God? You do when you turn down the voice of the Lord and say: "No, I will not take the Lord. I will not receive Him." When you say "No" to the preacher, "No" to the appeal, and "No" to the invitation, you grieve the Holy Spirit of God. Is it not an astonishing thing that this is the unpardonable sin? You can say "No" to God the Father and everything can still be open to you. You can say "No" to Jesus and everything will still be open to you. But when you say "No" to the workings of the Spirit, there comes a time when it is "No" forever. He does not say "Come" anymore. He does not appeal anymore. You are dead. You are lost. You are going to die and be lost forever. You are never going to be saved. Oh, there are unfathomable depths that I cannot understand. God said, "My Spirit shall not always strive with man." He gave them one hundred twenty years in Noah's day and then destroyed them off the face of the earth by the flood.

> There is a time, I know not when,
> A place I know not where,
> That marks the destiny of men
> To glory or despair.

Grieving the Holy Spirit

> There is a line by us unseen
> That crosses every path,
> The hidden boundary between
> God's mercy and God's wrath.

That is why in the Bible always the appeal of the Spirit is today, today. "To-day if you will hear his voice, harden not your hearts" (Heb. 3:15). "Behold, now is the accepted time; behold, now is the day of salvation" (2 Cor. 6:2). It is always *now*. There is no tomorrow in the Spirit of God, it is now. Come now, trust now, believe now, respond now. Open your heart to God now. Receive Jesus as your Saviour now. Grieve not the Holy Spirit of God, but make Him glad by giving your heart to the Lord.

Chapter 28

THE SWEETEST VERSE IN THE BIBLE

> And be ye kind one to another, tenderhearted, forgiving one another, even as God for Christ's sake hath forgiven you. (Eph. 4:32)

To me, our text is the sweetest verse in the Bible. "And be ye kind one to another, tenderhearted forgiving one another, even as God for Christ's sake hath forgiven you." (4:32). There is a chapter heading right after that, Chapter 5, but it is misplaced. It should have been two verses down. The context reads, "And grieve not the holy Spirit of God, whereby ye are sealed unto the day of redemption" (4:30). Then "Be ye kind one to another, tenderhearted, forgiving one another, even as God in Christ hath forgiven you" (v. 32). Then the passage continues even though there is a chapter heading between "Be ye therefore . . " (and it is the "therefore" that continues the thought), "Be ye therefore followers of God, as dear children; And walk in love, as Christ also hath loved us, and hath given himself for us an offering and a sacrifice to God for a sweet-smelling savour" (5:1, 2). The imagery pictures the golden altar of incense with its perfume, its ascending sweet-smelling odor, coming up to God. Together the verses make the whole passage, the entire thought, and it is necessary to see the total thought in order to understand fully our text.

CHILDREN OF LOVE

"Be ye therefore followers of God, as dear children." The Greek is *tekna agapeta*, "children of love." John wrote in his first epistle, "God is *agape*, God is love" (1 John 4:8). He is a love that is exalted, a special kind of love, *agape* love. God is *agape*. Then the Apostle

The Sweetest Verse in the Bible

Paul calls us here *tekna agapeta*. We are children of God, born in His love. We are wanted, we are desired, and we are prayed for.

Around the world many unwanted children are born. Sometimes as foundlings they are placed on a doorstep or in an ash can. Sometimes to get rid of them people send them to a home. But we are *tekna agapeta*, children born in the love, mercy, and goodness of God. We are desired, we are wanted, we are prayed for, we are welcomed. We are "dear children" of God.

IMITATIONS OF GOD

As children of God's love, Paul says, we are to be *mimetai* of God, "followers" of God. *Mimetai*, our words "mimic" and "imitator" come from it. As a mimeograph, we are to be copies of God, we are to imitate God. What an admonition! And yet, if we love the Lord, we will find ourselves unconsciously loving and following those precious characteristics that we see of God in Christ Jesus.

One day in the International Airport in New York City waiting for a plane, I met a man who was at the time the Governor of Maryland. He is a gifted political leader who delivered the keynote address at the Republican Convention that nominated President Richard M. Nixon. Learning that I was a pastor, he began to talk with me about the things of God and of his family (all who are Methodists). He began to talk about his mother, who must have been a very devout Christian woman. He said: "My mother had an unusual and strange habit. When she went down to the altar to kneel, to take the Lord's Supper, she always took off her jewelry and put it in her purse before she knelt before the Lord. Do you know that as the days passed and I grew up, I found myself taking off my jewelry. I would take off my ring, take off my watch, take off my jewelry when I knelt to take the Lord's Supper. Last Sunday morning, when I knelt there to take the Lord's Supper, my teenage boy was kneeling by my side. To my utter amazement, I saw him take off his jewelry — his ring and his watch." That is nothing but imitation. There is no special reason for it. It is indefensible by one who would seek to question why. It is but the fact that the father imitated his mother and he in turn was imitated by his son. How glorious it is to imitate God! That is the most wonderful originality in the world, to copy the Lord.

The sons of old Eli did not imitate their father. The sons of Samuel did not imitate their father. Absalom did not imitate his father David. But our Lord Jesus imitated His Father. He was an exact duplicate. "To see Me," He said, "is to see the Father."

Well, how is God? If one were like Him what would he be like? That is the point of text. He is kind, He is tenderhearted, He is forgiving. The Bible says so. It is as *ho theos en Christo*, which the King James Version translates, "as God for Christ's sake." What he actually said was "as God in Christ." That is what God is like. He is like Jesus. You see God in the Lord. If we were to mimic Him, we would be kind, tenderhearted, and forgiving.

BE KIND LIKE GOD

I speak first of the kindness of God.

> For the love of God is greater
> Than the measure of man's mind.
> And the heart of the Eternal
> Is most wonderfully kind.

When the prophet Gad came to King David to confront him with his sin of numbering the people of Israel, the prophet said, "You must choose between three judgments: seven years of famine, or to flee before your enemies as they pursue you three months, or three days of pestilence in the land." David, bowing before such a harsh judgment, said: "Let us not fall into the hands of men. Let us fall into the hands of God for He is merciful and kind. I choose three days pestilence." (See 1 Chron. 21:1-17.) The wonder of the story is that when the pestilence swept the land and the destroying angel came over Jerusalem, David saw him with his sword drawn over the city. David fell upon his face and, bowing before the Lord of judgment, pled for mercy in behalf of his people. When God sent David to the mount where Araunah's threshingfloor was located (Mount Moriah where Abraham had offered up Isaac), there David built an altar to placate the wrath and judgment of God. Later, on the same spot did Solomon build his temple, a place where God shows mercy, where God is kind. Why, the very location of it, the very erection of it, is a thanksgiving, a gratitude, and an acknowledgment of the goodness,

The Sweetest Verse in the Bible

kindness, and mercy of God. For the Lord stayed the plague in answer to David's prayer. God is kind, tenderhearted, and forgiving.

That explains to me why God does not destroy the wicked. These who plan murder, war, and violence; why does not God destroy them from the face of the earth? It is because He is kind and good. He makes His rain to fall on the field of a bad man as well as on that of a good man. He makes the sun to shine on the unjust man as well as on the just man. The Lord loves us all alike — good and bad. That is why Simon Peter wrote, "The Lord is not slack concerning his promise, as some men count slackness; but is longsuffering to us-ward, not willing that any should perish, but that all should come to repentance" (2 Peter 3:9). That is why the prophet Ezekiel cried out for God, "Have I any pleasure at all that the wicked should die? saith the Lord GOD" (Ezek. 18:23). God's judgment upon the wicked is delayed. The goodness and the kindness of God is seen in His longsuffering. Maybe tomorrow the evil man will repent. Maybe some day beyond tomorrow he will bow and give his heart to God. God is forgiving.

To me, that explains sometimes why grievous burdens are placed upon God's anointed, such as the slavery of Joseph in Egypt. Israel cried when Joseph's evil brothers came and said, "Is not this the coat of your son Joseph?" Many-colored, they dipped it in blood, a goat's blood. "Is not this your son's coat?" Jacob looked at it and recognized it immediately. He said: "Everything is against me. I have lost Rachel, the mother, and now Joseph, my son. I will go down to the grave grieving for my boy." But when Joseph was Prime Minister of Egypt and thereby saved the entire family from starvation, Joseph said, "Ye thought evil against me; but God meant it unto good" (Gen. 50:20). Even in our grievous burdens, God is kind, loving, remembering us for good.

Is that not the story of Moses in exile? As a shepherd for forty years God prepared him for service and finally spoke to him. Is not that the story of the tears of Hannah? Had it not been out of her broken-heartedness that she cried to God, there would have been no little Samuel lent to the Lord. Is not that the story of the Apostle Paul, deep bruised, incarcerated? Could those glorious letters, "The Prison Epistles," ever have been written without that suffering? Is not that the story of the Apostle John whom Domitian exiled to die on the stony, rocky isle of Patmos? On that lonely rock God rolled back the heavens as a scroll and John saw Him and the vistas of the apocalyptic age yet to come. Could that have happened anywhere else or under any other circumstances? Even our burdens are the kindnesses of God.

If one could go back through the sweep of human history and pick out one event and there stand in the glory of that magnificent, epochal hour and look on the face of a great general in his triumph, or something like that, what event would he choose? Ah, some of us might say, "I would like to have seen Alexander the Great when he stood triumphant over the dissolution of the Persian Empire." Or someone might say, "I would like to have been in Waterloo and there to have looked upon the face of the Iron Duke of Wellington in his victory over Napoleon Bonaparte." I would not blame you. What significant events those are!

BE KIND LIKE JESUS

But if I had my choice, do you know what I would like to see? Rather than seeing all of the generals in all of the hours of their triumph, I would have loved to have been there when the Book says that while the throngs and the multitudes were pressing Jesus on every side, there walked up to Him a leper. How could a leper get to Jesus when He was thronged and pressed by the multitudes on every side? The reason is most obvious. According to law when a leper left his colony of lepers, wherever he walked he had to cover his face with his hands and cry, "Unclean, unclean!" Wherever he walked, the people fell away from him. Always there was that empty circle around him. He could walk anywhere and the multitudes would part. That is how he got to Jesus. He just walked right up to the Lord. The throngs around Him, aghast, fell apart. But the Lord did not move. The Saviour stood right there where He was in the center of that icy, chilling, ever-present, empty circle. The leper came easily to Him and the Book says, "And the Lord touched him." He put His hand upon him. I would guess it was half the cure, just the feel of the sweet, loving, human hand of the Lord. Would not it have been great to have been there?

Or when the disciples were interdicting the mothers who were bringing their children to Him and the Lord said: "Forbid them not. Suffer them to come to Me. Of such is the kingdom of heaven." And He took them in His arms and blessed them. Would not you have loved to have seen that? Or when the crowds were hungry and the disciples said, "Send them away." Jesus said: "No. We shall feed them." And He fed five thousand men plus the women and children. Or when the blind man cried out and the friends around him said: "Hush, He has not time for such as you. He is a busy man." The Lord stopped and said, "Bring him to me." The kind and tender-hearted Jesus was moved with compassion. He was that way in all His life.

And He was that way in His death. When those who had crucified Him railed on Him, walked back and forth before Him and blasphemed Him, and when the thief by His side reviled Him, Jesus said, "Father, forgive them, for they know not what they do." He was kind, tender-hearted, and forgiving. When He saw His mother standing there He said to John the beloved apostle, "Behold your mother." Speaking to His mother from the cross He said, "Mother, behold your son." From that day John took her to his own home. No wonder the centurion, who was a hard man, said. "Truly, this man is the Son of God." Christ was kind in life. He was that way in death.

And He is that way in heaven today — kind, tender-hearted, and forgiving. The eloquent author of the Book of Hebrews says so: "For we have not an high priest which cannot be touched with the feeling of our infirmities; but was in all points tempted like as we are, yet without sin. Let us therefore come boldly unto the throne of grace, that we may obtain mercy, and find grace to help in time of need" (Heb. 4:15, 16). He knows all about us. Tried, tempted, suffering, no one goes through any experience, not even you, but that Jesus has drunk of the same bitter cup. He tasted even death for every one of us. The kindness, the tenderheartedness, the sympathy, the understanding, and the compassion of our Lord is placed to our account.

CHRISTIAN PEOPLE ARE TO BE KIND LIKE JESUS

We are to be like our Lord. We are to be *mimetai*, mimics, imitators of God. "Be ye therefore followers of God, mimics, imitators of God, be ye kind one to another, tenderhearted, forgiving one another, even as God for Christ's sake hath forgiven you." How we need this!

One of the most outstanding sermons of Dr. Truett was entitled, "The Need for Encouragement." "Be ye kind one to another, tenderhearted, full of sympathy and understanding."

In the autobiography of Frank Rutherford we read that he preached his heart out to his people. The intensity of truth burned in his soul in the church where he preached. One day after he had poured out his soul, he went to the vestry. Not a soul spoke to him. The janitor finally came in. His only remark was, "It is raining outside," and he went out and closed up the building. The pastor went home without an umbrella, drenched in the rain, and into his little room. He lost his heart and his ability to minister. He left the ministry. I read that and I thought, why could not just anyone have said some word of encouragement?

> It takes so little to make us sad.
> Just a slighting word, a doubtful sneer,
> Just a scornful smile on some lips held dear
> And our footsteps lag though the goal seem near,
> And we lost the joy and hope we had.
> It takes so little to make us sad.
>
> It takes so little to make us glad.
> Just a cheering clasp of some friendly hand.
> Just a word from one who could understand.
> And we finish the task we so long had planned.
> We lose the fear and doubt we had.
> It takes so little to make us glad.

Be kind, tender-hearted, full of sympathy and understanding.

I read in the life of Sir Walter Scott that when he was a little boy he was dull and slow in his lessons, and he was discouraged. One day, so Sir Walter Scott relates, he sat down by Scotland's sweetest singer, Bobby Burns, who read to him some of the lines of poetry he had written. He put his hand on the head of the little lad and encouraged him. Sir Walter Scott said he went back home and wept for joy. There was a marvelous change in his life because of that one word of encouragement.

One time I heard Gypsy Smith describe one of the most moving incidents in a little boy's life. He had gone to hear Dwight L.

Moody preach and Ira D. Sankey sing. After the service was over he went up to Ira Sankey, Moody's singer. Sankey, talking to the little waif of a gypsy boy, somehow by inspiration, and by a revelation from God, put his hand on the head of the little forlorn boy and said to him, "Some day God will make of you a great preacher." It was just a sentence. It was just the warmth of a hand. It was just a smile — kind, tender-hearted, sympathetic. But that kindness changed Gypsy Smith's life.

By common human experience in my pastorate I have learned that most people are won to Jesus because someone loved them into it. They prayed them into it. They visited them into it. They will say to me: "Pastor, so-and-so told us about the Lord. He told us about the church. He told us about Jesus and here we are. The friendship of his dear family won us to Jesus and to this church." I guess God meant it to be that way. There is a human equation that we cannot escape. Maybe that is one reason that He said to us, "Be ye kind one to another, tenderhearted, forgiving one another, even as God for Christ's sake hath forgiven you." We are to be mimics, imitators, *mimetai* of God.

Chapter 29

AWAKE AND ARISE

Wherefore he saith, Awake thou that sleepest, and arise from the dead, and Christ shall give thee light. (Eph. 5:14)

The noted reformer, Martin Luther, one time avowed that some texts are little Bibles such as John 3:16 or Revelation 3:20. But there are also some texts that are complete sermons. This text is one, addressed to the individual Christian, addressed to us individually, addressed to the church, the congregation of the Lord, and addressed to the lost. "Wherefore he saith, Awake thou that sleepest, and arise from the dead, and Christ shall give thee light."

A Duality Constantly Seen in the Bible

This is an astonishing thing for the apostle by inspiration to write, for in Ephesians 2 he said: "And you hath he quickened, who were dead in trespasses and sins; . . . and were by nature the children of wrath, even as others. But God, who is rich in mercy, for his great love wherewith he loved us, Even when we were dead in sins, hath quickened us together with Christ" (vv. 1-5). Now I can understand those words. A man who is dead cannot raise himself, he must be quickened. The life-giving power must be extraneous; it must come into him from the outside if he is to live. "You who were dead in trespasses and sins hath God quickened." When we were dead God quickened us together in Christ. A corpse cannot raise itself because it is dead. Now look closely at that amazing text. It says, "Awake thou that sleepest, and arise from the dead," as though we raised ourselves, quickened ourselves, to life in God.

All of this presents that constantly recurring dualism that one will ever find in the grace, the revelation, the truth, and the work of the Lord. That duality is always there with God and man — God in His part and man in his part without which neither is complete. Paul will write in the Book of Romans, "By faith Abraham was justified" referring to Genesis 15 where Moses wrote, "Abraham believed God and his faith was counted for righteousness." But on the other hand, James the Lord's brother will write, "Abraham was justified by works," and he will cite Genesis 22 where Abraham, in obedience to the mandate of God, offered up Isaac as a sacrifice. The reformer, Martin Luther, when he studied James said, "It is an epistle of straw and it ought to be taken out of the Bible." No, for both the epistles of Paul and of James are true. By faith Abraham was justified; he trusted God, casting himself upon the Lord, and God wrought for him that God-kind of righteousness that we call salvation and redemption. But also the confirmation of that faith was found in the works whereby Abraham offered to God his son Iasaac. He was justified by works.

That duality is found throughout the revelation of God. It is even in Christ. He is man as though He were only man. He is God as though He were God alone.

That duality is seen in our salvation. There is an atonement that only God could work out for us. But there is also an acceptance, a belief, a trusting that is possible only to the man. God has a part and man has a part. Both are vital and significant in our redemption.

That is also true in our work and service for God. God has to bless. He must sanctify our service. The Lord's presence must be with us. The other part is that I must offer to God a dedicated life — my hands, my heart, my soul, in the work and ministry that rightfully belong to Jesus. Both of them are vital. Both of them are needed. God must quicken us from the dead, but we also must arise from the dead. "Awake thou that sleepest, and arise from the dead."

A little girl and her brother were late for school. They had been playing along the way and forgot the time. Still some way from school they heard the school bell ring. The little girl said, "Brother, let us kneel down here and pray that God will not let us be late for school." But the little brother replied, "No, sister, let us run just as fast as we can and let us pray as we run." Our work must be like that — a blessing from God and an effort from man.

That is the way a man ought to live before the Lord. He can pray, "O God, give me a house for my home." Then he ought to say, "Amen" with a hammer and a saw. He could pray, "O God, give me a job." Then let him say "Amen" reading all the want-ad columns and knocking at the door of an employer. We may pray, "Lord, save the world." Then we ought to say "Amen" giving to missions. You may pray, "Lord, strengthen and bless the church." Then say "Amen" by rolling up your sleeves and pouring your life into it. I may pray, "Lord, strengthen me in the faith and in Christian commitment." Then I should get ready to take a part in the kingdom of God. Any place is a good place to serve Jesus. It is a duality always of God's blessing and man's dedicated effort. "Awake thou that sleepest, and arise from the dead."

Awake Individually

First, the text is addressed to us individually, as members, as Christians, as disciples of the Lord. So many of us are awake to the world. If a man sees the possibility of a profit, how quickened he is! How ready he is to turn night into day to gain it. If we are invited to entertainment, to dinner, or to amusement, how ready we are to be present, to be awake! But when God calls we are lethargic, sleepy. "Awake thou that sleepest, and arise from the dead." There is no other way to do God's work. A man can talk in his sleep, and he can walk in his sleep. I have heard preachers that I felt preached in their sleep. But one cannot work in his sleep. He must be quickened and awakened. The Lord found Moses tending sheep. He found Gideon at the threshingfloor. Elijah called Elisha while he was plowing. Jesus called Peter while he was fishing. He called Matthew at the receipt of custom. There is no such thing as serving God in lethargic indolence. "Awake ye that sleep, and arise from the dead."

This exhortation is addressed to all of us. It is not just for those who are elected to committees. Why, it is unthinkable that if I am not chosen, or if I am not placed on a committee, therefore I have no assignment in the kingdom of Jesus. It is addressed to all of us. All of us are elected. All of us are appointed. If one saw

Awake and Arise

a house on fire, would it be proper to wait for an appointed committee? If one saw a man fall in the river, would he wait for an appointed committee? Is it not glorious that the famous text does not read like this: "God so loved the world, that He sent an appointed committee"? Someone said that a camel is a horse that a committee put together. We all are elected. We all are chosen. God has assigned us. "Awake thou that sleepest, and arise from the dead."

Could I take the text and bring it especially in review before our teachers, our leaders, our sponsors, these who have accepted responsibility in the church? We may not do our work with genius. We are not all geniuses, we are not all ten-talent people. But we can do our work with enthusiasm and inspiration. In the Greek language there is a word *entheos,* "in God." On that word the Greeks built *enthousiazo,* "inspired by God." In the English language the derivative is spelled "enthusiasm." I may not be a genius for work, I may not have ten talents to lay at the feet of Jesus, but what I do I can do quickened, awakened, inspired with zealous, dedicated commitment.

So many of our people will stand before a class or before a group like wooden poles. One could make them in a carpenter's shop. They are like those totem poles in Alaska, just there, dead, unquickened, and asleep. "Awake thou that sleepest, and arise from the dead." Doing what we do, we ought to do it with zeal, enthusiasm, and inspiration. The text encourages us that in defeat, difficulty, despondency, despair, or disappointment we still are to be awake, to be raised, and to pour our lives into the assignment God has given us. There is no one but who has his heartaches, defeats, discouragements, despairs, and disappointments. Pick out someone that you think would be the least and most unlikely ever to know grief, or heartache, and he will be the one to have the hurt the deepest and the most grievous of all. There is no one of us but who has his hurt and disappointment. But, "awake thou that sleepest, and arise from the dead" in spite of it. God has assigned us to the task. We commit ourselves to it.

In Alaska, years ago, a preacher and his wife came to begin the work in Juneau, which is located in the panhandle of the state. It sometimes rains there more than one hundred inches a year. The pastor and his wife began to work in Juneau, and as the days passed the rain fell, and fell, and fell. The wife, oppressed in spirit, began to sit by the window and cry. Some of the people learned of it and came to her and said: "Do not do that. Get up and get out in the rain, do something."

Get out! And she did. She and her husband went berry picking in the rain. Alaska is covered with berries and all of them are edible. There is not a poisonous berry in Alaska. Some of them taste like cantaloupe, some of them taste like watermelon; some of them are on little bushes. There are blueberries, blackberries, green berries, and purple berries. I never saw so many berries in my life. They also went out in the rain and caught king salmon. They also went out in the rain and shot ducks. They went out in the rain and did whatever anybody else did out there in the rain. And they did the work of God in the rain. The time is never perfect, it is never just right. There are always handicaps and discouragements. But get out and go.

Awake As a Church

The text also is addressed to the church, to the congregation. "Awake thou that sleepest, and rise from the dead." It would apply first to our services of convocation and assembly. There is private prayer — there is also public prayer. There is private reading of the Bible — there is also public reading of the Bible. There is private worship — there is also public worship. There is private praise — there is also public praise. We are under a mandate and a commandment of God to assemble together publicly and openly in public worship. It is here that we are commanded publicly to confess our faith in the Lord, coming down that aisle before men and angels. It is here that the author of Hebrews commands us not to forsake to assemble ourselves together. When we thus serve the Lord, our worship ought to be done in a quickening spirit. It ought to have life and movement in it. It should have in it marvelous interest and the moving power of God.

Satan, when he was cast out of heaven, was asked, "What do you miss most?" The devil replied, "What I miss most is the blowing of the trumpets in the morning when the hosts of heaven were gathered for the worship of God." That is the way we ought to have our services here. They ought to be with the blast of the trumpet. Let us wake up! We do not honor God by being dead.

The more sanctified we are the more alive we ought to be. The more quickened we are, the more flaming we ought to be. Sound the trumpets! "Awake thou that sleepest, and arise from the dead."

That applies not only to our services, our public convocations, but the text also applies to the work of the Lord, the whole outreach of the church. Look at this Old Testament story: And the Lord said to Moses when they came down to the Red Sea, "Speak unto the children of Israel that they go forward." Get up and go. March! Move! There were two and one-half million people in that camp. For Moses to get word to the people, he had to send out runners. I can easily imagine the runners and the reception they had. Here is a runner who says, "God said move." And the man says: "Why man, look at that sea full of fish. I cannot go. I am duck hunting and I am fishing." The runner says: "But God says move. God says march." And I can see the runner come to another house and the man says: "But my wife is sick. You know I cannot move with my wife sick." The runner says: "God never said anything about your wife being sick. God said move!" The runner comes to another man who is putting up a hot dog stand and says: "Man, do not you know that the Egyptian army is passing this way? I am getting ready." And the man says: "You are getting ready? Hot dogs and hamburgers for the Egyptians?" "Yes," he says. "I am neutral. I am not for Israel and I am not for the Egyptians either. I am for selling hot dogs and hamburgers." "God said move. God said march." And then another man will say: "Look out there. There is the sea. And we are facing the sea. You mean march into the sea?" And the runner says: "I do not know anything about getting drowned. God never said anything about getting drowned. All we know is, God said march! God said move! And we are moving!" That is the church. The Spirit of the Lord says to the pastor, to every member of the church that has God in his soul: "Let us march. Let us move. Let us go! Go!" "Awake thou that sleepest, and rise from the dead."

AWAKE THE LOST

Last, the text is addressed to the lost. "Awake thou that sleepest, and arise from the dead." There is something to awaken to, there is something to arise to. There is light, life, and salvation and it is offered before the judgment. If we refuse to arouse ourselves, to awaken ourselves, if we continue before God lethargic, indolent, indifferent, there is a judgment to awaken to. At 6:00 one morning a freight train pulled into the town of Gans, Oklahoma. The engineer pulled the whistle over and over and over. Some must have wondered why at 6:00 in the morning he was trying to arouse the town. At 6:04 a terrible tornado swept the town and destroyed it. The sounds of eternity are rushing upon us. "Awake, arise!" There is something to awaken to, to arise to. It is not just I; it is also you. It is not just you, it is also the whole family of mankind that some day shall stand before the judgment of Almighty God. "Awake, arise!"

The gift of salvation and the light of Christ shall shine upon you, for the awakening, for the arising, for the receiving, for the taking. Awake, arise, and the light of Christ shall shine upon you. To me, there is no more beautiful verse in the Bible than the one Paul wrote in 2 Corinthians 4, "For God, who commanded the light to shine out of darkness, hath shined in our hearts, to give the light of the knowledge of the glory of God in the face of Jesus Christ" (v. 6). Awake, arise, and the light of Christ shall shine upon you.

> O come to the Light, 'tis shining for thee;
> Sweetly the Light has dawned upon me,
> Once I was blind, but now I can see:
> The Light of the world is Jesus.

"Awake thou that sleepest, and arise from the dead, and Christ shall give thee light." Life, triumph, victory, blessing — now and in the world that is yet to come. We all own for the taking. In His name, for His sake, in His grace, love and power we offer that eternal redemption, that heavenly inheritance of God's presence and glory to you now. "Awake thou that sleepest, arise from the dead, and Christ shall give thee light."

CHAPTER 30

FILLED WITH THE SPIRIT

And be not drunk with wine, wherein is excess; but be filled with the Spirit. (Eph. 5:18)

In Joel 2:28, 29 we find the marvelous prophecy of this day of grace and outpouring of the Spirit in which we live. "And it shall come to pass afterward, that I will pour out my Spirit upon all flesh; and your sons and your daughters shall prophesy, your old men shall dream dreams, your young men shall see visions: And also upon the servants and upon the handmaids in those days will I pour out my Spirit." The prophet says there is a great day coming when the Spirit of God will not fall upon just a leader here or there as upon a Samson, a David, or an Isaiah, but it will be poured out without measure upon all flesh: sons, daughters, old men, young men, and even upon slaves (translated "servants and handmaids"). There is no distinction in the outpouring, in the empowering of the Spirit of God.

There is no finer illustration of that outpouring of the Spirit than seen in John Jasper. Many learned professors of homelitics (the art of preaching) write that the greatest genius in the ministry that America has ever produced was John Jasper, a Negro slave. As he sorted out tobacco with his hands in the warehouse, the Holy Spirit of God came upon him. He became one of the greatest preachers in American history. Upon a visit I made to Richmond, Virginia, the Foreign Mission Board sent a young man out to the airport to take me to the board meeting. Driving into the city down a freeway, we came to a big bend in it. As I looked at the bend in the road, I asked, "Why should not the freeway go straight?" He told me that when the highway department condemned all the property by eminent domain for the building of this great expressway, they came to the church, the Sixth Mt. Zion Baptist Church in Richmond. It was the church of John Jasper. The people of Richmond said: "Do not touch one brick of this church. It shall stand here as a monument to the preaching of the slave, John Jasper." When one drives into the city of Richmond down the freeway, he will make a great bend, and there in the bend stands the Sixth Mount Zion Baptist Church, a monument to a slave, John Jasper. Upon all: your sons and daughters, old men and young men, even upon servants and handmaids, even upon the slaves, God shall pour out His Holy Spirit.

This text illustrates for us but another instance of the glorious manner of the revelation of God, the burden of the prophetic message. The Scriptures always portray the hope of a great day that is coming. "And it shall come to pass afterward, that I will pour out my spirit upon all flesh." However the immediate and the near term prophecy may be, dark, lowering, or judgmental, yet the manner and burden of the prophetic message is always that there is a greater day ahead. There is victory and triumph.

In the kingdom of God there is necessarily (and I think it is a part of the very character of the Almighty) advancement, progress, and development. God never recedes, He never retracts; rather He necessarily and inexorably moves on. Every age and every dispensation is the foundation for a greater one that is to follow, even to the consummation of the end of the world. God's creation is followed by redemption. His redemption is followed by sanctification. His sanctification is followed by glorification. God intends that the saints shall inherit the earth. That is why the Scriptures say that the elect are never to be discouraged or troubled. Convulsions of nature and of nations, the dissolution of social institutions in war and desolation — these things are but preliminaries to the final triumph of God in Christ Jesus. "Fear not, little flock; for it is your Father's good pleasure to give you the kingdom" (Luke 12:32). The whole spirit of the triumphant prophetic message and the revelation of God is optimistically triumphant. It is always up. There is a great day coming!

A Prophecy for Today

The prophecy is of a special and a deepening interest to us because it refers to the day, the age, in which we live. Continuing

Filled With the Spirit

the passage of Scripture we shared in Acts 2, the Pentecostal chapter, Simon Peter stood up and said, "But this is that which was spoken by the prophet Joel" (v. 16). It is this age, it is this day. This is the great hour of which the prophet spoke, and our lives are enmeshed in it. Pentecost was a time set in heaven, just as the Incarnation, the nativity of Christ was a time set in heaven. Paul will say, "When the fulness of the time was come, God sent forth his Son, made of a woman, made under the law" (Gal. 4:4). The time was set in heaven. When the Romans had made the empire one and the Greeks had provided a common language and the Jews had Moses read in every city, in the fullness of time, Christ came to be born of a woman. It was a time set in heaven. His crucifixion was at a time set in heaven. He is the Passover Lamb. The resurrection was at a time set in heaven. It was prophesied that on the third day He should rise from the dead. The ascension into heaven, and the second advent, the return of Christ, a time known but to God, are times definitely set in heaven. So also this outpouring of the Holy Spirit was a time known to God, prophesied by Joel, and set in heaven. As such, the day of Pentecost is a one time experience. It is something that happened in God's program, His kingdom development that will never happen again. There will never be another incarnation. Christ came one time to be born in a manger. Christ will never be crucified again. It was a one-time experience. So also there is one time that the Holy Spirit of God was poured out upon the earth. It marks the beginning of a new era, a new government, a new age of grace, a new dispensation, which was introduced by the messenger, John the Baptist, the forerunner. He said, "I indeed baptize you with water unto repentance: but he that cometh after me is mightier than I, whose shoes I am not worthy to bear: he shall baptize you with the Holy Ghost, and with fire" (Matt. 3:11). And before the Lord ascended to heaven He repeated that Johannine prophecy. "For John truly baptized with water; but ye shall be baptized with the Holy Ghost not many days hence" (Acts 1:5). The baptism of the Holy Spirit, the pouring out of the Holy Spirit, was a once-for-all set date in heaven, and it came to pass at Pentecost.

John said, "I baptize with water but He shall baptize with the Holy Spirit." Jesus is the Baptizer in the sense that He poured out this ascension gift. In Luke 24:49 the Lord said, "And, behold, I

252   Ephesians: An Exposition

send the promise of my Father upon you: but tarry ye in the city of Jerusalem, until ye be endued (clothed) with power from on high." The baptism of the Holy Spirit is the ascension gift of Christ. In that sense He is the Baptizer. When He returned to heaven after His death, burial, and resurrection, when He returned to glory, He poured out upon this world the Spirit without measure. In that sense He is the Baptizer pouring out the Spirit. But since Pentecost the Baptizer is the Spirit who baptizes us into the body of Christ, into the church. "For by one Spirit are we all baptized into one body" (1 Cor. 12:13). Christ is the Baptizer in the sense that He poured out the Spirit, the ascension gift from heaven, on the one day of Pentecost. But since that time the Holy Spirit is the baptizer and He baptizes us into the body of Christ, the church.

When a man trusts Jesus as Saviour, looks in faith and repentance upon Christ, the Holy Spirit baptizes him and adds him to the body of Christ. He becomes a member of the household of faith. That is a one-time operation. It happens when you are saved. You are added to, you are baptized into, the body of Jesus.

Could one be added and then taken out? Could he be placed in the body of Christ, then removed, and then reinstated? Can you be saved and then lost, saved and lost, added and taken out, made a part of the body of Christ, and then cut off? It would be like cutting off your foot and then putting your foot back on. Such an idea is fanciful in anatomy. It is no less fanciful in Holy Scripture. There is no such thing in the Bible as being added to the body of Christ and then taken out of the body of Christ and then added to the body of Christ, lost and found, back and forth. For by one Spirit are we all baptized into the body of Christ. That is the work of the Holy Spirit when we are saved.

This act of the Holy Spirit is positional. It is something God does for us. Like writing our names in the Lamb's Book of Life: I could not do that. It is something God does. So the baptism of the Holy Spirit is something God does for us. When we are saved we are added to the body of Christ.

But what is it that happens to us experientially? The thing that we feel? In recounting the experience of the apostles and their converts in Acts and in the epistles, without exception there is a nomenclature that the inspired writers use, and they never vary from it. They never use the word "baptize" to speak of the Holy

Filled With the Spirit

Spirit. The only time "baptize" is found in the epistles with reference to the Holy Spirit is in the passage in 1 Corinthians 12:13, "For by one Spirit are we all baptized into one body (the body of Christ)." What is the word they use? Without exception it is the word "fill." "And they were all *filled* with the Holy Ghost" (Acts 2:4). The baptism places us in the church, in the body of the Lord, like the symbol of water baptism by which we are baptized into the fellowship of the church. No one becomes a member of the fellowship of the local church who does not find himself walking with the Lord through the waters of the Jordan. There is an experiential part of salvation. That is something we feel and share. But there is something else God does in heaven in which I do not share. When God writes my name in the Book of Life I do not feel it, I do not even see it. I just know He promised that He would do it up there in heaven.

BE FILLED, COME ALIVE

The experiential part of the pouring out of the Holy Spirit is being filled with the Holy Ghost. The apostles never depart from the word "filled." At Pentecost they were filled with the Holy Spirit. At Samaria they were filled with the Holy Spirit. At Caesarea they were filled with the Holy Spirit. At Ephesus they were filled with the Holy Spirit. The disciples were filled with the Holy Spirit. Paul was filled with the Holy Spirit. Stephen was filled with the Holy Spirit. There is never an exception to it. Always that one word "fill," and that is the word of the text: "Be not drunk with wine, wherein is excess; but be filled with the Spirit."

The Greek word here, *plerousthe,* is translated "filled." It is in the imperative mood, an imperative of command. There is never a commandment that we be baptized with the Spirit, but there is a commandment that we be filled with the Spirit. It is imperative. We are to be quickened, we are to be alive. A dead, boresome Christian is a travesty on the name of Christ and an insult to God. That is true also with a preacher, a deacon, and a choir. Our services ought to be the most gloriously interesting of any convocation in the earth. There ought not to be any movie you ever saw, any show you ever attended, any game you ever went to, that rivals the intensity of the interest of the services of God. To the preacher, to the deacon, to the choir, to the teacher, to the leaders, to every member is the command, *plerousthe,* "be filled with the Spirit." We ought to sparkle for God. We ought to be alive for God. People ought to feel the spiritual fire in us when they touch us.

Be Filled — Continuously

"Be filled with the Spirit," *plerousthe.* The verb is present tense. There is no other way in the English language for us to translate the verbal system of the Greek but by the use of tense. Yet the Greeks never used tense as we do in English. In English we cannot talk without pigeonholing everything in a tense. Our verbs have to be past, present, or future. One cannot speak English without using tense to describe the time of action. But the Greeks did not do it that way. They used their verbal system to describe kinds of action. For example, the whole aoristic, verbal system in Greek refers to just the fact of a thing. What we would call the present tense in Greek actually means a continuous action and the present tense is used here in this text. We are to be filled with the Spirit continuously. Oh, our poor human nature! We are up and down. When we are up we can touch the feet of the angels. Then the next day we are so down, so dead and so unresponsive, it is as though we never did know the Lord. But we actually are to be happy, glad, praising God — and serving Jesus all the time, today, tonight, and on Monday just like on Sunday and Saturday. It is *plerousthe,* present tense. It moves, it continues.

Be Filled — All of You

It is plural, *plerousthe.* The verb includes everyone. We all ought to share in that marvelous, quickening presence of the Spirit of God. The professional man, the steam fitter, the fellow who picks up the garbage or sweeps the floor, the lawyer, the doctor, all of us, the pastor, the people, the seers, those who labor in teaching in their pedagogical ministry, all of us are to be filled with the Spirit. There is to be a quickening power that moves in all of us. People ought to be able to see it in us.

Be Filled to Utter Abandonment

Not only imperative mood (a command), not only present tense (continuous), not only plural in number (it includes us all), but it also is passive voice. That is, the subject is acted upon. It is something that happens to the subject. "Be ye filled with the Spirit." It is something the Spirit does to us.

Paul uses here in the text an illustration that is not easily understood the way it is translated. "Be not drunk with wine, wherein is excess, but be [*plerousthe,* passive voice], filled with the Spirit." The comparison that he is making is as when a man is under the influence of alcohol. He is *asotia.* The literal word *asotia* is "abandonment." He is just someone else, a different personality. He gives himself over wholly and completely to something else. When he is under the influence of alcohol, he is a different man. He is a different someone else and one could hardly recognize him. Why, the fellow is ordinarily so neat, nice, and natty, and now he is disheveled under the influence of the spirits of alcohol.

When I was at the Panama Canal I thought, "What a miracle this great canal is! The mechanism of the running of the canal and its gates after two generations is identical to what the American engineers first erected. One reason it is such a notable miracle is that one government after another attempted to build the canal and failed ignominiously. One can see the futile attempt in the ground about eight hundred yards away — the big scar is still there. But the American engineers were sent there and they completed the construction of the canal, one of the outstanding engineering feats in all of the history of mankind. Looking upon it, I thought of the song the American engineers sang after they had achieved the marvelous result:

> Don't send us back to a life that's tame again,
> We who have shattered a continent's spine.
> Easy work, oh, we couldn't do that again,
> Haven't you something that's more in our line?

Now the stanza that all of you know:

> Got any rivers you say are not crossable?
> Got any mountains you can't tunnel through?
> We specialize in the wholly impossible,
> Doing what nobody ever could do.

What a spirit in those American engineers! It is the exact spirit commanded by the Apostle Paul, *plerousthe,* "be filled with the

Spirit," doing what you never thought was possible. It is a marvelous, glorious prospect!

Be filled with the Spirit. Do the impossible for God. It is something God does for us, in us, and with us. Lord do it now.

Chapter 31

CHRIST LOVED THE CHURCH

Husbands, love your wives, even as Christ also loved the church, and gave himself for it;
That he might sanctify and cleanse it with the washing of water by the word,
That he might present it to himself a glorious church, not having spot, or wrinkle, or any such thing; but that it should be holy and without blemish. (Eph. 5:25-27)

This word of the apostle, "Christ also loved the church, and gave himself for it," is an identical pattern of thought though couched in different language, that Paul spoke to the same church leaders at Miletus, the pastors from the church at Ephesus. He said in Acts 20:28: "Take heed therefore unto yourselves, and to all the flock, over which the Holy Ghost hath made you overseers, to feed the church of God, which he hath purchased with his own blood." The word translated "feed," in the Greek, is *poimaino*, the word meaning to feed or to tend or to shepherd a flock. We are to shepherd the church of God which He has purchased with His blood. The Greek word for shepherd is *poimen*.

What kind of a church is it for which Christ died? And what is Paul talking about when he speaks of Christ loving the church and dying for it? There is in the Bible the generic idea of the "church." We use the general idea of a thing when we speak of "the state," or "the home," or "the school," or "the church." There is the idea of "the church." That is in the Bible. "Upon this rock I will build my church" (Matt. 16:18). In this text is also the idea of the institution, the idea of the church. There is also in the New Testament the word used to refer to the redeemed of all ages. In Hebrews 12 the author will say, "But ye are come . . . to the general assembly and church of the firstborn, which are written in heaven (vv. 23a). This is the church invisible and triumphant, the great congregation of the redeemed who shall worship the Lamb, the Lord Christ, in glory.

But the church that we know and the only church with which we have anything to do and the church to which the apostle belonged is always a local congregation. "Christ also loved the church (the local church), and gave himself for it." He died for it. In the New Testament where we read of it, and in life when we have anything to do with it, the church is always the local congregation, the assembly of Christ. The New Testament will speak of the churches (plural) of Judaea, the churches (plural) of Syria, the churches (plural) of Galatia, and the churches (plural) of Macedonia. John addresses the Book of Revelation to the seven churches of Asia. Always the church in our life and experience, in New Testament life and presentation, is the local congregation, this church.

When Jesus ascended into heaven, the church was left as a residium, a residue, a correlary of the ministry of Christ. There was no New Testament, there was no writing, there was nothing except the church. Christ gave it the ordinances, its discipline, and its great commission. When He went to heaven the ministry of our Christ was seen in a church that He left. Then at Pentecost He poured out upon the assembly the ascension gift of the Holy Spirit, the promise of the Father, the breath of God, the Holy Spirit. The church already had the ordinances, it had the discipline, it had the commission, it had the teaching. It had everything except the breathing, empowering, enabling Spirit of God. Upon the ascension of the Lord into heaven, the ministry of Christ continued in the pouring out of His Spirit upon the church. It was a local church, a church one could see, visit, and join. Then under the guidance, the surveillance, the direction of the Lord from heaven, the Apostle Paul was called openly, personally by the Lord. Through him and his fellow apostles, churches were founded all over the Roman Empire. These are the churches Christ loved and gave Himself for.

In the Revelation John says that he heard a great voice back of him which sounded like a trumpet. Being turned he saw a seven-branched lampstand. The lampstand, John says, represents

Christ Loved the Church 259

the churches of the Lord Jesus Christ. When John turned to look he saw the Son of God, the Saviour, walking in the midst of the seven-branched lampstand. That is, he saw the Lord walking among His churches. "Christ also loved the church, and gave himself for it." This is the church of our experience and of our lives; we know no other. A man could not join the invisible church or belong to the invisible redeemed, triumphant, glorified congregation of the Lord. It is not here, nor do we ever see it or know it on earth. The only church that we know is the church that is presented to us through the New Testament which, without exception, is a local congregation, the assembly of Christ's believers. When I was a boy I went to a little church in a small village. I went to Sunday school and as a child was converted and baptized. The little church was white with a cupola on top and a bell that they rang at Sunday school time.

This church where I now preach and pastor is the church of my life and my heart now. I love this church. I love its walls, just the way it looks. Some day, because of its age, we shall have to build another house. But I do not look forward to that with gladness. When the day comes to tear these old walls down, there will be a whole lot of my heart that will crumble with them. I love this church.

> I love Thy kingdom, Lord,
> The house of Thine abode,
> The Church our blest Redeemer saved
> With His own precious blood.
>
> I love Thy church, O God!
> Her walls before Thee stand,
> Dear as the apple of Thine eye,
> And graven on Thy hand.

In 1950 Dr. Duke McCall, who was then the Executive Secretary of our Southern Baptist Convention, and I made a preaching tour to the mission fields of the world. We went around the world and were gone four months. Mostly we were in the dark places of the earth where humanity is helpless and largely hopeless. Yet in those darkest places, in a jungle, in a forgotten, underprivileged country where the flotsam and jetsam of people are just poured out in waste, we would find a little church, a dedicated missionary, and a little flock of the Lord's people. Sometimes the church house would be made out of mud, sometimes made out of thatch, but I never saw it anywhere in the earth but as I looked upon it, my spirit was raised by what it meant and what it means. To look upon the dedicated people there brought joy and gladness to my heart. The people loved the Lord and were my brothers in Christ.

If one were looking for a man to go to a stone-age tribe in the Amazon Jungle and there spend this life teaching the natives, if we were looking for a man to run a hospital under the Arctic Circle, if we were looking for a man to teach in a school in the back country of Africa, if we were looking for a man to work in the slums of a great city like Calcutta, where would one find him? I mean a man of high heritage, noble culture, and splendid education, a man who would go and bury his life without any thought of recompense or reward, a man who would labor in an inhospitable environment and yet keep his spirit bright. Where would one find a man like that? I can tell you. You will find him in the church. Wherever it is in the earth, it is there a colony of heaven, pointing the way to glory.

"Christ also loved the church, and gave himself for it; that he might sanctify and cleanse it with the washing of water by the word." He loved it, gave Himself for it, presides over it today from heaven, and walks in its midst. Paul is talking about this church, our church, that He might sanctify and cleanse it with the washing of water by the Word. The term that is astonishing to me is the word translated here, "washing." It is the Greek word *loutron*. In the Old Hebrew Testament it is *kiyor*. It is the name for the big laver. In the Tabernacle and later in the Temple was found the brazen altar. Beyond the altar was the laver where the priest washed before he entered the sanctuary of God. That is the word Paul uses here, the *laver* of the Word. Our Lord washes His church with the *laver* of the Word.

CHURCH ORDINANCES ARE TO BE WASHED
IN THE LAVER OF THE WORD

The church ought to be a teaching church, a studying church, a learning church. The church ought to be one that is washed in the laver of the Word. How desperately that is needed and how earnestly our church should seek to achieve it! The church is to be an understanding church. It ought to be a studying church. It ought to be a Scripturally knowledgeable church.

Here is an illustration of how we fall into doctrinal aberration when we do not study and learn what the Bible has to say. I was holding a crusade in a city that was located near the largest air base in the world. The chief chaplain at the air base was Southern Baptist. In the crusade I was with him on many occasions. One time he said to me, "Why do not you Southern Baptist pastors teach your people the Word of God, the truth of the Lord?" "Well," I said, "I suppose we try but we do not do it well." He said: "That is true. It is not done well. I want to give you an illustration. This week I went to see a couple on the air base, an Air Force man and his wife. They said to me 'Our child is still-born and we want you to come to baptize our child.' I said, 'Baptize your still-born child? What church do you belong to?' They replied, 'We belong to a Southern Baptist church. We come from the south.'" Then the chaplain said to the bereaved couple, "What makes you think that your still-born baby will be bound forever in hell if I do not baptize him?" And the couple replied, "We have friends in the complex on the base where we live and they have told us that if we do not baptize the still-born baby its soul will spend eternity in damnation and hell." And the chaplain said to me, "Why do you not teach your people the Word of God?" I said to him, "Chaplain, it grieves my heart that such a thing could ever be." The tragic, sad point of hurt lies in the factual truth of the accusation against us. There are uncounted thousands of our people who are not conversant with the Word of God. This constitutes for us an assignment and a challenge. Christ loved the church. He gave Himself for it that He might bathe it in the laver of the Word. Oh, that we might be knowledgeable! We must learn and receive the revealed Word of God with an assurance that comes from heaven itself.

The ordinances are to be administered according to the Word of God. The ordinances belong to the church. They do not belong to the Congress, to the courts, to the Chamber of Commerce, or to the civic club. They belong to the church. To present them and to administer them according to the revelation of the Word of God is a part of this washing in the laver of the Word. They are so simple and so significantly meaningful according to Matthew 28:19, 20. One, two, three, the ordinances follow that order. First, "Go ye therefore and make disciples." We are first to be saved. We are to be Christians first. Second, "baptizing them." We are to be baptized, buried with the Lord in the likeness of His death, and raised with the Lord in the likeness of His resurrection. "Teaching them to observe all things whatsoever I have commanded you." Third, we are to take the Lord's Supper according to the instruction of the Lord. Paul said, "I praise you, brethren, that . . . keep the ordinances, as I delivered them to you" (1 Cor. 11:2). They are meaningful symbols of spiritual facts. They portray the redemption and the resurrection of our Christ as well as His triumphant return. "As long as you eat this bread and drink this cup, you show forth the Lord's death till he comes." As the dipper holds the water, these ordinances hold and shape the truth.

It has been said that heresy, aberration, and doctrinal inexactitude always begin in a false interpretation, presentation, and administration of the ordinances. If a church can keep the ordinances doctrinally correct as it is in the Bible, the church will be correct in every other area of doctrinal life. The church is to be washed in the laver of the Word, administering the ordinances according to the revelation of God.

CHURCH SUPPORT IS TO BE WASHED IN THE LAVER OF THE WORD

Supporting the church is to be done according to the Word of God, washed in the laver of the Word. Do you suppose the Lord gave us a vast world mission assignment and then left us without any knowledge of how we are to sustain it and to support it? That is why the church so often turns to so many different ways to support itself. I listen on the radio as I go over the city and sometimes a man will say: "This vial of oil I have blessed. I have seen it heal the sick. I have seen it make short legs come out and be as long as they ought to be. I have seen withered hands anointed with this oil and be straightened out. I have seen cancers that were healed, blind eyes opened, and deaf ears unstopped with this oil." Then he says: "You send me $12.00 and I will send you a bottle of this holy ointment. Put it on wherever you ache and wherever you are sore and it will heal you." Just think of raising money for

Christ Loved the Church

God like that! Or they will say: "I have a little prayer cloth over which I have prayed. Put it whever you hurt and it will heal you. Send me a gift, I will send you a prayer cloth, and it will make you well." I have to bow my head and ask the Lord to forgive me in how I react. Is that what I ought to do to raise support for the work of the Lord? Are we going to bless vials of oil, little pieces of red cloth, and a thousand other like things to finance God's church? No! "Christ also loved the church, and gave himself for it." He washed it in the laver of the Word.

We are to support the work of God according to the Word of God. First Corinthians 16:1 says, ". . . as I have given order to the churches of Galatia, even so do ye." The Apostle Paul continued, "Upon the first day of the week let every one of you lay by him in store, as God hath prospered him." On the first day of the week a proportion of my money is to be set aside for God. It belongs to God. It does not belong to me. It is not mine. It is His. Some of us can give more; our proportion is greater. Some of us less; our proportion is smaller. Some of us are more able, some of us are less able, but if we do as God says in the Word, we all can share our part and God will bless us.

Sometimes a man says, "I can give half of what I have." Sometimes there will be a man who will say, "I can give ninety per cent of what I have and live on the rest." Somebody one time said, "You know, I might be able to give a fifth but I tell you it would be hard for me to give a tenth." I would settle for that! God's way is to begin with a truth. "On the first day of the week let every one of you lay by him in store, as God has prospered him." This is a proportion that I set aside for the Lord. Our people believing the Bible as they do would always start with a tenth. This belongs to God. Then as the Lord would make me able and as He would press upon my heart the need for other purposes in the kingdom, I would try to give to that also. But the truth is God's proportion and it is sacred for Him. Do as God says.

CHURCH MEMBERS ARE TO BE WASHED
IN THE LAVER OF THE WORD

Last, by the Word of God I am to come into the assembly of Christ, being a part of it, joining myself to it. This is a part of the commandment, the expectation, and the call of God. The Lord added to the church those who publicly, openly gave their hearts to Him. The Lord added to the church such as should be saved. The Lord has commanded us openly to be a part of the household of faith. If I refuse, then the church ceases to live for me and for Christ. It does not live apart from my public, open acknowledgement and association. "Ah, but Pastor, you do not understand. I can worship God out here in a part of the family of God in some mountain retreat somewhere." I would not argue. I am just saying that it is not that way in the Bible. From the beginning there has been always that public association with the assembly of God's people. It has never been otherwise since New Testament times. Without the assembling of God's people, the church would die. It would disappear.

In the Old Testament the blood of the Passover was openly displayed. Those who belonged to God were publicly set apart. In the New Testament a public confession is a part of the experience of salvation itself. "If you will confess Me before men I will confess you before My Father in heaven," said Jesus (Matt. 10:32, 33). The Apostle Paul put it in the heart of our experience of salvation: "If thou shalt confess with thy mouth the Lord Jesus (openly, publicly), and shalt believe in thine heart that God hath raised him from the dead, thou shalt be saved. For with the heart man believeth unto righteousness; and with the mouth confession is made unto salvation" (Rom. 10:9, 10). I cannot understand many of the deep mysteries of the secrets of God, but some things I can easily see, such as why it is that God would purpose for us openly and publicly to associate ourselves with the house of faith and with the church. In Revelation 12 we read, "And they overcame him (the great adversary) by the blood of the Lamb, and by the word of their testimony" (v. 11). When a man comes forward and stands before men and angels, something happens to his own heart and something happens to those who see and hear his confession of faith. The man is avowedly a publicly professed believer in Christ and he belongs to the church of the Lord. Thus the church grows and is blest.

There were two lawyers, one was named Will and one was named Tom. In the town where they lived there was a tabernacle revival meeting. One night down the aisle went the lawyer Will, gave his hand to the preacher and his heart to God, accepted

Christ as his Saviour, and stood there before the congregation under the tabernacle confessing his faith in the Lord Jesus. Early the next morning Will got up to go down to his office to gather together his personal belongings to move out, thus dissolving the partnership. For he said in his heart: "My partner, Tom, is such a bitter critic of the church and of Christ and of God, I do not think I can stand it. His ridicule, his sarcasm, and all of those bitter things he says about God will be more than I could take, so it is best for me to gather my things, move out, and dissolve the partnership." So he got up early in the morning to go down to the office to gather his things and to move out. On the way down the street he met the last man in the world he wanted to see. He met his partner, Tom. Tom looked at him and said, "Will, why are you up so early and where are you going?" Will replied, "Tom, last night I found God. I gave my heart to Christ and I am a Christian now. Tom, I know how you feel about God, about Christ, about the church, and about the people of the Lord. You are bitter and sarcastic and I just do not think I can live under such criticism. So I got up early this morning before I thought you would be down, to gather my things and to dissolve the partnership. That is why I am on the way this morning." Tom replied: "Will, you did not know it nor did anyone know it. But last night I went to that meeting and stood outside the tabernacle. I saw you go down the aisle and give your hand to the preacher, standing before the people, confessing your faith in God. You and I have been partners all these years. We have always stood side by side. We have been through numerous cases, trials, and difficulties. Will, when I saw you standing up there by yourself last night it just seemed to me that I ought to be standing by your side. The reason I have come early in the morning is that I thought maybe you would teach me how to be a Christian, to believe in God, and be saved." "And they overcame him by the blood of the Lamb, and by the word of their testimony."

There is no little child who publicly confesses his faith in Christ but that people are affected by it. The house, the home, the friends, the neighbors, all, God blesses through that testimony. It is according to the Word. "Christ also loved the church, gave himself for it," and washed it in the laver of His Word. Will you do it God's way?

Chapter 32

THE HEAVENLY MYSTERY

> This is a great mystery: but I speak concerning Christ and the church. (Eph. 5:32)

The letter of Ephesians is an encyclical. It is actually addressed to all of the churches. The copy of the manuscript we have, when the New Testament was collected, happened to have Ephesus written in the address. In this letter that discusses the body of Christ, the church, Paul delineates two important mysteries. One of them is in the third chapter of the book. "If ye have heard of the dispensation of the grace of God which is given me to youward: How that by revelation he made known unto me the mystery (Greek *musterion*) . . ." (vv. 2, 3). To us a mystery is an enigmatic saying, a development or situation that baffles us. We do not understand. The word in the New Testament, however, has an altogether different meaning. A *musterion*, translated here "mystery," is a secret in the heart of God that was not revealed until God chose to disclose it. Paul says here that in the dispensation of the grace of God given to him, by revelation there was made known the mystery of the church, namely, that the Gentiles should be fellow heirs and of the same body and partakers of the same promise in Christ by the Gospel. The mystery, the secret kept in the heart of God, was that there should be created a new thing, a new body. It should be composed of Jew and Gentile, bond and free, male and female, old and young, rich and poor, altogether in one new living organism. The prophets did not see that. The church is not in the Old Testament. Paul avows that the church is a mystery, a secret kept in the heart of God until it was revealed to His holy apostles. The church is a New Testa-

The Heavenly Mystery

ment creation. It is something not revealed in the old covenant, the Old Testament, but the secret was revealed to the apostles when Christ called them to found the churches. That is the first mystery that Paul speaks of in this letter to Ephesus.

The second mystery concerns its nature. "This is a great mystery: but I speak concerning Christ and the church." What is that great mystery? Paul goes back to Genesis 2 and the creation of Eve. Having cited it and quoted from it, he says that is the mystery that is revealed in the creation of this new living institution, the church of Christ. Genesis 2:21 says, "And the LORD God caused a deep sleep to fall upon Adam, and he slept: and he took one of his ribs." (That word "rib" is one of the strangest translations I have ever seen. The Hebrew word translated here "rib" is the ordinary Hebrew word for "side." It is used commonly in the Old Testament — the "side" of the ark, the "side" of the tabernacle, the "side" of the temple, the "side" of the house. Yet the translation here is, "And he took one of his *ribs*." It is not translated "rib" anywhere else in the Bible. Why they chose to translate it "rib" here, I cannot find out.) The reading should be: "And he took [out of the side of Adam], and closed up the flesh instead thereof; And the [side], which the Lord God had taken from man, made he a woman, and brought her unto the man. And Adam said, "This is now bone of my bones, and flesh of my flesh: she shall be called Woman (*isha*), because she was taken out of Man (*ish*). Therefore shall a man leave his father and his mother, and shall cleave unto his wife: and they shall be one flesh." Then Paul adds in Ephesians the words, "This is a great mystery: but I speak concerning Christ and the church."

THE MYSTERY OF ORIGIN

First, the mystery of the church is a mystery of origin. The Lord took out of the side of Adam and made the woman, born in the wound and the scar of Adam. The church was taken out of the suffering, the sorrow, the blood, and the cross of our Lord. We were born in His redemptive grace. The mystery of our origin is out of the suffering and death of our Christ, from the wound and the scar in His side.

As you think of that, is it not an astonishing development that out of the execution and the indescribable suffering of Christ should be born this holy and heavenly institution, the church? Notice the contrast between the death of Christ and the death of the other philosophers and religionists who have founded great and lasting movements in the earth. Gautama Buddha, "the enlightened one," died in 483 B. C. at the age of eighty. He was traveling northeast of a sacred city of the Hindus on the Ganges River. Having eaten a large meal of pork, he fell violently ill and died. The rajahs cremated his body and buried him with noble honor. Confucius died at the age of seventy-two, five years later in 478 B. C. He became ill, went to his bed, lay there for seven days, and died. Neither one believed in God. Neither one believed in prayer. Confucius was buried in Shantung with honor and reverence. In about 400 B. C. the civil war between Sparta and Athens ended. There was a political reaction and in 399 B. C., at seventy years of age, Socrates died a beautiful and pleasant death — humanely he was drugged. The vote had been two hundred eighty-one against him and two hundred twenty for him. As he died he quietly philosophized with his friends. His last words were: "I owe Aeschaelus, the god of healing, a cock. Do not forget to pay it." In A. D. 632 Mohammed became violently ill with headaches and fever. He died unsensationally in his bed. He was buried in Medina, the most sacred spot in the earth to the Islamic worshiper outside of Mecca. Look at these deaths: the death of Buddha, the founder of Buddhism; the death of Confucius, the founder of Confucianism; the death of Socrates, the founder of Platonism; and the death of Mohammed, the founder of Islam. In no instance is there any redemption or grace ever attached to the death of any of them.

But the crucifixion and the agony of our Saviour was different. It is set apart. It is unique. It is the unsimilar and unduplicated. In the death of Christ there was born the redemption and the atonement of His people. Out of His suffering, from the scar in His side, there was taken and there was born the church. "This is a great mystery, but I speak concerning Christ and his church."

A Mystery of Nature

The mystery of the church is the mystery of nature. The Lord God looked over all of His creation but there was not found anything or anyone to be a real companion for Adam. "And the LORD God said, It is not good that the man should be alone; I will make him an help meet (suitable, fitted) for him" (Gen. 2:18). And the Lord God brought before Adam all of His creation in the living world; the fish, the fowls, and the beasts of the fields. And Adam named them. Then God adds again, "But for Adam there was not found an help meet for him" (2:20). So the Lord God made for Adam a help mate, a companion suitable for him, and brought her to him.

This is an identical thing as we are told of God in the creation of the man in the first place. As the Lord God had finished His work, the stars were shining in the heavens. The chalice of the firmament was ablaze with His glory. The earth was an arc of beauty and wonder. And yet, in all of God's fullness of creation, in the infinitude of His glory, in the handiwork, the lace work of His hands, there was nothing that loved Him in return, that thought His thoughts. An ocean cannot think God's thoughts. The Milky Way cannot express love to God. They are without response. They just glorify Him in their beauty and in the wonder of their infinitude. But for companionship, for responsive love, how could one look to an ocean or a star or a sidereal sphere? "And God said, Let us make man in our image, after our likeness" (Gen. 1:26), that He might speak our thoughts, that He might love and commune with us. So God made the man in His own image for fellowship, companionship, and response. It is that identical thing here in the story of Adam and the woman God made out of his side. There was not found in all of God's creation an help meet for him.

There was a little girl who wanted her mother to sleep with her. The mother said: "No, child. Here is your teddy bear. Now you just cuddle up with your teddy bear and go to sleep." And the little child replied: "But, Mother, it cannot cuddle back to me. I want somebody who can cuddle back to me." Somehow inanimateness does not respond.

Once I read the story of a little girl named Naomi who was born blind. Her mother had died and her father was rearing her. The father said that many times he would wake up in the middle of the dark of the night, and there standing by his bed as close as she could get, was that little girl standing in her little white nightgown, her hair flowing over her shoulder. She was standing there in the dark, for the days and the nights were alike to her. She just wanted to be close. "It is not good that the man should be alone; I will make him an help meet for him." And out of his side God created the woman and brought her to the man and he said, "This is now bone of my bones, and flesh of my flesh" (Gen. 2:23). "This is a great mystery, but I speak concerning Christ and his church."

We are the same in nature with our Lord. He took our nature and we possess His. In the beautiful and eloquent passage in Hebrews 2 the author writes: "For verily he took not on him the nature of angels; but he took on him the seed of Abraham. Wherefore in all things it behoved him to be made like unto his brethren, that he might be a merciful and a faithful high priest . . . in that he himself hath suffered being tempted, he is able to succour them that are tempted" (vv. 16-18). He took our nature. He was made one with us. He was born of a woman. He had a human mother. He grew up in an inhospitable world. The sun and its heat, the rain and its cold beat upon His head. The ground yielded for Him briars and thistles. He was crowned with thorns. He knew what it was to hunger, to thirst, to sorrow, to be hurt, to grieve. He was made like one of us. He took our human nature and He has given us His divine nature.

In the eloquent 1 Corinthians 15 the apostle writes, "And as we have borne the image of the earthy, we shall also bear the image of the heavenly" (15:49). We shall be like Christ. We shall see Him face to face, as He is. This house we live in will be buried, planted. It is planted in dishonor. It is raised in glory. It is planted in weakness. It is raised in power. It is planted a mortal body. It is raised a spiritual body. We have His nature. As the Apostle Peter wrote in his second letter, 1:3, 4, ". . . through the knowledge of him (Christ) . . . whereby are given unto us exceeding great and precious promises: that by these ye might be partakers of the divine nature." This is now, "bone of my bones and flesh of my flesh." We are like Him.

A Mystery of Vital Union

The mystery of the church is also the *musterion* of vital unity. We are members of His body, of His flesh, and of His bones. We are no longer two, but one flesh. "This is a great mystery, but I speak concerning Christ and his church." It is the mystery of a vital unity of oneness. There is no relationship in life comparable to that between a man and his wife. With invisible and enduring bonds, they are joined together. They share in the joys and sorrow, in the triumphs and successes, and in the defeats and despairs of life. They are one, one flesh. "This is a great mystery, but I speak concerning Christ and his church." We are one with Him. We are vital to Him. He cannot be without us. There could be no head without a body. There can be no Saviour without the saved. There could be no king without his subjects. There could be no shepherd without his flocks. We are vital to Christ. He needs us, His people, and we are one with Him. We are crucified with Him, we are buried with Him, we are raised with Him, we are ascended with Him, we reign with Him. If He is triumphant, we shall be triumphant. If He is victorious, we are victorious. If He inherits the kingdom, we are joint heirs.

This is the deep, abiding, spiritual meaning of the two ordinances of His church. In baptism we are buried and raised with our Lord. In the Lord's Supper we are identified with Him. Listen to Paul as he writes: "The cup of blessing which we bless, is it not the *koinonia,* the communion (the fellowship) of the blood of Christ? The bread which we break, is it not the communion, the *koinonia* (the sharing) of the body of Christ? For we being many are one bread, and one body: for we are all partakers of that one bread" (1 Cor. 10:16, 17). We are one with Him by an invisible bond. However it is with Christ, it is with us, for we also are one with Him. If He fails, we fail. If He is defeated, we shall be defeated. If the victory does not belong to Him, it shall not belong to us. But if He triumphs, we also shall triumph with Him. "Therefore shall a man leave his father and his mother, and shall be joined unto his wife and, they two shall be one flesh." "This is a great mystery, but I speak concerning Christ and his church."

A Mystery of Destiny

The mystery of the church is finally the mystery of an ultimate, a final, and an enduring salvation and assurance. We are one with Him to care, to nurture, to cherish. "For no man ever yet hated his own flesh, but nourisheth it and cherisheth it even as the Lord the church." "For we are members of his body, of his flesh, and of his bones." Even as Christ nourishes and cherishes the church, so every member of the body of Christ is treasured and loved by Him. Tell me, did you ever read in the Bible of the Lord saying: "Take these poor away. Take this flotsam and jetsam out of my sight. Take these sick and these ill, take them away"? The Scripture always says, "And he healed them all." Precious in His sight is every member of His body.

John the Apostle said that what Jesus did and what happened to the Lord were signs. They were deep, spiritual teachings. Here is one John describes. When the soldiers of the crucifixion came to Jesus and saw that He was already dead, they did not break His legs. When they had come to the other crosses they broke the legs of the first criminal, and of the other which was crucified with Him. But when they came to Jesus, He was so manifestly dead, they broke not His bones. John said, "And he that saw it bare record, and his record is true: and he knoweth that he saith true, that ye might believe. For these things were done, that the scripture should be fulfilled, A bone of him shall not be broken" (John 19:35, 36). This is a sign fulfilled in our Lord's body, the church. There shall not be one of the least of the members of the body of Christ that is lost or that is broken. It will not be. We may be the most hopeless and the most unworthy of God's children, but we belong to Christ. We are members of His body and as such He nourishes and cherishes us.

Look at our destiny: Christ caring for us, loving us, cherishing us, nourishing us, that He may present us to Himself some day a glorious church, having neither spot nor wrinkle, but holy and without blemish. This is our ultimate and final destiny.

One of the members of our church, a dear sainted woman, was in one of our hospitals. In a terminal illness she died. But the doctors used chemicals, tubes, medicines, massages, and all of those apparati and brought her back to life. When she came into consciousness for just awhile, she exclaimed, "Oh, and now I must die again!" What a strange persuasion some have that when our life is done and our task is ended that we then are to be plunged into a terrible "yonder," a horrible "out there!" If the human arrangers can just delay by five more breaths our escape, then may all of the science of the physicians, the chemists, and the pharmacists be brought to bear that we may take these five more breaths. O Lord, no! When the task is done and the life is ended and age has taken our faculties away, why is it not the comfort of the Christian that he be translated in victory, in triumph, to an upper and more glorious world, joined to Christ in glory? Our translation is our coronation day. It is a great consummation toward which all life inevitably moves.

For those outside of the Lord, death is a blackness. It is a despair, it is a defeat, it is an awesome prospect. It is death forever. But to the child of God, joined to the body of Christ, death is a triumph. It is our ultimate victory that some day all of us shall enjoy, shall experience. We cannot be lost. We belong to His body. We are members of His very frame. The Lord said, "And I give unto them eternal life; and they shall never perish" (John 10:28). If a man's head is above water, his feet cannot be drowned. If our Lord is in heaven, we cannot be lost though we are the very soles of His feet and the humblest and most unworthy of the household of faith. If He lives we also shall be saved and shall live with Him. We cannot be lost. Christ does not lose part of His members. We are joined to Him.

Trust God to see you through. He never lost a battle nor will He ever lose one of His members. His body shall be full and complete and we shall be a part of it. Bone of His bone, flesh of His flesh. Do you belong to Him? Have you given your heart to Jesus? Will you say: "Here I come to join myself to God. Here I am."? Make that choice and decision now in your heart. Find out the secret hid in the heart of God. Understand the great mystery. Become a part of Christ in His church.

Chapter 33

HONORING OUR PARENTS

> Children, obey your parents in the Lord: for this is right.
> Honour thy father and mother; which is the first commandment with promise;
> That it may be well with thee, and thou mayest live long on the earth.
> And, ye fathers, provoke not your children to wrath: but bring them up in the nurture and admonition of the Lord. (Eph. 6:1-4)

There is hardly a Greek word used in this passage but that is fraught with deep and significant import. "Children, *hupakouo* your parents." *Hupo* is the preposition for "under." (We spell it "hypo," beneath, under.) *Akouo* is the word "to hear." When the two are used in composition, *hupakouo,* it means to hear with submission, with bowing, with yieldedness, and thus "to obey." Children, listen in submission, in yieldedness, in obedience to your parents.

"Honour thy father and mother." The Greek word for "honor" is one of the most beautiful words in the language: "*Timao* thy father and mother." *Tim-e* is a word implying preciousness and dearness. It refers to something that is of great value and of great price. From the word *tim-e,* which means preciousness, dearness, of great value in price, came the word *timao* meaning "to honor, to reverence, to hold in infinite respect and esteem." "*Timao* thy father and mother." You see, a child could obey his parents out of fear. He could be recalcitrant, reluctant, unyielding and unwilling. But God says that the child is to obey the father and the mother in respect, in honor, in reverence. When you see that happen in life, it is like a breath of heaven.

Honoring Our Parents

One time I was preaching in Jacksonville, Florida, and the pastor there took me to one of the famous restaurants on the Eastern seaboard. As we walked into the lobby I saw beyond the cashier's desk a large portrait of a fine looking woman. The pastor said to me, "When we are seated, remind me to tell you the story of that woman." After we were seated at the table, I brought to his attention his promise to tell me that story. On a small, unprosperous farm in South Georgia there was a father, a mother, and a boy. The father died, and the mother took the boy to Jacksonville. They opened a little eating place downtown. They were such fine people that God blessed them. Their little restaurant flourished. They were persuaded to go to the edge of the city and build a very spacious and luxurious eating place. Before the restaurant was completed, the mother died. Just before her death she called her boy to her side and said: "Son, I want you to promise me one thing. When the beautiful restaurant is opened, will you promise me that in it you will never sell wine, or beer, or liquor?" The boy replied, "Mother, I promise." When the luxurious restaurant was completed and the customers began to come, there also came the representatives of the brewery and of the winery and of the distillery. They said to that boy, "You cannot run a luxurious restaurant like this unless you sell beer, wine, and liquor." In each instance the boy took the representative to the lobby and pointed to the picture of his mother and said: "I promised my mother before she died that I would never sell alcoholic beverages in this beautiful place. Before I break that promise, I will go back to the plow handles on that farm in Georgia." He honored his mother and God blessed her boy. One of the finest restaurants on the Eastern seaboard is that restaurant. It has the best reputation and serves the most delectable food. Honor, *timao*, hold in reverence and respect, in endearment and in preciousness, thy father and mother, "which is the first commandment with promise."

The first commandment: Thou shalt have no other gods before me. The second commandment: Thou shalt not make unto thee any graven image, neither shalt thou bow down thyself before it. The third commandment: Thou shalt not take the name of the Lord thy God in vain. The fourth commandment: Remember the Lord's holy day and keep it sacred for the worship of God. The fifth commandment is the first one with promise, Honor thy father and mother, reverence in endearment thy parents. What is the promise? "That it may be well with thee, and thou mayest live long on the earth."

This promise is a magnificent illustration of the value the Lord God places upon filial duty and devotion. The commandments were given for the shaping of the nation. The Lord could see as only God can see that the prosperity, perpetuity, and permanence of a nation lie in the filial devotion and respect of the children in the home. If there is want of respect in the home for the authority of parents, there will be want of respect in the nation among the citizens for the laws of the country. Bad children make bad citizens. The dissolution of the home makes for the decimation of the state. So the Lord wrote, "Honor thy father and mother in filial reverence, that it may be well with thee, and that thou mayest live long on the earth."

The word "fathers" has a generic meaning. The Bible, for example, will use the word "meat" to refer to all food. So the word "fathers" is used here in the sense of parents — fathers, and mothers. "Ye parents, provoke not to wrath, to exasperation, your children." Do not drive your children away until in frustration and despair they turn to do most anything. It is not unusual that a girl in a home will be so frustrated and in such despair that she runs off and marries the first boy who comes along in the hope of getting away. And, often a boy is driven out because of the uncompromising and sometimes uncaring attitude of his father and his mother. Ye parents, do not *parorgizo* your children, driving them to extremities, to bitterness. Provoke not your children to wrath, but rather *ektrepho* them.

It is sometimes strange how words are translated. In Ephesians 5:29 *ektrepho* is translated "nourish." Here the word is translated, "bring up." Bring up the children, nourish the children in the *paideia*, the discipline of act, the corrective instrumentality of bringing them up in the *nouthesia*, the appeal of word. First, *paideia*, by discipline by act. And then, *nouthesia*, by word and by appeal.

There are then two things in this passage that Paul has written. One, authority and respect in the home, reverence for parents. And the other, authority and respect before the Lord, reverence for our Lord. Children obey your parents "in the Lord," and ye parents bring them up in the nurture and admonition "of the Lord."

Authority and Discipline in the Home

First, then, is the authority and discipline in the home, and the answering respect and submission on the part of the children. The home defeats itself and the end for which it was created is destroyed, when there is lack of discipline on the part of parents and when there is no concession to authority on the part of the children. We mentioned that the Lord gave this to the nation, to the state. The situation in the home inevitably spills over into the state. I can illustrate the disciplinary necessity in the home by the disciplinary necessity in the state. As the ends of the home are frustrated for lack of discipline and concession of authority on the part of the child, so the ends of the state are destroyed, hopelessly so, when there is lack of authority, the enforcement of law, on the part of a magistrate, and when there is refusal to obey the law on the part of a citizen.

That is why I could never enter into the psychology, the thinking, of the desperate, violent, and revolutionary militants who seek to burn and to destroy, to overthrow, to root up. They offer nothing in place of what they sarcastically call "the establishment." They just destroy. They just ruin. They plunge the nation into anarchy. What I cannot understand is this: if they destroy the establishment and are successful in uprooting the order of our civilization and society, would it not be the same thing with whatever they substituted in its place? Would they not also burn and uproot that? Their program means nothing but a continuing anarchy. And that anarchy begins in the home. If there are to be obedient, law abiding citizens in the state, there must be yielded, obedient, submissive children in the home who reverence their parents and who accept the discipline and the authority of father and mother as a part of the law of God and the way of the just and blessed life.

But the parent must represent the right kind of authority. They are to *ektrepho* the children, nourish them, not to beat them into submission. I read a statistic last week of how many children (and they number so many) are killed every year by brutal, disciplinary beatings on the part of father and mother. *Ektrepho,* bring up the child, nourish the child in infinite patience, love, sympathy and compassion. Do not beat the child. Bring the child up in the *paideia,* discipline, firmness, and in *nouthesia,* the appeal, the word of exhortation of the Lord.

The child that is placed in your arms is so helpless, so immature, so without experience. Without your guiding and loving hand, the child would perish. You can do with a child as you choose. It is like a polished piece of metal on which you can engrave anything. It is like a page of a book upon which you can write anything. The child is like molding clay. You can shape it into anything.

I am not saying that environment is everything, for heredity also has a vast control over all that we do and all that we become. But, I am saying that you can take a child and, in teaching, you can make a child most anything: a cannibal, a communist, a convict. You can teach him how to cheat, how to steal, and how to lie. The child is largely you. Heredity, the spirit in the child, the makeup of the child, the background of genes in the child, has a lot to do with how the child turns out. But, under God, what that child becomes is largely what you teach him.

This is why the Lord said to Eli, "There will be destruction in your house because you refused to restrain your sons, Hophni and Phinehas" (1 Sam. 3). Is not it an unusual thing that that message should have been given to the little boy Samuel? "Samuel, Samuel," God called. And he said, "Speak, Lord, thy servant heareth." God replied, "I will destroy the house of Eli, the high priest at Shiloh. I will destroy the house of Eli because he did not discipline and did not restrain his sons, Hophni and Phinehas." Both of the boys were killed by the Philistines and, as you read the Scriptures, in the years that followed, the entire house of Eli was utterly destroyed. Ah, the responsibility that God lays on the father and the mother when the child is born in the home!

Authority and Discipline Before the Lord

Not only is there to be authority and discipline in the home, but also that authority and discipline is to be "in the Lord." Twice is that emphasized in this passage. Children, obey your parents *in the Lord.* There are two facts that are so salient in American society today. I wonder if they are related. Fact number one: the F. B. I. tells us that so much of the crime in America is done by young people below twenty-five years of age, and much of that figure by boys eighteen years of age and under. Is not that an astonishing thing, that the criminal element in America should be young people? Last year alone more than a million boys and girls entered careers of crime. That is the first fact. The criminal element in America is mostly youth. Fact number two: There are something like fourteen million children in America, between the ages of four and fourteen, who have no religious education whatsoever. They are not Mormons, they are not Catholics, they are not Jews, they are not anything. Is there any correlation or relevance between those two facts? Is it not the wisdom of God when He addresses the father and mother to nourish the child and to bring up the child in the *paideia*, the discipline, and in the *nouthesia*, the words of admonition of the Lord?

So many times do I see parents who say: "It is not my proposal to influence my child Godward, or upward, or Christward, or heavenward. I will just let the child choose for himself whether he loves God or not, or reads the Bible or not, or goes to church or not. There is no inclination on my part to influence the child. I want him to choose and decide for himself." Coleridge and a friend once were speaking of this and were looking at Coleridge's garden. It was full of weeds. The man said to Coleridge, "Why don't you dig up those weeds and plant flowers?" He said: "I don't want to prejudice the garden in favor of flowers. We just let it grow up as it is." *If you do not guide those children heavenward, Godward, Christward, churchward* you will be the only one who is neutral, who is not influencing them. Do not think otherwise but that the world will have its influence and its say. The infidel will have his influence and the criminal element will have its influence. The pimp, the procurer, the bookie, the chisler, the dope pusher will all have their influence and say. The streets of the city offer no diplomas, they confer no degrees, but they educate with terrible precision. If there is any hope for the citizenship of a nation, for the future of a government, and for the very fabric of society itself, it lies in the godly nurture and admonition of these children under loving endearing hands of their fathers and their mothers.

Take the child, and encourage the child to pray, to love God, to read the Bible, to attend church.

> You ask me why I go to church;
> I give my mind a careful search.

Because I need to breathe the air
Where there is an atmosphere of prayer.

I need the hymns that churches sing;
They set my faith and hope on wing.

They keep old truths and memory green,
Reveal the work of things unseen.

Because my boy is watching me
To know whatever he can see

That tells him what his father thinks.
And with his eager soul he drinks

The things I do in daily walks,
The things I say in daily talks.

If I with him the church will share,
My son will make his friendships there.

The Child's Immortal Soul

When we kneel and work, minister and help, pray and guide, teach and nourish, admonish and appeal in the life of a child, literally, we are touching eternity. The soul of that child is immortal. Once the child is born, his life never ends. The soul and the life of a child are forever, immortal, eternal. Here is a letter I received written by a grandmother.

Dear Dr. Criswell:

In January of this year of 1971 I was in Baylor Hospital with my six-year-old grandson who was fighting a losing battle with leukemia. We were listening to your Sunday morning message concerning a new world and a better world up there in heaven, which made a great impression on the little boy Cary Lee. So much was he impressed that it caused him to ask many questions. He asked how anyone would get to this better world. I explained the best I could. Later he asked if he might come to God all by himself. The next day he said that God had talked to him and asked him not to be afraid, and told him that He would be coming for him soon. The lad smiled as he told me how warm and soft

God's arms felt around his shoulders as God spoke to him. He wanted me to tell his mother, 'Mommy, please don't cry when I go away.' He asked that we give his clothes to his little friend, his art supplies to the church, and 'Please don't give my little shoes away.' He assured me everything was all right and talked about God coming for him calmly and unafraid. He was laid to rest Easter Sunday in Palmer, Texas, after two years and two months of battle with pain and suffering.

Thank you so much for that message, and I am thankful for a loving God who is able to help a little boy understand and accept God's plan for his life. If you have a copy of that Sunday's message, I would appreciate one very much. May God continue to bless you in your work.

Sincerely,
Ethel Davis

There are many letters that come to me, as you know, from the television and radio service. Some write, "We have found the Lord." Others say: "I have given my life to God. I have entered the ministry." Others will say, "I am now being appointed a missionary." So many beautiful things are written to me as God blesses the outreach of this word over television and radio. But, I have never received a letter that humbled me more in all of my life than that letter. A little boy, facing death, found in the message that assurance and that comfort and that hope, that, if we look up in faith and trust to Christ, the Lord will see us through. Calmly and unafraid, he accepted that sentence from heaven as the will of God for his life.

Am I not correct in this judgment? That when you hold the life of a child in your hands, you are holding eternity, destiny, and immortality? That is why we have the inspired Word: "And ye parents *ektrepho,* nourish, bring up the children, in the *paideia,* the discipline, in the *nouthesia,* the word of appeal in the Lord."

Chapter 34

STRONG IN THE LORD

Finally, my brethern, be strong in the Lord, and in the power of his might. (Eph. 6:10)

All of Paul's epistles are divided into two parts. The first part is doctrinal. He expounds the will and mind of God. The second part is always practical admonition. In the long list of precepts by which Paul concludes the second half of this letter to the church at Ephesus, he finally comes to this magnificant passage of rhetorical grandeur. So splendid is it that the passage is actually lessened by exegesis and exposition. But we shall look at it closely.

Words of Strength

Let us look at some of the words Paul uses. The reason we look at these words is that they mean far more if we can see the exact syllable that the Holy Spirit inspired and then place it in our language and in our thoughts. It is most difficult to take a word from one language and make it mean exactly what it originally meant in another language. "Be strong in the Lord." The command, "be strong," is the present tense, second person, plural, imperative mood and passive voice of *endunamao*. *Endunamao* actually and literally means "to clothe oneself with power." In the passive voice the subject is acted upon. In the King James translation one might think it refers to self effort. Make an effort to be strong in the Lord. There is no approach to the real idea one would gain from that translation. It is in the passive voice. The subject is acted upon. We are "to be strengthened in the Lord." That word is used regarding the Apostle Paul in Acts 9 after he was saved, went into Arabia, and then returned to Damascus. Acts 9:19 says that "he

Strong in the Lord

was strengthened," *endunamao*. That is, the power of the Lord God came upon him. That word is used in Romans 4. Paul is describing Abraham who was a hundred years old and his wife who was ninety years old. "He staggered not at the promise of God through unbelief" (that he should have a son by Sarah) and (then the word is used) he *endunamao* "was strong in faith" (v. 20). God helped him to believe. That is the word here in Ephesians: *endunamao*. We are strengthened. It is something God does for us, something that human nature in itself cannot do. We are strengthened in the Lord and in the power of His might.

What is the difference between power (*kratos*) and might (*exousia*)? *Kratos*, translated here "power," is manifest power or dominion. In those marvelous doxologies, as in 1 Peter 4:11, it is written, "To whom be praise and *kratos*." *Kratos* there means "dominion." In Revelation 1:5, 6 we read, "Unto him that loved us, and washed us from our sins in his own blood, . . . to him be glory and *kratos*," that is, "dominion," "manifest power."

On the other hand, *exousia*, translated "might," is inherent power. In 2 Thessalonians 1:9 Paul speaks of the day when the Lord comes in "the glory of his power," The word used is *exousia*, "inherent power." Be strengthened therefore in the Lord, in the *kratos*, "the dominion," and in the *exousia*, "the inherent power of God."

"Put on the whole armour of God, that ye may be able to stand against the wiles of the devil." "Wiles" is one of the most interesting words in the translation, but it is a limping kind of translation. The word is *methodeia*, "method." *Methodeia* literally means "to follow after a thing systematically; to learn it, to follow it, to write it down, to analyze it, to systematize it." The word came to have an evil meaning, as to follow after with cunning deceit and trickery. *Methodeia* refers to the systematic evil of Satan. Someone once asked me: "In the temptations of the Lord, Satan promised Jesus the kingdoms of the world and the glory of them if He would fall down and worship him. Did Satan have that power and glory to give to Christ?" My answer was very plain and simple, "Yes. It was no temptation or trial at all if Satan did not have the glory to offer." Paul, in 2 Corinthians 4 calls Satan the god of this world. Do you believe that? Look around you. Do you see anything more universal than death? Satan is the god of this world. Do you see anything more universal than sin, pain, or suffering? This world, in the heavenlies, in the celestials, is afflicted with *methodeia,* a systematic methodical trickery of evil presided over by the spirits of the abyss under the leadership of Satan.

Conflict at the Heart of the Universe

My brethren, there is conflict at the very heart of this world. "For we wrestle not against flesh and blood, but against principalities, against powers, against the rulers of the darkness of this world, against spiritual wickedness in high places." All of those are names of hierarchical, evil angels in the heavenlies. There is conflict and war at the very heart of the universe. We cannot escape it, we cannot flee from it. If we go to the moon we will find that conflict among us there. If we finally get to Mars we will find that same conflict among us there. If we explore the heavens and build space stations in the sky they will be used for war and for purposes of destruction. The history of the world is written in blood, every page of it. In the days of the Hittites, the Elamites and the Sumerians; in the days of Tiglath-pileser, Shalmaneser, Sennacherib, Ashurbanipal; in the days of Nabopolassar and Nebuchadnezzar; in the days of Cyrus and Xerxes; in the days of Phillip of Macedon and Alexander the Great; in the days of Cassander, Antiochus, Lysimachus, Ptolemy, and Seleucus; in the days of Pompey, Caesar, and Hannibal; in the days of Attila and Genghis Khan and Kubla Khan; in the days of Charlemagne, Napoleon, and Wellington; in the days of Bismarck, Kaiser Wilhelm II, Hitler, and Tojo; there is nothing but the usual story of conflict and war. "In the days of peace, prepare for war." There is conflict at the very heart of this universe. All history is surely written in blood.

Why is the story so tragic? Because of personal pride. Sin began in the heart of Lucifer when he lifted himself up against God in pride. Nebuchadnezzar said, "Is not this great Babylon which I have built for my glory and for my excellent majesty?" That is pride. Alexander the Great sat on the banks of the Indus River and wept because there were no more worlds to conquer. That is pride. Imagine the thrill that Hitler felt when the youth of Germany by the hundreds of thousands raised their hands in salute and then called in thunderous tones, "Heil Hitler!"

Why is war so universal? Because of a yearning for national supremacy. Hamilcar took his little boy, Hannibal, and made him swear undying hatred and destruction of the Roman empire. That is desire for national supremacy. Japan, in the Second World War, fought for her place in the sun, for national supremacy. There is something inherent in the human spirit that drives toward oppression, conquest, and domination.

> Sound, sound the clarions, fill the fife.
> Let all the trembling world proclaim —
> There is more glory in one hour of strife,
> Than in an age without a name.

When Clovis, king of France, had his army baptized, his warriors held up their fists above the water to wield their battle axes as never before. It was to say, "This arm is unbaptized." And they fought as furiously as they ever had done before. Conflict and strife is at the very heart of the universe.

CONFLICT IN THE HEART OF MAN

Conflict and civil war is also in the Christian life and in the Christian faith. "Finally, my brethren, be clothed in the power of God and in the *kratos* of His *exousia*. Put on the whole *panoplia* (translated here 'armour'), put on the whole *panoplia* of God that you may be able to stand against the *methodeia*, . . . (the system of destruction of the devil)." For our war, our fights, and our conflicts are not against flesh and blood. Our enemy is not something one can seize with his hands and choke it to death, or take a sword and cut it asunder, or fire a sub-machine gun and mow it down. Our war is against principalities and powers and rulers of darkness, spiritual thrones and influences in even the heavenly places.

The Christian warfare, therefore, is internal. It is in us. It is a civil war in our own souls. In Galatians 5 and in Romans 8, Paul will describe the two natures on the inside of you. You are two, you are not one. You are two natures, two persons. And these two persons war against one another, the apostle said. Sometimes people think that because of the depravity of their own souls, even after they are Christians, after they are saved, that they have not been genuinely saved. It is the opposite. Because you have that conflict and that war in your soul is a sure sign that you are saved. This war is in ourselves. The battlefield is in the world around us. Worldliness: how does one grasp it, or hold it, or shoot it, or murder it, or cut it, or decimate it? Worldliness is an influence. It is a spiritual reality. It is an atmosphere and we live in it. The world does not lend itself to praise, to piety, or to prayer. Worldliness is the enemy to God and we live in the heart of worldliness. The conflict reaches into the realm of the spirit world above us, beyond us, around us, beneath us, and within us. The very world, unchained and invisible, wars against the child of God. Why was the Lord driven out into the wilderness? Because He had taken upon Himself our nature and had to be confronted with the trials of the Evil One. The Christian warfare is inside and it is outside and it is spiritual and of a spiritual nature. We have to be tested.

How To Be Strengthened

In presenting that conflict Paul says, "Finally, my brethren, *endunamao,* be strengthened." How? How does a Christian wage war and fight and how does he stand against such insuperable opponents and enemies and decimating avengers as those found in spiritual hosts? Could it be that we can war with physical strength? The time was when a man was judged and his value was ascertained by his physical strength. Can you imagine how the exploits of Samson must have thrilled the people of his day? I can remember when I was a boy that every boy talked about who could whip whom. Even the adults were somewhat like that. But physical prowess is a passing, insignificant nothingness. The Prussian monarch with his seven-foot grenadiers today would but make for a submachine gun a bigger target. Physical excellence is nothing. As I go around the world and look at these walled cities, I cannot help but think, "Just exactly what would that physical strength be against a modern atomic bomb?" The physical confrontation is nothing. The height of the wall emphasizes its insignificance and the vanity of the purpose for which it was built. The strength cannot be physical.

Shall we war with weapons of the intellect and of the mind? I do not deny that brilliance of intellect charms and captivates. The Greeks had a saying, "*Gnosis esti dunamis,*" "Knowledge is power." Socrates taught that if one actually knew, he actually

Strong in the Lord

would be perfect. Having known, having been taught, being knowledgeable, he would always make the right decision. That is the basic philosophy of Socrates. Do you not wish that could be so? Oh, that warfare could be nothing but a matter of teaching, of knowledge, of understanding. The problem lies in that our minds and our intellect are just as fallen as our anatomical frame.

Actually, the mind can understand nothing. Our cognitive faculties are of no consequence and significance. There is not a vital question that I can ask and the mind can answer. The mind, the understanding, the intellect cannot enter into beginnings and origins. The mind and the intellect and the understanding cannot even enter into the mysteries that we see around us. For example, how do beautiful flowers appear out of mud and mire? You see it but you do not understand it. It is a mystery into which the mind cannot enter. One cannot burnish a lampstand and make it give light. All the lampstand can do is to hold up the light. Nor is there light in the mind itself. It is but a lampstand in which God places the light of His truth and grace and redemptive glory.

How am I to be strengthened in the warfare of the soul and of the life and of the world? *Endunamao,* be clothed in the might and in the power, in the dominion and in the inherent strength of the Lord. Our strength must be something that comes from God. Our victory is not something we can achieve for ourselves in our weak and fallen natures. A brawny muscle may be able to tunnel through a mountain, a brilliant intellect may be able to grapple with mathematical problems, but in facing the warfare in which we are engaged, we need God's help in our souls. This warfare is beyond appeal to our human ableness and endowment. If we win, victory must come from God.

If God is to do it, how? The Scriptures plainly reply. "God has spoken once and twice have I heard it, that power belongeth to God." "All authority, all power is given unto me in heaven and in earth." That *kratos,* that dominion, and that *exousia,* that inherent authority and strength, God gives to us. There is no sweeter passage in God's Book than John 1:12, 13 "But as many as received him (believed in Him, trusted Him, took Him), to them gave he power (the authority, the privilege) to become the sons of God; . . . born, not of blood, nor of the will of the flesh, nor of the will of man, but of God." It is a strength from the outside, from heaven, a strength in the Lord. It builds itself upon the rock of Christ. It sees things invisible and eternal. It endures as beholding Him who is invisible, and it triumphs in the power of the Lord. It kneels in prayer. It communes with heaven. It searches the Word of God for the divine secrets and the mysteries of His revelation. It appeals to us all in the call and work of the Lord. The humblest, the most unlearned and untaught, the poorest, the finest, the most intellectual, the most academic, the most elevated, the most cultivated, the most gifted — from all of us that appeal to God needs to be made. "Be strengthened in the Lord."

I remember the marvelous address of Admiral Nimitz as he stood on the battleship *Missouri* in Tokyo Bay the second day of September, 1945, when Japan capitulated and the war was done. He was the head Admiral, the chief of all the Naval operations in the Pacific. He closed that wonderful address with words something like these: "Close to my headquarters in Guam, in a little green valley, there is a military cemetery. I look out my window on that little valley and I see those ordered rows of white crosses. I walk among those fallen comrades: soldiers, marines, and sailors; and I read their names." Then he named a long list of men — ordinary American boys. And he said: "They fought together as comrades in arms. They died together. And now they sleep together in death. This day our victory, our triumph, is the fruit of their dedicated lives." That is exactly what God calls us to in the warfare of the Lord. We are humble, ordinary people locked together in a common determination — brothers in arms in Christ.

> Am I a soldier of the cross,
> A follower of the Lamb,
> And shall I fear to own His cause,
> Or blush to speak His name?
>
> Must I be carried to the skies
> On flow'ry beds of ease,
> While others fought to win the prize
> And sailed thro' bloody seas?
>
> Are there no foes for me to face?
> Must I not stem the flood?
> Is this vile world a friend to grace,
> To help me on to God?

> Sure I must fight if I would reign,
> Increase my courage, Lord;
> I'll bear the toil, endure the pain,
> Supported by Thy Word.

"Finally, my brethren, *endunamao*, be strengthened, be clothed in the *kratos*, in the dominion, and in the *exousia*, in the power of the Lord." That is your invitation from God. Join hands with Christ and march to glory and to victory with Him.

Chapter 35

WAR IN THE SPIRIT WORLD

> For we wrestle not against flesh and blood, but against principalities, against powers, against the rulers of the darkness of this world, against spiritual wickedness in high places. (Eph. 6:12)

Let us look first at the text, the words the apostle was inspired to use. *Pale* is the Greek word for "wrestle." It is not an impersonal antagonism or act; it is most personal. Wrestling is a contact sport, and *pale* means face to face combat, hand to hand, foot to foot, wrestling unto death. This personal confrontation is emphasized by Paul's use of the word *pros*, we wrestle not "against." In the Greek the verse reads first *haima* then *sarkos*, first "blood" and then "flesh." *Pros* means "face to face." "We wrestle not against flesh and blood, but against," and then he names here a hierarchy of evil, fallen spirits and angels.

One order of evil angels Paul calls *archas*. It means "the head ones," "the leading ones." Another order Paul calls *exousia*, translated here "powers." The word refers to an order characterized by inward ableness and endowment. In themselves they are powerful, *exousia*. Another order of evil angels Paul calls *cosmokratoras*. *Cosmos* is "world," and *kratas* is "powers." Placed together the word refers to the world rulers of darkness. Is not that a strange revelation? The invisible and unseen rulers who lie back of the turmoil and conflict we see in this world are evil and fallen angels. Sometimes one persuades himself that surely the leadership of the world must lie in gracious and good hands. Then he picks up any newspaper and reads of an outbreak of violence and war. Conflict, *cosmokratoras*, the rulers of this world, are back of it all. Another order of evil angels Paul calls *pneumatika*. The word refers to spiritual beings of wickedness. *Epouranios*, translated here "high places" is literally "in the heavenlies." The whole earth is covered with these unseen and invisible enemies of darkness. The idea is staggering and terrifying.

Paul is saying: "Your enemies are not material, they are nonmaterial. They are not visible, they are invisible. They do not have body and form, they are spirit." A material antagonist, Paul would avow, is nothing. It is trivial, insignificant. The church for three hundred years lived and prospered under vicious and violent attacks and persecution. There has been no era in Christendom, in the history of the church, when the church was so under attack as in the first three Christian centuries under the fierce persecution of the Roman Empire. Material antagonists are nothing. They are insignificant and inconsequential. Paul knew what it was to have material, physical, and corporeal enemies. He says that in Ephesus "I fought with wild beasts." He spoke of having been beaten five times with forty stripes less one and thrice beaten with Roman rods. Physical warfare to the apostle was not even to be spoken of. The real enemies that he faced were invisible and unseen. Not flesh and blood, but *archas, exousias, cosmokratoras, pneumatika,* the hierarchy of invisible, evil, and fallen spirits. There is a revelation in the whole Word of God that outside of us and beyond us there are those that attack us, waste us, and destroy us.

EVIL REVEALED THROUGHOUT THE BIBLE

In the Garden of Eden, beyond the gates, is a subtle and sinister spirit. The story of sin and evil does not begin in Eden. The story begins in the age of the ages beyond the foundation and creation of the world. When Eden is presented in the pages of the Bible, outside the gate there is already present an evil, diabolical, and fallen spirit. He uses the serpent to beguile and betray our first parents.

In the story of Job one sees all of the providences that overwhelm him: the wind that blew his house down, the fires that burned up his property, the thieves that took away his flocks and his herds, and the disaster that destroyed his children. To Job, as to us, they look like providences of life. These things happen because unseen, unknown, and invisible to us there is an incorporeal enemy. He accuses Job in the presence of God Himself. He afflicts the sainted man of the east.

In Zechariah 3 the prophet saw Joshua, God's high priest, who ministered before the Lord. He saw him standing before God dressed in filthy garments and Satan standing at his right hand to oppose him, an invisible and unseen enemy to us, but nonetheless real.

In His temptation the Lord is driven into the wilderness to face an antagonist. It is the devil. We wrestle not against flesh and blood, but against incorporeality, against the unseen, invisible world that presses us on every side.

In the revelation of God that unseen and invisible world is itself a scene of violent conflict and war. Apparently through the ages there is war, antagonism, and conflict at the heart of the universe and we are an inexorable part of that violent confrontation. In Daniel we are told of Michael standing as a prince for God's people, Israel. He is opposed by the princes of the nations of the world. Think of that! The mighty archangel Michael was so opposed that he could not bring to Daniel an immediate answer to his supplication and prayer of intercession. Michael, opposed by the princes of darkness! In the Revelation there is war in heaven. Michael and his angels war against the dragon and his angels. The conflict endures to the consummation of the age. In the revelation of God there are two opposing hierarchies, two opposing ranks of soldier angels, two groups of celestial beings created before God created us. They are the hosts of heaven and they are divided into two parts: those who remain unfallen and those who have fallen into evil and rebellion. We speak first of what the revelation will say about those who are unfallen, who are still faithful to the Lord, the angels of glory, the hosts of heaven, these who follow in the train of our Lord.

ANGELS OF GLORY

Some of those angels are named seraphim, a Hebrew word meaning "the burning ones." The seraphim stand in the presence of God and do obeisance, covering their faces with their wings and covering their feet with their wings. With wings on their backs, they hover in the presence of God crying: "Holy, holy is

War in the Spirit World

the Lord of hosts. The whole earth is filled with His glory." The seraphim pay homage to the exaltation of God.

Cherubim are another rank of angels. They were the ones who were placed at the eastern gate of the Garden of Eden when our first parents were driven out. Their figures were woven in tapestry in the Tabernacle and in the Temple. Two of them faced the mercy seat above the Ark of the Covenant, and their overarching wings touched. They are depicted in Ezekiel 1 and 10. In the Book of the Revelation, what a disappointment to see that word *zoa*, translated "beasts." It ought to be translated "living ones." The four of them represent all of the story of the history of mankind in the earth. They are the cherubim. Wherever the cherubim are presented, they are symbols and tokens of God's love, grace, mercy, and forgiveness. They are the ones who in God's grace and mercy represent us and the mercy and love of God that He sends down to us.

One angel is called the "archangel." In 1 Thessalonians 4 the apostle says that we are to be raised from the dead by the voice of the archangel. There is only one of them in the Bible called by that name, and that is Michael. Five times we see his name in the Bible: three times in the Book of Daniel, one time in Jude, and one time in the Revelation. Michael stands as the guardian angel for the people of the Lord; he is the archangel.

Gabriel presents himself to Zechariah the priest, the father of John the Baptist, as the messenger who stands in the presence of God. Four times is Gabriel named in the Bible: twice in the Book of Daniel and twice in Luke. In all four instances he is identified with the redemptive work of Christ.

Besides the seraphim, the cherubim, the archangel, and Gabriel the messenger of the Lord, there are innumerable hosts of other angels. In the Scriptures so often they are presented as being uncounted, innumerable, infinite in number. The Scriptures say that they were created by God from before the beginning of the foundation of the world. When the Lord created the universes, when He flung them out into space, into orbits and galaxies, the angels magnified the handiwork of God. They exhibited the glory of the Lord. The Scriptures say that when the Lord created the world, the angels were there to rejoice and sing together and to look with wonder and astonishment upon the handiwork of God. They are innumerable. In Hebrews 12 it says that we shall some day come "to the general assembly and church of the firstborn, [whose names] are written in heaven, and to an innumerable company of angels." In the Revelation they are described as ten thousand times ten thousand and thousands of thousands. The Greek word used there is "myriad." In the English language "myriad" means "an uncounted number." Myriad times myriads times myriads and then thousands times the myriad; thus, the number of angels in the ranks of God are infinite.

They are also powerful. In the story of the seige of Hezekiah and Jerusalem under the iron hand of Sennacherib the bitter Assyrian, there is an interesting revelation. The people of the Lord prayed earnestly. That night in answer to the prayers of Hezekiah and Isaiah the prophet, only *one* angel passed over the hosts of the Assyrians and 185,000 dead corpses were counted the next morning. Just *one* angel did it. When I think of that I am astonished at what the Lord said in Matthew 26:53. Turning to Simon Peter, Jesus said: "Put up the sword. For could I not ask my Father and He would send me more than twelve legions of angels?" Each legion manned at the full accompaniment would be 6,000 men. Twelve legions would be 72,000 angels. Only one angel, passing over an army, left 185,000 dead. The power of the angels of God!

In Hebrews 1:14 angels are called "ministering spirits" sent from God to shepherd, to guard, and to keep God's saints. For those of us who place our trust in the Lord, these angels by the uncounted millions are ministering spirits to sustain, to care for, to keep, to help, and to guide. It was an angel that ministered to the Lord after the forty days of temptation. It was an angel that comforted the Lord in Gethsemane. It was an angel that opened the iron door prison for Simon Peter in the Book of Acts. It was an angel that stood by the Apostle Paul in the hour of great trial and ultimate deliverance. It was an angel that gave to John, the sainted apostle on the isle of Patmos, the apocalyptic revelation. When John fell down to worship him, the angel said: "No, for I am thy fellow-servant and of those who keep the faith in the Lord." Is not that an astonishing thing? When John sought to worship at the feet of the angel, the angel identified himself with us and called us fellow servants. They work with us. They live with us. They guide and guard and keep us, the angelic hosts of glory, the ministering spirits of heaven.

EVIL ANGELS

Do you not wish we could stop there? But the Biblical revelation does not stop there. At the heart of heaven itself is evil. At the heart of the universe is violent and internal conflict. There are other angels, other princes, and other spirits. They are as evil, dark, bitter, and implacable as the angels of God are merciful, sympathetic, and shepherdly. They are evil spirits. They are fallen angels. "For we wrestle not against flesh and blood, but against principalities, against powers, against the rulers of this world of darkness."

First and above all is the prince of the power of the air, Lucifer, *diabolos*, our accuser. Satan is his name and he is the most powerful of all the princes that God created. He is above all of them. That is why in the Jude epistle we read, "Yet Michael the archangel, when he disputed with the devil about the body of Moses, durst not bring against him a railing accusation" (v. 9). Even Michael the archangel dare not confront Satan. But he said: "The Lord rebuke thee." The prince that is the most powerful of all that God made is Lucifer. His name is Satan, *diabolos*.

The presentation of Satan in the Middle Ages is sheer, unadulterated, gross caricature. In those medieval plays he was always introduced as someone who had horns, a forked tail, a red suit, and a leer upon his face. I presume that pleases him because it hides his actual identity. Nothing could be further from the truth. Satan is called in 2 Corinthians 11 "an angel of light." And in 1 Corinthians 4 he is called, "the god of this world." He is brilliant, he is gifted, he is shrewd, his strategy is almost unassailable, unapproachable.

And apparently he always wins. He won in the Garden of Eden, and he wins over the human race. Death is universal. Pain, misery, and heartache are universal. He presides over the dark, sullen, joyless stream of humanity that continues on in its tormented way until finally it loses itself in the darkness of the grave. Apparently Satan wins — always. The ultimate end of every life is to die, to fall into the arms of corruption and death. This is the strategy and the victory of Satan, the archenemy of God, the accuser of the brethren, the invisible and the implacable, incorporeal enemy of the human race and of God.

But he is not alone, In Revelation 12 we learn that when Satan fell he took with him one third of all of the angels of glory. Our minds cannot enter into that nor does the Revelation explain it. What happened? It was that way, the Book says. One third of the angels of God left their habitation and chose to be with Lucifer. What a prince he must have been and still is, walking in the midst of the glory of fire and the jewels of God! Lucifer was cast away and one third of the angels rebelled with him. When he was cast down, they were cast down with him and became evil spirits called "demons" in the Bible.

There are two kinds of demons. Why there are two kinds, I do not know. Some angels are in prison, bound down in darkness and waiting the great Judgment Day of Almighty God. But some of them are free. Why some are in prison and others free I cannot learn. But those that are free are these that are named here in Ephesians 6:12. These *archas* and *exousias* and all of the rest of that order are here with us. In Acts 10:38 Jesus went about doing good, "healing all who were oppressed of the devil." When I see this I might suppose that I am reading fantastic legends and fairy tales in the Bible. It is unthinkable and beyond imagination that such should be in the earth. But in experience, daily I see it and come in contact with it. There are souls, people, who are oppressed by these evil spirits.

Oppressing Spirits

There was a young man in our church whose father came to me and said, "Pray for my boy that he not be sent to the electric chair, but that he be sent to prison because he needs to be incarcerated the rest of his life." I visited the young man before he committed the crime that sent him to a life sentence in prison. He stabbed a cab driver to death with a knife for no cause and no reason. As I talked with the young man, I sensed in him a spirit of habitual criminality. He was possessed. There was something evil in his soul.

Such evil possession can be seen in the leaders of violence and corruption. They do not respond to a gentle, sweet, and redemptive appeal; rather they give themselves to the destruction of the race. They push and peddle wares that destroy boys and girls, and they do it with no compunction of conscience. They are leaders of vice and corruption. They have another spirit in them.

War in the Spirit World

Evil spirits dwell in other areas of life where things are not so violent. There are those who have a spirit of thievery; they are kleptomaniacs. They are compulsive thieves. What they get in theft is of no necessity in their lives, yet they are driven to steal. They are possessed. There are people who are compulsive liars. Some people are given to exaggerate. Ah, how many of us exaggerate an ordinary situation when actually the reality is nothing at all. Some have a spirit of lying, of misrepresentation. They are seized with it. There are those who are possessed in a thousand ways. Some have a violent temper, one that is uncontrollable, inexcusable. Where does that come from? The physical frame, the body, is just clay made out of dirt. But there is a spirit that possesses it and uses it.

What is our deliverance? We have no strength in ourselves. There is no man who lives who is equal or able to face Satan. He is far superior to any of us. Nor in my humble judgment are we equal to any of the fallen spirits who follow in the destructive and disastrous train of Satan our arch-antagonist. Then why are we not ultimately destroyed? How do we have any hope whatsoever? How is it not for us just one long story of doom, disaster, and death? Our hope lies in the deliverance of God and in the presence of the Holy Spirit in our hearts, in the Lord and His merciful care. There is no hope, there is no strength, and there is no comfort outside of casting ourselves upon the mercies of God. We cannot war in ourselves. "Take therefore the whole *panoply* of God that ye may be able to stand."

In Matthew 17, on the top of the Mount, the Lord is with Elijah and Moses. The two Old Testament saints are speaking to Him about the death that He should accomplish in Jerusalem. He is suddenly glorified, transfigured. At His feet are Peter, James, and John. I do not blame Simon Peter for saying: "Lord, stay here on this glorious mountaintop. Let us stay. What joy, what gladness, what happiness, and what ecstasy! Let us just stay!" But life always summons us back down to the valley. When the Lord came down there were the other nine apostles. A father had brought to the nine a demented, possessed boy, and had asked the disciples to heal him, to cast out that evil spirit of destruction and waste and they could not do it. They were helpless. The Bible plainly reveals why.

While Peter, James, and John were up there with the Lord, the nine were quarreling about who was greatest in the kingdom. I presume they were talking about that inner circle of the three disciples taken by the Lord up there. They were quarreling about whether they were greater than the rest. As a result, before the evil spirit that afflicted the boy they were helpless. Power had gone from them. The Lord said, "Bring the boy to Me." He healed him, delivered him, and cast out the evil spirit. When the crowd had melted away, the disciples gathered around Jesus and said: "Master, why could not we deliver that boy? Why could not we cast out that evil spirit? Why could not we heal him? Why?" And the Lord told them why and then ended it with the verse, "But this kind can come forth by nothing, but by prayer and fasting." You cannot do it in yourself. There is no deliverance in us, nor strength nor help. This work is done in prayer and in fasting, in casting ourselves upon the mercies of God.

If the war is won, God has to win it. If there is strength to do it, God has to give it. If there is help, it has to come from heaven and this is the message of the sainted Apostle Paul. For our enemies are not material or corporeal. They are not *haima* and *sarkos;* they are not blood and flesh, but they are invisible spirits. They are unseen. They are spiritual and God must help us. We must cast ourselves upon the mercies of the Lord. May He be kind and good to us who need Him so. May He strengthen and comfort and help us.

Chapter 36

THE PANOPLY OF GOD

Finally, my brethren, be strong in the Lord, and in the power of his might.
Put on the whole armour of God, that ye may be able to stand against the wiles of the devil.
For we wrestle not against flesh and blood, but against principalities, against powers, against the rulers of the darkness of this world, against spiritual wickedness in high places.
Wherefore take unto you the whole armour of God, that ye may be able to withstand in the evil day, and having done all, to stand.
Stand therefore, having your loins girt about with truth, and having on the breastplate of righteousness;
And your feet shod with the preparation of the gospel of peace;
Above all, taking the shield of faith, wherewith ye shall be able to quench all the fiery darts of the wicked.
And take the helmet of salvation, and the sword of the Spirit, which is the word of God. (Eph. 6:10-17)

In our text we pick out the phrase, "the whole armour of God," the *panoply* of God. the Greek word is *panoplia. Pan* is "all," *hapla* is "weaponry" or "armor." Paul here names all six of the pieces of armor and weaponry that a Roman legionnaire wore into battle. For many years Paul was chained as a prisoner to a Roman soldier. The apostle refers to that chain numerous times in the Scriptures. For example, he referred to it as he stood before King Agrippa pleading the cause of Christ. Agrippa said, "Almost (in a little) you would persuade me to be a Christian." Paul replied, "Not only in a little but in everything, in much, could I wish that both you and all who hear me this day be such as I am except for this chain." Acts closes with Paul's address to his Jewish people in Rome. He said, "For the hope of Israel I am bound with this chain." In the years that Paul as a prisoner was chained to a Roman soldier, he daily looked upon the armor the soldier wore, and he names all of it here in Ephesians 6.

The soldier was girt about with a large, heavy belt that braced him and held the armor in position, making it possible for him to be free and unfettered in his attack. One of the kings of Gaul (now France), had welded around him an iron band which was to keep him from gaining weight the rest of his life. The Roman soldier had a girdle, an iron belt that kept him trim and held his armor in place.

There was the breastplate which was no decoration, but a grim reminder of the vital organs that had to be carefully protected.

There were the heavy shoes, the *caliguli*. Do you remember Caligula, the Roman emperor? His name means "little shoes," "little boots." The boots were made of hobnails, and were heavy in order to grip the road or the field so that the soldier might have a firm footing.

The shield covered his entire body. The helmet protected his head. The sword he used to face the enemy. It was the short, Roman, two-edged sword, an offensive instrument so deadly that it overwhelmed the civilized world. With his shield the soldier brushed aside the ranks of spears as he fearlessly attacked his enemy face to face. There was no match in the ancient world for the Roman legionnaire. Now that brings us to an observation of the Christian faith.

In symbolism and in type, in the New Testament and in history, Christianity is always martial. Is that not an astonishing thing? Martial imagery is so often used to describe the faith. The symbolism of the Christian life is filled with war and conflict, but it is not actual steel and iron that the Christian uses in spiritual warfare. It is the steel and iron of the spirit. Paul will say in 2 Corinthians 10, "For the weapons of our warfare are not carnal, but mighty through God to the pulling down of strong holds" (v. 4). We do use an actual sword or an actual spear but the imagery is that of the weapons in war. This imagery has been a part of the Christian faith from its inception.

The Panoply of God

The Christian religion was born in persecution, martyrdom, suffering, imprisonment, bloodshed, and in death. It was so in the life of Christ. He suffered execution. It was so in the lives of the apostles. All of them were martyrs except one. It was so in the story of the early Christian church. For the first century the church endured unspeakable persecution, and still does so today in many areas of the world as it has through all of the centuries preceding. As a Spartan was born for soldiery, so a Christian is born into conflict. His destiny is to be assailed and his duty is to attack. The Christian should be like David, who is described as running to meet Goliath. Why did he not stay in the sheepfold? Because of the nature of the faith. That has always been true. Listen to these hymns:

> Lift up your heads, ye gates of brass,
> The bars of iron yield.
> Let the King of glory pass,
> The cross is in the field.

> Till every foe is vanquished
> And Christ is Lord indeed.

> Soldiers of Christ arise
> And put your armor on.

> Lead on O King Eternal;
> Henceforth in fields of conquest
> Thy tents shall be our home.

> My soul be on thy guard,
> Ten thousand souls arise.
> Fight on my soul till death
> Shall bring thee to thy God.

> We are living, we are dwelling
> In an age on ages telling,
> Sworn to be Christ's soldiers ever,
> Strike! let every nerve and sinew
> Tell on ages, tell for God.

> March on, O soul with strength,
> As strong the battle rolls!

> Arise, O youth of God,
> March on to victory.

302   *Ephesians: An Exposition*

In these hymns I am pointing out to you that there is a facet of the Christian faith that is supremely martial. It speaks of war and conflict and into that conflict, as Christians, all of us are born. Therefore, when I read that we are to take the whole *panoply* of God: a girdle, a heavy belt; the breastplate of righteousness; our feet shod with the preparation of the Gospel; the shield of faith; the helmet of salvation, and the sword of the Spirit, I am seeing a symbolism of the Christian faith that has always characterized it.

THE SHIELD OF FAITH

Let us look at the shield of faith. Having put on the whole *panoply* of God, we are to add to it the shield of faith. To possess the helmet, the breastplate, the belt, the shoes, the sword — all these are not enough. One must also be protected by a shield. Having put on the armour of God, we are above all, (*epi pasin*) besides all the other to take the shield of faith. The reason for this is because the armor in itself could not protect the soldier. "Take the shield of faith," wherewith ye shall be able to quench all the fiery darts, or missiles, or javelins, or arrows of the wicked one. A man's armor in itself could not protect him from that. He needs a shield.

In the story of Paris, the prince of Troy who abducted Helen, is also found the story of the army hero, Achilles. Achilles had been dipped by his mother in the sacred river Styx and was invulnerable except for the heel by which she held him. In the Trojan War precipitated over Helen, Paris, the prince of Troy, shot an arrow full of poison and it struck Achilles in the heel and he died. In ancient warfare there were tiers and tiers of archers. An ordinary arrow, when its force was spent, lay dead and harmless, but many of those arrows were tipped with poison. They were fiery darts. Paul refers to the shield which will protect from the fiery darts of the wicked one. The armor itself, as I said, is not enough to protect the soldier. He also needs a shield.

Do you remember how King Ahab died? When he went into the war against the Assyrians, he was protected by armor next to his body. On the outside he was dressed in peasant clothes to disguise himself from the enemy. The Scripture says that as the battle raged, there was a man who took a bow and drew it back at a venture, that is, without aiming. The arrow speeding on its way

The Panoply of God

entered between the joints of Ahab's armor and pierced his heart. His blood ran out in the chariot and the dogs licked it up when it was washed. Thus Ahab died.

There must be some other instrument of protection besides the armor that the soldier wears. Paul calls that something else the "shield of faith." Faith protects the head against doubt. Faith protects the heart against the love of the world. Faith protects the hand that wields the sword.

Faith Shields the Head Against Doubt

Faith protects the head, the intellectual processes by which as reasonable creatures we cannot help but weigh the evidence for or against God. We are either for or against Christ and for or against the church. Recently a poll was taken of students in one of the universities of America. They were asked to write in order three questions that they faced in religion. The three questions they listed were in this order. First, the student asked: "Is there a personal God? Does He really exist? Is He personal or is He just cosmic law?" The second question that perplexed them in the faith, in religion, was: "Is Christ divine? Is He different from other men? Is He unique and separate? Is Christ diety?" And the third question, "Is it necessary to belong to the church or to any other religious organization?" These were not the mouthings and the rantings and the ravings of atheists or even of agnostics. These are the perplexities of university students as they look at the evidence for religion.

Is there a God? Does He speak? Does He talk? Does He understand? Does He answer? When the heavens are black, is He still there? Does He pity? Does He have sympathy? What is God like? Is Jesus Christ divine? Is He deity? Is He God? Is He different from other beings who also are different? Were He incarnate deity, would history be as it is? His own brethren, the Jews, ask: "How could He be the Messiah when the world continues on just the same? For the Messiah will change the world." Is it necessary to belong to the church? I have said that, to me, the tragedy in Russia is not the locking or closing of the churches, but the tragedy is that the great masses of the Russian people do not even miss the church. It means nothing to them.

How does one answer those questions? These thoughts are intellectual doubts. How does one answer them? There is no answer except by faith. "For he that cometh to God must believe that he is (that He exists), and that he is a rewarder of them that diligently seek him" (Heb. 11:6). There are no arguments in the Bible regarding God. It just begins, "in the beginning God." The only comment ever said about the existence of God in the Bible is, "The fool hath said in his heart, There is no God." One cannot prove God intellectually. There are numerous arguments which could be made for God, but finally and ultimately the man that comes to God comes to Him by faith or he never comes at all. God is a reality only to those who by faith accept Him, believe in Him, trust Him.

The same is true with Christ as a divine Saviour. All of the arguments in the world cannot prove the deity of Christ. "No man cometh unto me except the Father draw him." It is the spirit of God that convicts a heart and brings a soul to Jesus. One cannot accept Jesus only intellectually and be saved. He needs faith. It is something a man accepts as a gift from God or he never accepts it.

It is the same regarding the church. If the church has any meaning and any message, it arises in the spiritual response of faith in the hearts of the people. If a man does not want to come, if he does not want to respond, there are no intellectual arguments in the earth that can draw him or convince him. These things are by faith. Paul says, "Above all, take the shield of faith." Above all we must take the shield of faith without which our minds are incapable of accepting, receiving, and believing in God.

Look at the alternative. By faith I accept God, by faith I accept the Lord Christ, and by faith I believe in the destiny of His church. If I do not, if I refuse, what are my alternatives? They are simple and plain. When I turn aside from God and His promises and His people, I turn to face nothing but a dismal night of darkness and ultimate despair. Two university students shut themselves in a room and took their lives. They left a note which said: "We have decided to go together. There is nothing left." The daughter of a rich family took her life announcing: "I am sick and weary of social life. It is empty and it is nothing to me." These things are not unusual or peculiar. When I turn aside from the faith, I have no alternative but to face the darkness of despair and inevitable hollowness of nothing. Life has no meaning without faith. It has no purpose. It reaches toward nothing. This is modern existentialist, philosophical despair. That is why Paul says: "Above all, take the shield of faith." Take the shield of trust and believe.

Faith Protects the Heart Against Love of the World

Not only is faith protection of the head, the mind, against intellectual doubt, but it is also the protection of the heart against the love of the world. James, the Lord's brother, pastor of the church at Jerusalem, wrote in James 4:4, "For the friendship of the world is enmity with God." They are diametrical opposites. One cannot serve God and the world. It is one or the other. The love of the world is the glamour and the glory of Satan. Lucifer offered it to Jesus if He would bow down and worship him. One who becomes enmeshed in the world, caught up in the love of the world, is therein taken away from God. The rich young ruler could not enter in because the gate is too narrow for the man who loves the world. One cannot hold the world in his heart and still enter into the kingdom of God. The gate is not wide enough. The road is not broad enough.

The love of the world is that evil influence that takes one away from God. The love of the world is the influence that makes us think more of ourselves than we think of others and of God. The shield of faith is to guard us against the waywardness of our hearts, lest we lose ourselves in the glitter, the glamour, and the glory of the world. There is no sadder sentence in the Bible than this one that Paul writes in the last chapter of his last letter: "Demas hath forsaken me, having loved this present world" (2 Tim. 4:10).

Faith Protects the Hand That Holds the Bible

The shield of faith protects our hand that wields the sword of the Spirit, which is the Word of God. The sword of the Spirit is the sword given us by the Spirit, the Word of God. Oh, what a tragedy when we lose our conviction and our persuasion that this is the divine, inspired Word of God from heaven! We immediately become like hollow reeds that bow before every breeze of passing fancy when we lose the conviction that this is the revelation of

God. Without this sword of the Spirit, the church turns into a social club. Without the Scriptures religious faith turns into speculative philosophy, and the whole experience of the Christian religion can be defined in simple "do-gooding." Like any other club or association that is dedicated to the social amelioration of the sad lot of men, the church has no answer from heaven. If it has no revelation from above, it has nothing to offer more than any other altruistic organization. It has no marching, thrusting drive of the power and Spirit of God. It has lost it.

There was a man who came up to his pastor and said: "You know, before you came, I abhorred the flesh, the world, and the devil. But under your fine preaching I have come to love all three." The pastor had lost his shield of faith to protect the hand that wields the sword of the Spirit, the cutting edge of the Christian faith. The conviction and the commitment that this is the revealed Word of God is protected by the shield of faith. Hebrews 4:12, 13 says, "For the word of God is quick, and powerful, and sharper than any two-edged sword, piercing even to the dividing asunder of soul and spirit, and of the joints and marrow, and is a discerner of the thoughts and intents of the heart . . . but all things are naked and opened unto the eyes of him with whom we have to do." The living, quickening Spirit of God is found in the living, quickening Word.

The Christian soldier is to be like those of Nehemiah's day who built the wall of Jerusalem. In one hand they held the sword, and in the other hand they worked with the trowel. Giving ourselves to the Bible, the inspired revelation of heaven, and giving ourselves to the building up of His kingdom in the earth, we are to put on the whole *panoply* of God. *Epi pasin*, above all, besides all, we are to hold the shield of faith.

Faith Gives a Glorious Victory

Always in the Bible without exception there is ever that reaching out and assurance of a final consummating victory. The Bible is a book of realism, grim realism. It presents its heroes exactly as they are. It presents human nature and human history exactly as it is. But always with this note, namely, that the whole story is moving toward some glorious consummation of victory. It may begin in blood, it may begin in martyrdom, it may begin in suffering, it may contain imprisonment and persecution, but always it reaches out toward a glorious triumph. The note of victory is never absent in the Word of God. The Bible says there is a greater day coming, there is a finer day tomorrow, there is something to be glad about, to be uplifted about. There is singing and rejoicing and gladness. That is the Christian faith!

The apostles saw Jesus crucified, but they also saw Him raised from the dead, so they looked up. They knew imprisonment and persecution but they also saw iron doors open. Even the sainted Apostle John who outlived them all, the only one who was not martyred, was shut out as a broken old man to die in exile on Patmos. How does the story end? It begins, "I, your brother in tribulation was on the isle of Patmos for the faith, for the gospel of Christ. . . ." But it ends with the angels and all creation saying: "Hallelujah, for the Lord God omnipotent reigneth. The kingdoms of this world are become the kingdoms of our Lord and of His Christ. And He shall reign forever and ever. Hallelujah! Hallelujah!" That is the Christian faith. In exile, in triumph, in imprisonment, in crucifixion, in death, there is still singing, rejoicing, and victory in the presence of the great God, our Saviour, the Lord Jesus.

That is the faith of the Apostle Paul. He knew the enemy and described him. In a thousand forms and disguises he is always Satan, Lucifer, the accuser. But Paul also knew the power of Christ. Christ is power embodied. Christ is omnipotence incarnate. He was powerful in His life: healing the sick, casting out spirits, raising people from the dead. He was powerful in His death, securing our atonement and forgiveness of sin. He was powerful in the resurrection, tearing up for us the bonds of the grave. He was powerful in His ascension. "He is able to save to the uttermost them that come unto God by him." And Jesus is (for Paul and I could pray for us all) powerful in His glorious return, personal and visible!

In the little book that I have our children read before being baptized, there is a question. The Lord's Supper ends with this verse: "For as oft as ye eat this bread and drink this cup you do show forth the Lord's death till He comes." The question is "What does that mean, 'till He come'?" A child never fails to answer that question in the spirit in which it is presented. What does it mean — "till He come"? The child replies, "That means that Jesus is coming again." Then I always ask: "Do you believe that? Do you believe you will see Jesus some day?" And the child always answers: "I do." He is coming! He is returning. That is the glad triumphant note that Paul calls "the blessed hope."

Once Jesus was despised. But the day is coming when every tongue shall confess Him as Lord. Once He was rejected, but one day every knee shall bow before Him in adoration. Once He was led as a lamb to the slaughter, but one day His voice shall shake the foundations of heaven and earth. Once He was crowned with thorns, but then shall they bring to Him and place on His brow the diadem of all God's heaven and earth. Once He had eleven men to follow Him, but then shall He appear in glory, descending with ten thousand times ten thousand of His angels and His saints!

> All hail the power of Jesus' name!
> Let angels prostrate fall!
> Bring forth the royal diadem,
> And crown Him Lord of all.
>
> Ye chosen seed of Israel's race,
> Ye ransomed from the fall;
> Hail Him who saves you by His grace,
> And crown Him Lord of all.

This is the incomparably glorious prospect upon which the Christian faith ever looks. This is the note that closes the Book of Ephesians. It is the triumph that closes the Book of the Apocalypse, the unveiling of the appearing of the Son of God.

Take the shield of faith as your own. Give your heart and life to the Lord Jesus. Put on the whole *panoply* of God. Let this word of truth bring forth in your life a response of faith in Jesus.